£35

Tabula Bonorum Angelorum Invocationes

Clavicula Tabularum Enochi

Sourceworks of Ceremonial Magic Series

Volume 1 - Practical Angel Magic
of John Dee's Enochian Tables

Limited Edition of 1500 copies

Of which this is number..122..

In the same series:

Volume I - Practical Angel Magic of John Dee's Enochian Tables

Volume II - Keys to the Gateway of Magic: Summoning the Archangels

For further details of forthcoming books in this series, edited from classic magical manuscripts, see www.GoldenHoard.net.

Practical Angel Magic of
John Dee's Enochian Tables

from four previously unpublished manuscripts on Angel Magic
being a complete transcription of Tabula Bonorum Angelorum Invocationes
in manuscripts BL Sloane 307 and 3821 and Bodleian Rawlinson D 1067 and D 1363

as used by Wynn Westcott, Alan Bennett, Reverend Ayton, Frederick Leigh Gardner, and
other senior members of the Hermetic Order of the Golden Dawn

Stephen Skinner & David Rankine

GOLDEN HOARD PRESS
2004

Published by Golden Hoard Press
BM Avalonia
London WC1N 3XX, UK.
www.GoldenHoard.net

First Edition

British Library Cataloguing in Publication data

Dee, John, 1527-1608
     The practical angel magic of John Dee's Enochian tables:
     from three previously unpublished manuscripts on angel
     magic, being a complete transcription of Tabula Bonorum
     Angelorum Invocationes in manuscripts BL Sloane 307 and
     Sloane 3821 and Bodleian Rawlinson D1067. – (Sourceworks of
     Ceremonial magic ; v. 1)
     1. Enochian magic 2. Angels
     I. Title II. Skinner, Stephen   III. Rankine, David
     133

ISBN 0954763904

Cover Design by Valentina Kim

Printed in Singapore

*"Whilst heaven endureth, and earth lasteth, never shall be razed out
the memory of these Actions"*

- the Angel Raphael speaking to John Dee
28 March 1583

Dedicated to the memory of Alan Bennett
who carried the flame of the Tradition

Contents

The Invocations of the Kings, Seniors, Angels and Spirits

The Keys to the Portals

Ashmole's Prayers

Appendices

Bibliography

List of Tables & Illustrations:

Acknowledgements

We wish to thank the staff of the British Library and Bodleian Library for their assistance in preparing this volume. Folios from Sloane MS 307 have been reproduced with permission from the Trustees of the British Library, for which we are duly grateful.

"...the nature of angels and spirits...is neither inscrutable nor interdicted. ...it is no more unlawful to inquire the nature of evil spirits, than to inquire the force of poisons in nature, or the nature of sin & vice in morality." *The Advancement of Learning*, 2nd Book, VI, 2, Bacon 1605.

Introduction

The four manuscripts transcribed in this book are highly significant manuscripts in the history of magic. In researching them we have come to a number of conclusions about:

a)   The precise methods used in angel magic both by Dr John Dee and other practitioners both before and after him.

b)   The origin of these methods, which shows little or no practical line of demarcation between evocation and invocation.

c)   The line of transmission from magician to magician of these techniques which appears to partly re-write the history of Western Magic, specifically with reference to the transmission of the final angelic invocations of Dee.

d)   In tracing this line of scholar magicians we have discovered that in every age some of the most prominent players were major members of the establishment, politicians, lords, legislators, and even royalty.

e)   A small part of just one of these manuscripts (Sloane MS 307) was used as *Book H*, the key to the Enochian system, by founding and higher-grade members of the Golden Dawn. Even this small extract was later suppressed. The Golden Dawn only used part of Dee's magical techniques. Here for the first time is printed the whole key to the Enochian system as originally discovered by the senior initiates and founders of the Golden Dawn.

Traditional Approaches to Western Magic

First we need to look at how the history of magic has been viewed in Western Europe over the last thousand years. It has almost always been explained or examined in one of five basic ways:

1.   By assembling a collection of biographies of magicians or isolated historical events like Faust's pacts, Cellini's evocations or Mesmer's parlour tricks.

2.   By associating magic with Neoplatonism or the Hermetic texts that circulated in Europe during the Renaissance. This academic approach looks at magic as if it was a cultural trend, a poor relation of science, or the discredited remains of pagan practice and philosophy.

3.   By associating magic with movements like Rosicrucianism, the Illuminati or Freemasonry, and from that association implying a continuous history of hidden brotherhoods up to and beyond the Hermetic Order of the Golden Dawn. This was a popular Victorian view.

4.   By looking at magic from the perspective of its persecutors, as exemplified in the witch trials. This approach also includes the Faustian view that magic consists of selling one's soul to the devil, a view popularised and promoted by the church, and a theme that was later taken up in literature.

5.   By examining the craft of village cunning men and wise women, and the development of local witchcraft and leechcraft. From the mid 20th century this strand blends into modern witchcraft, which draws its substance from a number of other sources as well.

None of these approaches (with the exception of modern witchcraft) says much about the actual magical practices used by magicians, what happened to their workbooks, what practical results they obtained, and how they handed this knowledge on. Let us examine each in turn:

1.   The first approach consists of simply supplying a series of biographies of well-known real and fictional magicians such as Faust, Abramelin, Dee, Barrett, Crowley or even Casanova. This gives the impression that romantic individuals cropped up every so often, and that there was no continuous history of the subject, in

the same way as there is for example a continuous history of art, architecture or literature. All too often we see gaps of decades, even centuries, between each episode. Most Victorian histories, including that of Eliphas Levi, fall into this category.

2.   The second approach, and one often taken by scholarly writers like Frances Yates, is that magic is part of the gradual evolution of human knowledge. These writers explain magic as if it was part of a late flowering of Neoplatonism, or the result of the injection of Christianised Kabbalah into the mainstream of European thought by the likes of Pico, Reuchlin and Bruno, rather than something which had been established just as strongly long before these cultural influences reached Renaissance Europe.

The usual thesis is that magic fell out of use, or certainly out of respect, from the coming of the Age of Enlightenment in the early 17th century onwards, and from thence forward science became the main pursuit of the intelligencia. This view is contradicted by the facts, not only by Newton's well-known interest in alchemy and angelic theology, but by records of the consistent and carefully documented practice of magic right up to the current time.

3.   The third, and one of the more appealing views of magic, was that it was the rationale of a number of well known societies and fraternities who passed on its practice from one century to another. This transmission of magical theory and practice however has not been via secret societies, except in a few scattered instances. On the whole, Rosicrucians, Freemasons and Illuminati were not magical groups, nor were their members magicians, except in a private capacity.

The vast literature concerning secret societies like the Illuminati, Masons or Rosicrucians, clearly shows that they were in most cases more concerned with fraternal networking and political causes than with magic. If the history of Masonry, for example, is examined closely it will be seen that the system of elevation by degrees, passwords and secret handshakes made more social, political and commercial sense than magical sense. French Masonry was heavily intertwined with politics, and the Rosicrucian movement hoped to create a climate for the formation of a political utopia among the intelligentsia of Europe, particularly in the Germanic states.

The only exception to this was the Hermetic Order of the Golden Dawn founded in the late 19th century, where the practice of magic took precedence over the other two objectives. Although these

Masonic activists of late nineteenth century England did find Masonry a useful way of preserving secrecy about their magical activities.

If we eliminate the modern (late 20th century) Rosicrucians' rosy view of history, which justified the inclusion of anyone they fancied, like Bacon, Newton or Shakespeare, as a member of their Fraternity, merely upon the basis of supposed sympathetic interests, then we are left with the letters and correspondence circulating at the time of the founding of the movement soon after 1612. From these you can clearly see that the Rosicrucians were much more concerned with a new political order, plus a bit of alchemy and the new Paracelsian medicine, than they ever were with the invocation of spirits or angels.

Aaron Leitch convincingly says of the Rosicrucians:
"It is most likely that the Brotherhood did not exist in any tangible sense. The Rosicrucians claimed to meet only at an "Invisible College" - and there are many subtle hints to suggest that this was meant as an allegory. The Rosicrucian manifestos were addressed to all free thinkers and spiritual seekers in the world; especially those who yearned for the dawning of a new age, the advancement of learning, and freedom from the oppressive Roman Church. The Invisible College was the common ground within the hearts of all who sought such goals. There is no known historical philosopher or Hermetic mystic, who we would call 'Rosicrucian' today, who ever claimed membership to such an Order."

It is safe to say that the handing down of magical technique has not occurred via the Rosicrucians, except in the sense that the movement united men of a like mind, some of whom were also interested in magic.

4.   Of all the approaches, the fourth is perhaps the most misleading as it draws its information from those who were most interested in persecuting magic. We look below in more detail at the attitude of the Church to magic. The idea that the practitioner of magic would sell his soul for knowledge or power has been around since the Middle Ages, but especially flourished under French and Italian Catholicism when grimoires like the *Grimoirium Verum* and the grimoire of so-called *Pope Honorius* made their appearance. These rely for their rationale upon the catholic view of damnation, rather than mainstream techniques of magic. The aim of most serious magicians was knowledge and not the endangerment of their soul. 'Pope Honorius' incidentally has no connection with

Honorius filius Euclid who authored the *Sworn Book*.

5.   The fifth approach looks at magic primarily from the local village wise woman and cunning man perspective, where a few (sometimes elderly and eccentric) occupants eked out a living constructing and deflecting charms, or providing herbal medicines. Some of the excellent writers who best exemplify this approach are Norman Cohn and Keith Thomas in *Religion and the Decline of Magic*. Thomas explains[1] that "popular magic and intellectual magic were essentially two different activities, overlapping at certain points, but to a large extent carried on in virtual independence of each other. Most of the magical techniques of the village wizard had been inherited from the Middle Ages, and had direct links with Anglo-Saxon and classical practice".

Such techniques were certainly passed on often by inheritance, but did not tend to enter the studies of the learned or more highly placed members of society, where the 'style' of magic was completely different. Thomas continues, "It was relatively uncommon for such persons to possess books, or for their activities to rest upon a body of self-conscious theory".

Modern witchcraft dating from the 1950s, as sponsored by such luminaries as Cecil Williamson, Gerald Gardner, Alex Sanders and Jim Baker is too recent and too eclectically constructed to throw light on the early development of magic, and so is excluded from this discussion. Of course the modern witchcraft movement draws on many of the above strands for its substance and has mixed many of these together.

Almost all of these studies look at magic from the outside. None of these approaches does justice to the evolution of magical technique in Western Europe as a separate and valid field of study that was practiced alongside astronomy, chemistry, physics or geography by some of the best minds of each age. The nature of angels (which seems irrelevant in our currently irreligious age) was just as important a study as the geometry of lenses or the mathematics of astronomy.

We feel that magic is worthy of such study, and we can demonstrate that in every age some of the best minds including clergy, scientists, lawyers, senior politicians, statesmen, and even royalty, right up to the present day, have been deeply involved in its study.

---

[1] *Religion and the Decline of Magic* page 271.

Definition of Magic

Magic is concerned with practical techniques for communicating with angels, demons (or daemons), spirits, and elementals, and questioning them or compelling them to assist the practitioner in very specific ways. We would like to group all of these entities (as they often were grouped in the 15th and 16th century) under the category of 'spiritual creatures', meaning entities not inhabiting the physical plane.

This is a much more useful distinction than that forced upon them by the doctrines of Christianity, where there is concern to separate the angels who 'fell' from those who didn't. In any case Christianity has always been confused about the theological status of elementals and other non-human spirits. The King James version of the Bible translated the words for all of these various creatures, which were quite distinct in the Latin and Hebrew texts of the scriptures, simply as 'devils', a slackness of the translators that has caused much confusion, bigotry and misery over the centuries.

Modern pagan movements have attempted to broaden the definition of magic. For example the gods and goddesses of various pantheons have been included in the list of spiritual creatures available for invocation. However, in the context of ceremonial magic, these entities were not often invoked *per se* by European magicians before the end of the 19th century. Since the Renaissance, the gods of the Greek and Roman pantheons were seen as part of the general literary and artistic heritage and education of post-Mediaeval Europe. To quote Daniel Driscoll, "in accepting astrology, Mediaeval Europe accepted the major gods of the [Greek/Roman] pagan pantheon; the pagan gods simply became...in philosophical terminology 'secondary causes'." Magicians like Ficino or Campanella invoked the planetary forces, rather than the ancient gods or goddesses associated with the planets.

Gods of pantheons outside of Greece or Rome hardly figured in the Renaissance intellectual landscape, or were conveniently re-classified as demons. Such a fate befell Ashtoreth (the Phoenician goddess of love and increase) and Baal (her Phoenician consort) both of whom turn up later as demons in grimoires such as the *Goetia*.

Other views have obscured the world view of early practitioners of magic. In the second half of the 20th century it was popular to subscribe to a psychological interpretation of magic, to the effect that entities such as demons are just 'dissociated complexes' or some other part of the vocabulary of theoretical psychology. Strangely this idea was probably initiated by Aleister Crowley's ultra rationalist introduction to his edition of the *Goetia* in 1912, long before Carl Jung's theories became popular. It is quite possible that this rationale was written by Crowley with his tongue firmly in his cheek, but more likely he was overcompensating to prevent the *Goetia* being rejected out of hand by his primarily Victorian readers. Crowley's later writings show that he thought of such entities as having considerably more independence of existence than he ascribed to them in this particular introduction. But this pernicious view, embellished by Jung's theories, still colours some modern thinking about magic.

To understand the thinking of magicians of earlier periods, you should not allow your views to be clouded by this particular theory that has been popular for so short a period. By making magic appear solely subjective, a lot of the 'sting' was taken out of the subject, and it has consequently been embraced by New Age thinkers. However, we do not subscribe to the idea of magic as either a form of access to the sub-conscious mind or as a form of therapy, and this idea certainly did not colour the theory or practice of pre-20th century magicians at all. In fact all of the theories of modern psychology are much more shallowly rooted than the age old theoretical framework of traditional magic.

In defining magic in terms of 'spiritual creatures' it may be objected that nobody believes any more in the objective existence of angels or demons on the grounds that if they are invisible, they must not exist, and are therefore not worthy of study. There are however many subjects that rely completely on belief in the invisible. Modern belief in such invisibles as radio waves, quasars or protons is endemic, and prefaced *only* on a theoretical framework, rather than on direct experience. All these things are known only through their effects, and none known by direct experience. The theory behind magic also relies upon the observation of effects. Magic has however also had, over the centuries, many instances of direct experience. The whole point of magic was not just to produce an effect, but often to move the invisible cause into the realm of the visible effect. It is therefore not logical to dismiss one set of beliefs (magic) but not the other (physics) on the grounds of invisibility, especially as both have measurable effects.

Lastly, some might instead argue that practitioners of magic are simply deluded by a sophisticated form of wish fulfilment. If magicians were simply gullible fools gratifying their own fancies, then you would expect to see a succession of successfully self-serving visions and comfortable answers. This is not the case: many answers received from 'spiritual creatures' are not as comfortable as expected, and often mischievous and uncooperative 'deceiving spirits' arrived rather than the expected angels. This suggests the action of an external agency rather than the results of self-delusion.

Dualist View of Magic

Dualism is the perception that the world divides neatly into black and white, good and evil. This has lead to concern about the difference between what has been called 'black magic' and 'white magic'. The difference has often simplistically been put down to good or bad intentions. In almost all cases the basic techniques of evocation or invocation are the same, and the operator's intention has little or no effect beyond defining the objectives of the ritual. In practice the type of entity called through by such techniques could be angel, demon or spirit, regardless of the intention or piety of the practitioners. So if the techniques and the results were the same, then for the practicing magician there was no question of a distinction. It is only a later interpretation imposed from outside which insisted upon a supposed difference characterised as black or white magic.

Dualism was the legacy of the increasingly repressive grip of Christianity. Adam McLean, in his excellent introduction to *A Treatise on Angel Magic* highlights the effect of introducing dualism into magic:

"Before this period [the Renaissance] magicians could work naturally to invoke spirits without any great inner qualms. They saw that such spirits were, after all, part of God's creation and worthy of the occultist's attention... [but] from that time on...the magician's healthy relationship to the realm of spirits, his personal exploration through ritual of the spiritual world, becomes diseased by a concern about 'evil'."

This is no more apparent than in John Dee's Spiritual Diaries (*Libri Mysteriorum*), where despite his undoubtedly pious intention to conjure angels, he often finished up talking with 'divells', 'deceivers' or other stray spirits. This caused him, and Kelly, a lot of heart searching, but they persisted. Dee's desire to talk with angels was driven by his belief that the angels alone would be able to give accurate answers to his probing questions, 'because they were closer to God'. His concern was one of degree of wisdom, knowledge and accuracy, rather than theology.

The fine theological distinctions between angels, demons and spirits were in practice of little use, and sometimes the baser spirits still appeared, treating Dee's painstaking pious prayer-filled preparations with the same reverence as the protagonist in the old joke: 'what happens when you show a cross to a Jewish vampire?'

The roots of this problem lie partly in the distinction between 'devil' and 'demon'. This distinction is *very* clear in the Greek (*Septuagint*) and Latin (*Vulgate*) versions of the Bible, but has been totally destroyed in the Protestant versions of the Bible, especially the King James version. The crux of the issue is the meanings of the two Greek words *daimon* and *diabolos*. These two terms are totally distinct and never confused in the Greek originals of the New Testament or the Greek translation of the Hebrew and Aramaic of the Old Testament.

Diabolos always translates the Hebrew words TzR or STN, Satan the name for the tempter or god's spiritual 'adversary'. But *daimon* translates a number of Hebrew words that apply variously to Pagan deities, apparitions, spirits, and even satyrs. The root of *daimon* is *daio* which means 'to distribute fortune', and it should never have been confused with the word for the ultimate spiritual adversary.

Diabolos occurs in the Bible just thirty-five times, while *daimon* in various forms occurs more than seventy times. English translations have confused these two terms totally, translating *both* as 'devil'. *Diabolos* is definitely a different word. This has lead to the confusion that has lumped all sorts of 'spiritual creatures' with the Devil himself, a categorisation that they do not deserve any more than angels do.

In fact Calmet, and a number of other theologians, were of the opinion that demons are identical with apostate angels. As such we are simply left with a range of 'spiritual creatures' of varying degrees of veracity and knowledge, including angels, spirits and demons, which are quite separate from the Devil himself. This confusion did not arise till the King James version of the Bible appeared in English. In a pre King James world, this is how John Dee and other scholar magicians perceived them.

It bears repeating that under the same king, some of the most ferocious English witch persecutions ever seen were launched.

Aristocratic Connections

The aristocracy has been an enduring thread throughout the history of ceremonial magic in England, from the 12th century to the present day. One of the amazing things about this type of magic is that, at every period it has attracted the very highest echelons of society, from English kings and queens, like Henry IV and Elizabeth I, who definitely owned and read grimoires, through titled Barons and Lords, including several Chancellors of the Exchequer and at least one Master of the Rolls, all of whom indulged in the practice of angel invocation, and who owned extensive libraries of rare manuscripts on these subjects. Queen Elizabeth even discussed, with John Dee, the detailed contents of a grimoire that she had inherited from Henry IV.

There was also a flourishing parallel tradition of local village wise women and men who practised 'wort cunning' and drew up charms, but the practice of angelic and demonic invocation was to a very large extent confined to the hands of the upper and professional classes. These techniques of invocatory angel magic have been passed on, not from local village witch to witch, not through secret fraternities, not as part of neo-Platonic or alchemic studies, but from one scholar magician to another, and quite often in a limited geographic area.

One of the strangest coincidences that we discovered whilst researching these manuscripts was the number of angel magicians who had connections with Worcester in Worcestershire. Almost all the main practitioners of angel magic in the 16th and 17th century (except the Napiers) came from nearby.

Just to instance a few:

John Dee had one of his rectory 'livings' located at Upton upon Severn, in Worcester, upon which he depended financially. This living was taken from him when he left England for the Continent, having absentmindedly forgotten to have the Queen's seal affixed to it.

Edward Kelly was born in Worcester, and went to Worcester College at Oxford.

Thomas Coke, who was the alchemy assistant to the 'Wizard Earl' Henry Percy Northumberland, and worked for a period for John Dee, also came from Worcester.

Elias Ashmole (who collected and preserved Dee's manuscripts and practiced angel magic himself) accepted the position of Commissioner for Excise at Worcester on 8th December 1645, after turning down a number of other more suitable positions in other areas. He was introduced to this position by John Heydon, himself interested in angel magic, who also had Worcester connections, and who wrote *Theomagia*, one of the now neglected books on magic.

Baron Somers and Sir Joseph Jekyll, angel magicians who we will meet in more detail later in this book, both came from and had their family seats and lands in the Worcester area.

A number of other participants in angel magic were also connected with this region. This connection even survives into the 20th century with Gerald Yorke, who had his family seat at Forthampton just south of Worcester. He was very knowledgeable about angel magic, and was the person responsible for collecting and preserving many of Aleister Crowley's papers, including those on Enochian magic. Interestingly he was also for a period the Dalai Lama's representative in the UK.

In the early 1970s, Gerald Yorke kindly granted access to all of these papers to one of the present authors. Another recipient of Gerald's generosity was Robert Turner, who in turn dedicated his edition of Dee's angel magic grimoire *De Heptarchia Mystica* to Gerald. So the Worcester angel magic tradition lives on.

Part 1 - A Short History of Angel Magic in England

Sources of Angel Magic in the Grimoires

The idea of invoking angels goes back a very long way to pre-Christian times. Even Jesus was thought by many people to have used the magic of angels to perform his miracles. One early Christian father, Gregory Thaumaturges wrote that it was commonly believed that "Jesus was a Magian;[2] He effected all these things [his miracles] by secret arts. From the shrines of the Egyptians He stole the names of angels of might." Gregory goes on to refute this view. The reason why he was thought to have stolen the names of angels, is in order to use these angels in his magic. As always, possession of the true name of a spiritual creature gave the magician power over that creature.

Angel magic survived the Middle Ages in grimoires in both Latin and Hebrew. Surprisingly, by the 12th century, the practical techniques of angel magic are almost all rooted in early grimoires, which until recently have usually been associated by scholars and modern practitioners exclusively with demonic magic.

The four hundred years from the 13th to 17th century is a period where the grimoire or handbook of practical ceremonial magic dominates magical procedure. Perhaps the most important grimoires of this period were, from our point of view, the *Sworn Book of Honorius [Liber Sacer sive Juratus]*, and the *Lemegeton* [which includes within it the *Goetia,* the *Art Theurgia Goetia* and the *Almadel*]. The oldest of these grimoires is probably the *Sworn Book.*

The Sacred or Sworn Book of Honorius

One of the earliest and most influential grimoires was *Liber Sacer sive Juratus,* which literally means *The Sacred or Sworn Book* of Honorius . The book was considered sacred by its author and many of its owners because it contained techniques for calling the angels, and for achieving the Beatific vision. The author is not the Pope Honorius of later Faustian grimoires but an altogether more interesting figure called 'Honorius filius Euclid of Thebes'.

---

[2] A magician.

The most familiar Euclid is Euclid of Megara[3] who devised the basic theorems of geometry that all schoolchildren used to be obliged to learn. Honorius, the author of the *Sworn Book* is referred to as the son of Euclid of Thebes (probably the Thebes[4] in Greece not that of Egypt). This is not the same Euclid, but a more shadowy figure who may well have originally written in Greek.

The book opens with the mention of a convocation or meeting at which 811[5] Masters of magic assemble to decide how to resist a papal plan to persecute magicians. This meeting, which caused the *Sworn Book* to be written, drew its adepts from as far afield as Athens, Tholetus [Toledo) and Naples, the later city being where the convocation was held.

The *Sworn Book* was written by Honorius at the request of this group of 811 Master Magicians, to preserve their secrets, and allegedly with the help of the angel Hocroell[6]. Even at this point we see magicians soliciting the help of angels in *intellectual* endeavour, a theme that will continue to repeat itself over the next 800 years. The date of composition of this grimoire is definitely before 1249[7], and the most likely date being during the papacy of Gregory IX (1227-41) a pope who attempted to suppress magic and persecute magicians, as he saw them as a threat to the authority of the church. They were a threat because they purported to converse directly with angels!

Three centuries later John Dee owned a copy of the *Sworn Book*, and undoubtedly drew upon it for the design of his key sigil, the Sigillum Aemeth. Perhaps it was also the source of the idea that prayers made to the angels could result in communication from such beings with superior knowledge and intelligence.

It is also very suggestive that John Dee gave his first public lectures on Euclid of Megara, and in fact contributed a Mathematical Preface

---

[3] We will refer to the geometer as Euclid of Megara, as that is how he was known in Dee's time, although subsequent scholarship has discovered that the geometer and the philosopher of Megara were not the same person.

[4] Modern day Thivali. Interestingly Thebes is only about 40 km from Megara, in Greece.

[5] The number 811 has a symbolic meaning being the Greek numeration of IAO, a Gnostic god name associated with Abraxas [I=10, A=1, O=800]. Although IAO was in use in a number of works on magic, it tends to suggest a Greek rather than a Hebrew origin for this grimoire. Some manuscripts state the number was 89 magicians.

[6] Possibly an angel of the zodiacal sign of Leo.

[7] William of Auvergne, Archbishop of Paris, made two references to the *Sworn Book* in his book *De Legibus.* Therefore it has to have existed before his death in 1249.

to the first edition of Euclid which he helped translate (with Henry Billingsley) and publish in English in 1570. Euclid resurfaces much later in 1651, when significantly a certain Captain Thomas Rudd (1583-1665) published just the first six books of the geometry of Euclid of Megara together with the same Preface by John Dee.

Both Rudd and Dee (who owned a copy) would have been familiar with the *Sworn Book* of Honorius son of Euclid of Thebes. Is it possible that their interest aroused in Euclid of Megara may have initially been caused by a confusion of this Euclid with the Euclid of Thebes?

In Dee's efforts to get intellectual satisfaction from the angels, piety and cleanliness were paramount considerations. This grimoire stresses the purity of its intent, and not just in order to preserve its owners from possible ecclesiastical prosecution. In the opening paragraphs it says "it is not possible that a wicked and unclean man could work truly in this art; for men are not bound unto spirits, but spirits are constrained against their will to answer clean men and fulfil their requests." This is a very important point. And later it explains that "we call this book the *Sacred* or *Sworn Book* for in it is contained 100 sacred names of God and thus [it is] sacred, for it is made of holy things...it was consecrated by God."

For Dee, the *Sworn Book* was very important. It was not just concerned with the invocation of angels, but was the origin of the Sigillum Aemeth (or Sigil of Truth) that is the key diagram engraved on the wax tablets used on his Table of Practice, and on the wax tablets used as supports under its legs[8]. This Sigil, which has a complex geometry, and should be coloured according to very specific rules, may even pre-date the *Sworn Book*. It also appeared in one of Kircher's books. The *Sworn Book* is therefore a prime example of a grimoire which provided some of the basic rationale, equipment, diagrams and techniques of angel magic.

The *Sworn Book* was very influential amongst a wider circle of Elizabethan intellectuals, and it is interesting to note that Ben Jonson (1573-1637), the playwright contemporary of Shakespeare, was also the owner of one of the main surviving manuscript copies of *The Sworn Book*.[9] It is well known that Jonson was interested in and well informed about alchemy, which can be seen from the detail in his play *The Alchemist*. However it is not so well known that he

---

[8] These tablets are still preserved in the British Museum, and can be seen today.
[9] British Library manuscript Sloane MS 313.

was also interested in and practiced the angel magic contained in the *Sworn Book*.

Giordano Bruno, who visited Dee, and probably read his copy of the *Sworn Book* when he was in England in the early 1580s, actually incorporated into his book on the Kabbalah, a character called 'Onorio' from Thebes: probably a sly reference to Honorius of Thebes.

Heptameron or Magical Elements

This book by Peter de Abano (1250-1317), may have been written around 1300, towards the end of his life. It contains the Latin versions of conjurations to be found in the *Goetia*, and therefore is probably one of the sources of that important grimoire. The *Heptameron* was first printed in English in 1655 [10], but was undoubtedly know to Dee perhaps in the Latin version of 1496. Like the *Goetia*, but unlike some of the other grimoires, it emphasises the importance of an inscribed circle on the floor, "for they are certain fortresses to defend the operators safe from the evil Spirits".

One of the interesting contributions that this grimoire makes to the contents of the present book is its list of angelic powers and objectives. These are very similar to those listed in the present work, and the source of some very interesting transcriptional mistakes in the manuscripts of the present work.

Armadel, Arbatel, Almadel

Note that the *Armadel*, the *Arbatel*, and the *Almadel* are three distinct and different grimoires despite the similarity of name. We will deal with them in order.

Armadel[11] might be the name of the author but it is more likely to be a common noun. This grimoire has been very influential in the history of angelic invocation. It opens with the seals of 7 angels: Michael, Anael, Raphael, Gabriel, Cassiel, Sachiel, and Samael, the first four [12] of which also appear on the opening page of Dee's manuscript of his very first *Liber Mysteriorum*[13]. Dee thought that

---

[10] The *Heptameron* was contained in the 1655 English edition of the *Fourth Book of Occult Philosophy* which was reprinted by Askin Publishers in 1978.

[11] A translation of a 17th century French manuscript of this grimoire by S L MacGregor Mathers was edited by Francis King and published by RKP in 1980. That edition seems however to be a bit scrambled in terms of the order of its chapters.

[12] Together with Uriel.

[13] This begins in December 1581.

the relatively unknown angel Annael (Dee spelt it with a double 'n') was the angel presiding over the whole world (at least during Dee's lifetime) and therefore the ruler of Michael, Gabriel, Raphael and Uriel, the angels of the four quarters, and the angels with whom Dee was most keen to communicate.

The *Arbatel* dates from 1575 and is also entitled *De Magia Veterum.* John Dee is known to have owned a copy of the Arbatel, to which he makes several references in his *Libri Mysteriorum,* especially to the spirit Och [one of the so called Olympic spirits who also occurs in other grimoires]. The *Arbatel of Magick* was included in Agrippa's *Fourth Book of Occult Philosophy*[14]

However the most interesting of these three grimoires from the point of view of angel magic is the *Ars Almadel.* This first appears in a 15th century manuscript in Florence[15]. 'Almadel' might be a word of Arabic derivation, with *Al-* being the definite article 'the', plus *madel* or *mandel.* Words from the major invocation[16] of the *Almadel* also appear in Dee's Enochian calls, suggesting that either Dee or Kelly may have used and adapted material from the *Almadel.* The *Almadel* invocation: "I [am] the servant of the highest the same your god Adonai Helomi & Pine" parallels Dee's Enochian "Lap zirdo Noco MAD Hoath Iaida" which translates "for I am the servant of the same your God the true worshipper of the Highest".[17]

In addition, Dee and other practitioners of angel magic have utilised magical equipment that was made of wax. The magic of the *Almadel* is worked using a fascinating piece of magical apparatus called an 'almadel' or possibly a 'mandel'. This is a square tablet of white wax, with holy names and characters written upon it with a consecrated pen. Its surface is inscribed with a large hexagram, which covers most of the top of the tablet, with a triangle in the centre. Four holes are drilled through the tablet, one in each corner. More wax from the same source is then used to fashion four candles; each with a small protrusion of wax (like a 'foot'), half way up the length of the candle.

The four candles are placed in candlesticks, and positioned in a

---

[14] This volume contained just two essays by Agrippa plus two of the grimoires mentioned above, another geomancy, and a commentary on spirits, a total of six separate books. A complete modern typeset edition of the *Fourth Book of Occult Philosophy* is due to be published in 2005 by Nicolas Hays.
[15] Florence II-iii-24.
[16] From Sloane MS 2731. See Peterson *Goetia* footnote page 153.
[17] From Sloane MS 3191 *48 Claves Angelicae* first Call.

square pattern with the 'feet' all facing inward. The almadel itself is then placed between the candles, so that it rests on the four 'feet' and is thus elevated above the surface of the table of practice. A small golden or silver talisman is then placed in the centre of the almadel. An earthenware censor is placed on the table directly underneath the almadel.

No less than four almadels must be made, each with its own four candles and an earthen censor. Each is ascribed to a different 'Altitude' or 'Chora', and there is a different colour for each of the four Altitudes. The same golden seal can be used in the operation of each of the Altitudes.

The colour of the almadel belonging to each Chora[18] differs:

first Chora	=	lily white.
second Chora	=	red rose.
third Chora	=	green mixed with a white silver colour.
fourth Chora	=	black mixed with a little green.

Once you have chosen which angels (and thus which Altitude) you wish to work with, you set up the almadel, light the candles, and burn mastic in the censor. The smoke will rise against the bottom of the wax tablet, and is forced to pass through the four holes. So you have candles surrounded by channelled smoke as your arena for the manifestation of the angel. It is within this smoke, and upon the almadel and its golden talisman, that the angel in question should manifest.

The equipment described by the angels for use in Dee's Enochian system of magic include an engraved wax tablet used as a support for the scrying stone in which the angel manifests (as well as four smaller tablets as support or insulation for the legs of the Table of Practice). It would seem that Dee's angel scrying equipment was therefore very much part of the *Almadel* grimoire tradition.

Art Theurgia Goetia

This book is the second part of the *Lemegeton*. This grimoire draws some of its angel seals from the first Book of Trithemius'

---

[18] Although this word is usual translated as Altitude it is probably from the Biblical Greek word, *chora* that means 'an empty expanse, a room or a space or territory (including its inhabitants)'. It is interesting to speculate that 'altitude' might correspond to 'aethyr' as well as to 'chora'.

Steganographia, which was written around 1500 although not published till 1606. The *Theurgia Goetia* is a very interesting name for a grimoire, as it incorporates in one title the evocation of spirits (*Goetia*) and the invocation of angels or other divine beings (*Theurgia*), helping to confirm our observation that the techniques of both these procedures are almost identical. Most importantly, the *Theurgia Goetia* gives the key method for calling and *manifesting* spiritual creatures, with details of the sort of deserted location required by the practitioner, and the use of the crystal stone.

Art Pauline

This forms Part III of the *Lemegeton* or *Lesser Key of Solomon.* The key angel magic idea derived from this grimoire was the idea of a wax 'Table of Practice' which no doubt helped in the concept or the creation of Dee's Holy Table.

Trithemius [1462-1516]

Trithemius was a very important influence on John Dee and many other magicians of his period. He was the mentor of Henry Cornelius Agrippa who wrote the *Three Books of Occult Philosophy,* a book that was probably the most influential and comprehensive book on magic ever written. He not only wrote a short but important text on the invocation of angels into a crystal, but also the *Steganographia,* or the art of concealed writing, which doubles as an intriguing text on angel magic. Dee was so concerned to secure a manuscript copy of this, that he paid a very high price for one.

Simon Forman (1552-1611)

The life of Simon Forman in some ways chronologically paralleled that of John Dee, but at a much less respectable level. Forman was primarily an astrologer and physician, however he too became involved in angel magic in 1589. He got so proficient at it that in Easter 1590, he even wrote his own guide to angel conjuration, with formulas for deriving angelic names, and prayers used to call them.

Enough has been said to demonstrate the continuity of tradition between the magic of the grimoires and the angel magic of John Dee. Let us now look at Dee's application of these different magical strands.

John Dee, Elizabethan Magus

John Dee [1527 - 1609] is the name that first comes to mind when the subject of angel magic comes up, but in fact he was only one of a long chain of relatively well-known English scholars, lawyers, lords and literary men whose taste for angel magic caused them to keep their own diaries of 'Actions with Spirits'. Dee's story is too well known to bear repeating here, but a few events need to be drawn out to show how he fits into the line of transmission.

Dee's character is summed up by the motto on his Coat of Arms, which appears at the end of his *Letters Apologeticall* that was published in 1599. The motto was *veritas praevalebit*, or 'truth prevails'. This sums up Dee's attitude to all his work. He was not concerned with appearances he believed fervently in the truth.

When popular opinion whispered about his being a sorcerer, Dee actually requested King James I to try him for sorcery, so that the truth would come out. Considering that James I was very adverse to any hint of witchcraft, Dee must have been either very certain that the truth would prevail. Or maybe it just betrayed a naïve trust in the perspicacity of the English legal system.

According to his own note (in Sloane MS 3188) he began his interest in angel magic and scrying in 1569 when he was 42. His first experiments consisted in invoking the archangels Raphael and Michael. From that date till his death in 1608 he pursued knowledge through communication with angels and spirits, as well as through the more conventional means of book collecting, experimentation and discussion with his peers. His own output of words was considerable. As we explain in the Bibliography, he was capable of keeping as many as three parallel diaries going at the same time, plus the writing of numerous books and correspondence. We however are interested in the survival and subsequent transmission of just one of his most secret books.

Tale of a Chest: the survival of four key books

Some years after Dee's death in 1608 a sale was held of his remaining books and furniture. At this sale was John Woodall (1570-1643) a 'Paracelsian surgeon' who later recognised and helped abate the causes of scurvy. One of the most influential medical books of the time was *The Surgeon's Mate*, written by John Woodall and first published in 1617. This was the first textbook in any language for the guidance of ship surgeons on long voyages.

Unique when it was published, *The Surgeon's Mate* is neither a comprehensive surgical nor a complete medical treatise, but a textbook to guide novice physicians and inexperienced surgeons who might be expected to treat medical and surgical emergencies peculiar to ships far from land for prolonged periods of time and under tropical conditions. Although Woodall's text was written chiefly for young sea surgeons, it was addressed to a much wider readership because of its treatises on gunshot wounds, gangrene and the plague. The book gained immediate success and was reprinted in 1639, 1653 and 1655. Because it was so universally used by ship surgeons sailing around the world, most of the copies were worn out or lost at sea in the course of time and only eleven copies are now known to exist of the many that were printed.

Woodall's other appointments included election as surgeon to St. Bartholomew's Hospital in 1616, and the promotion in the Barber-Surgeons Company to Examiner in 1626, Warden in 1627 and Master in 1633. At St. Bartholomew's he was a colleague of Sir William Harvey, the discoverer of the circulation of blood.

The year 1626 was noteworthy both for reform and Woodall's pocket. First, the Privy Council decided to pay the Barber-Surgeons Company fixed allowances to furnish medical chests for both the army and navy; and second, the Company requested Woodall to supervise their provision, in addition to his long-standing commitment to supply the East India sea chests.

Despite his dismissal as Surgeon General to the East India Company in 1635 for economic reasons, he retained a monopoly on supplying the Company's medical chests until 1643, the year of his death at about the age of 73, presumably in London[19].

Woodall was obviously a man obsessed by chests, particularly travelling ones, so it is not surprising that at the sale of Dee's goods he bought a particularly fine cedar wood chest 'about a yard & half long' (1.37 metres) with a 'lock & hinges, being of extraordinary neate worke'. Now this chest had a substantial secret draw which neither Woodall nor the next 3 owners were aware of, which is very strange considering Woodall's professional familiarity with chests.

When John Woodall died in 1643, the chest passed to his son Thomas Woodall, Sargeant Surgeon to King Charles II. Ironically John Woodall was also an intimate friend of Elias Ashmole, and so

---

[19] See 'John Woodall. Paracelsian Surgeon', in: *Ambix* 10 (1962), 108-118.

it is almost as if the contents of the chest were destined to eventually reach Ashmole's hands, but failed to do so at this point in time. Instead Thomas Woodall sold the chest, along with other household goods, to a 'joyner' (a carpenter who specialised in furniture) whose shop was on a corner of Adle Street[20] in the city of London.

Map of London in 1593 at the peak of John Dee's career. Adle Street is visible at the top right.

Robert Jones was a confectioner, who lived at the sign of the Plow (a public house) in Lombard Street, near to the present Bank of England. One day in the same year that Thomas Woodall died, he was taken shopping by his wife Susannah Jones, in search of 'household stuff'. They visited Adle Street and bought the chest from the joiner's shop.

---

[20] Adle Street used to be a westerly continuation of Silver Street, now disappeared. It is now called 'Addle' street and is not far from the Thames.

Twenty years after they bought the chest (in 1662) Susannah and her husband were moving it from its usual place when they thought they heard 'some loose thing rattle in it' at the bottom right hand end. Mr Jones therefore "thrust a piece of iron into a small crevice at the bottom of the chest, and thereupon appeared a private drawer, which being drawn out, therein were found divers Books in manuscript, and papers, together with a little box, and therein a Chaplet of olive beades, and a cross of the same wood, hanging at the end of them"[21].

They had found Dee's secret drawer and in it Dee's most precious manuscript books, papers and his olive wood rosary, 54 years after Dee's death. However they did not consider the books to be of any value, as they could not understand then. In due course their maid used up about half of the papers to light fires[22], and for other household uses. When the Joneses finally noticed this they decided to keep the rest of the books and papers rather more safely. It is intriguing to think, that despite the quantity of Dee's manuscripts which have survived the intervening 400 years, that a goodly proportion were destroyed by this unfortunate serving maid [from our calculations, perhaps as many as seven of the 28 manuscript books written by Dee were so destroyed].

Two years later Robert Jones died. A year later in 1666 the Great Fire of London burned out the area where they lived. The chest was too heavy to move, and so it was also destroyed by the fire, but Mrs Jones had the good sense to carry the books out of her house with the rest of her household goods, to the nearby open fields of Moorfields[23] about a mile away. After that she took much greater care of the books.

A few years later, Mrs Jones re-married, this time to a Mr Thomas Wale, one of the Warders in the Tower of London. She took the remaining books and papers with her. Mr Wale was however more curious about the papers and books than her first husband, and so sent them to his good friend the antiquary Elias Ashmole (1617 - 1692). Ashmole was an important scholar and collector of the period. It was later Ashmole's collection of artefacts that was to form the basis of Oxford's Ashmolean Museum, whilst his books helped augment the Bodleian Library in the same city.

---

[21] Ashmole's note written at the front of Sloane MS 3188.
[22] To light 'pyres', not to make pies as rendered by one commentator.
[23] Not 'Moon fields' as one commentator would have it.

In fact it was Ashmole's servant Samuel Storey who collected the parcel of Dee's manuscripts from the Wale's house on 20th August 1672 and delivered it to Ashmole who was then staying with Dr William Lilly at Hersham [near Esher] in Surrey.

Lilly was a close friend of Ashmole's, a well known astrologer, and also a practitioner of angel magic.

You can imagine Ashmole's reaction when he discovered that this collection of manuscripts contained four of Dee's key angel magic books in manuscript. He subsequently painstakingly copied these out by hand.[24]

Dee's Key Manuscripts

The manuscript books in the chest were:

1. *Libri Mysteriorum I - V*
2. *The 48 Claves Angelicae*
3. *Liber Scientiae, Auxilii & Victoriae Terrestris*
4. *De Heptarchia Mystica (Collectaneorum Liber Primus)*, and
5. *A Book of Invocations or Calls*

The first manuscript was Dee's Spiritual Diaries for 1581 to 1583, a day-to-day record of his scrying with Edward Kelly[25]. The other four were the fruits of that scrying.

Ashmole later bound the last 4 books up in one volume (Sloane MS 3191), which were therefore separated from the day by day scrying of the Spiritual Diaries, as he could see that they were the end result of Dee's system, rather than the painstaking scrying that produced it.

On the 5th September the same year (1672) when Ashmole had returned to London, Thomas Wale called upon him, at his office in the Excise Office in Broad Street (just a short walk from where his wife had originally found the chest). They made a deal and Ashmole exchanged a new copy of his *Institution, Lawes & Ceremonies of the most Noble Order of the Garter* for Dee's five manuscript books. Ashmole undoubtedly got the better part of the bargain, and, probably feeling a little guilty, also offered Thomas Wales' son a job as one of his Deputies at the Excise Office (the predecessor of the

---

[24] These copies by Ashmole are now Sloane MS 3678 in the British Library.
[25] Now published as *John Dee's Five Books of Mystery*, edited by Joseph Peterson, Weiser, 2003

modern government department of Customs & Excise) for the then good salary of £80 per year.

Of the 4 manuscripts that Ashmole bound together, three are now well known (see the Bibliography for details of their modern editions), but the last book has remained obscure.

A Book of Invocations or Calls

The last of the books found in the chest is the one of importance to us. This last manuscript was described by Ashmole (in Sloane MS 3188) as "a booke of invocations or Calls, beginning with the squares fill[e]d with letters, about the black cross". It does not have a title, but is sometimes referred to as the *Booke of Invocations or Calls,* or by the title of the table found at the beginning, *Clavicula Tabularum Enochi,* or as *Tabula Bonorum Angelorum Invocationes.* It is also sometimes referred to and as *The Book of Supplications or Invocations.* All these are different names for the same manuscript.

It was written in Latin and had just over 9000 words, and as we shall see below, is in fact the immediate predecessor of the manuscript that is here transcribed, which is more than ten times longer. The Latin manuscript is now bound up in the British Library as part of Sloane MS 3191 and begins at folio 58r with the opening lines:

"Fundamentalis ad DEVM Supplicatio, et Obtestatio pro Angelorum Bonorum, benigno, habendo Ministerio"

This is however only the title of the first prayer. This manuscript consists of:

a.   A circular diagram of the 49 Angelorum Bonorum or Good Angels.

b.   Two Angelic Tables containing 624+20 letters, from which were drawn a number of angelic names and names of god. The first table in the manuscript is marked as incorrect, and the second table noted as corrected Die Luna [Monday] 20 Aprilis, 1587 by the angel Raphael. These tables are the key to the whole manuscript[26].

---

[26] This corrected Table appears again in only one of the manuscripts of our present book, which is Sloane 307. In this form it represents the most correct version of this table, from Dee's point of view, and is in many ways different to the uncorrected version copied by Mathers and presented in the published Golden Dawn papers, and many later books on Enochian Magic based on these.

c.   An opening 'Fundamental Prayer to God and entreaty for the benign ministry of the Good Angels. This, like the following invocations, *specifically includes Dee's name* as the supplicant[27]:

"I, John Dee, your unworthy servant...most humbly and faithfully ask you to favour and assist me..."

This inclusion makes it certain that these were the invocations that Dee prepared or received and which he used for his own personal invocations.

d.   A list of the names of the 24 Seniors[28] assembled from the central 20 letters of the preceding Angelic Table. These 24 Seniors are grouped according to the 4 compass directions, East, South, West and North, 6 per direction[29]. The manuscript includes four Addresses or prayers to the Six Seniors of each of the four compass directions

e.   Next there are lists of 128 lesser Good Angels (together with an equivalent number of corresponding Malevolent angels to balance them). It is instructive that although later writers have characterised Dee as high minded and only interested in angels of light, in fact when you get to the heart of his system you see that he is equally prepared to deal with both Good and Malevolent spiritual creatures, without being unduly worried by the dualism introduced by the Church's thinking on the subject.

For Dee it was a question of getting accurate information, and in doing so he saw that the universe was balanced, not lob-sided. Each group of 16 angels (plus 16 malevolent angels) was qualified to perform certain specific tasks, or give specific information.

This list of angelic competencies is important for several reasons. First it led to some scribal errors, which have enabled us to identify the relationship of the three manuscripts used in the transcription of the present book. Secondly it is interesting to see the list of magical objectives in which John Dee was interested, and for which these angels were supposedly skilled[30]. In brief these were:

---

[27] This feature does not occur elsewhere amongst Dee's papers. Therefore these invocations were obviously of the utmost personal importance to him.

[28] 'Seniors' is a term mentioned by Dee as being specifically derived from *Revelations,* the Apocalypse of St John. In fact it appears as the 24 'elders' in chapter 4, verse 4 of the King James Version (which was only published after Dee's scrying sessions). Dee seems as interested in *Revelations* with its frequent mention of angels, as Aleister Crowley was in it, with its mention of the Beast 666.

[29] An interesting, but probably coincidental, similarity is that the main ring of the Chinese feng shui compass is also divided in the same way into 24 equal sectors.

[30] See also Appendix 1.

i)   Medicine and the cure of sickness (or in the case of the 16 malevolent spirits, the bringing of sickness).

ii)   The discovery, collecting, use and intrinsic powers of metals, also the combining of stones and their powers [in short alchemy in the widest sense].

iii)   Skill in Transformations.

iv)   Comprehending the species and uses of the living creatures in each of the four Elements.

v)   Skill in dealing with mixed natures and other natural secrets (Natural Magic).

vi)   Changing of place.

vii)   Mechanical Arts

viii)   Understanding the secrets of all men, including their inclinations, actions, circumstances, and good or evil deeds.

This list is strangely limited, and indicative of Dee's desire to use the angels to further his scientific knowledge. The last objective could however have been of use in Dee's brief as an 'intelligencer' or spy.

The Present Manuscript

It is clear that the present manuscript is a working expansion of the *Book of Invocations or Calls,* the last of the four manuscript books found in Dee's secret chest. It is for this reason that we have gone into so much detail concerning its provenance.

Someone had access to this manuscript either before it was 'lost' to the world in the chest in 1608, or after it was recovered in 1662. They translated its contents out of Latin and then expanded the invocations more than tenfold. They also included considerably more explicit detail as to how the angelic names were derived from the Table, and how they were to be used. Also, very importantly, whilst Dee included both the correct and an uncorrected Table of the Good Angels at the front of the Latin manuscript, the present English text discards the incorrect material and just provides the corrected Table of Practice. This Table thus supersedes all other versions of these Tables, and particularly those used by the Golden Dawn. The Golden Dawn version, via Regardie has been subsequently repeated by many modern authors. The cells in the Tables in those books sometimes include both correct and incorrect letters within the same square. It is clear that Dee did not do this.

Dating and Du Bartas

In the first page of the prologue to the present manuscript, mention is made of a writer called Du Bartas and his works, and elaboration is called for to provide further context for the manuscripts. Guillaume De Salluste, Seigneur Du Bartas, lived from 1544-1592. In 1578 at the age of 34 he published his seminal work *La Semaine; ou, Creation du Monde* a hugely successful epic rhyming poetic work describing creation and the early Biblical tales of *Genesis* over a period of seven days, but mirroring the Creation from a Protestant viewpoint.

La Semaine was translated into Latin and many modern European tongues and widely distributed, being a 'blockbuster' bestseller of its time. This was probably the best-known literary treatment of the Fall story before Milton's, which eclipsed it. The Fall story of course helped to introduce the problems of duality into the practice of magic. *La Semaine's* seminal influence on his classic work the *Inferno* was acknowledged by Dante Allegheri.

During the period 1579-92 Guillaume De Salluste worked for the French diplomatic service, being stationed between the courts of Queen Elizabeth I of England, King James of Scotland, and the King of Denmark, a position that was doubtless helped by the widespread influence of *La Semaine*. De Salluste also published a translation into French of Ovid's *Metamorphoses* in 1586, which has magical overtones, and a work entitled *Urania or the Heavenly Muse* in 1589.

It is very easy to speculate that this influential figure would have been interested in, and quite possibly involved with magicians of the time, as he certainly moved in the same circles as John Dee. Because our present text specifically mentions Du Bartas, it provides us with a tentative dating. As 1605 was the first publication date in English of *La Semaine*, this is probably the earliest date the present manuscript could have been written[31]. At that date, Du Bartas would have been a controversial reference, and therefore most likely to have been included if the manuscript was written just after 1605.

The Contents of the Manuscript

It seems from examination of changes and corrections in both

---

[31] Of course it is possible that the present author might have seen an earlier French edition.

manuscripts, that Sloane MS 307 is the earlier manuscript, and that Sloane MS 3821 is a copy made for Elias Ashmole. Sloane MS 307 is the only manuscript which contains the key table at the beginning, and therefore it is likely to have been the original copy. The handwriting of a few pages of prayers at the end of Sloane MS 3821 is certainly Ashmole's. Ashmole had painstakingly copied many of Dee's works himself.

In the front of Sloane MS 3821 is a contents list written in another 17th century hand. This clearly shows that *The Practice of the Tables* is just the first part of this manuscript, and the rest, though apparently related, is not part of it. In fact the later section clearly relates to another set of magical operations which we plan to cover in a future volume in this Sourceworks of Ceremonial Magic series.

It is worthwhile transcribing the items in this contents list. Numbering has been added to provide clarity:

1   The Practise of the Tables – fo[lio]. 1.

2   Operations of the East Angle of the Air by Invocation made to the Royal Spirit Oriens – fo[lio]. 217[32].

3   Celestial Confirmations of Terrestrial Observations by certain select powerfull Contractures[?] drawn from the Seven Sarzod[?] Intelligences – fo[lio]. 245.

4   Humble Supplication to Almighty God[33] - fo[lio]. 281.

5   Enoch's Prayer[34] - fo[lio]. 286.

6   Michael Nostradamus's Epistle to his Son in his *Book of Prophecies* from Salon [dated] Mar 1 1555 and to Henry the 2[n]d King of France June 27. 1558[35] – fo[lio]. 297.

7   A Select Treatise as it was first discovered to the Egyptian Magi...from ancient to modern Ages – fo[lio].323.

---

[32] This consists of operations for each of the four Angles of the Table (under the jurisdiction of Oriens, Paymon, Egin and Amaymon) and operations for the 7 days of the week running from Saturn to Venus in the traditional weekly order. This has a different folio sequence, and has not been included in the present work, but will form part of a future volume.
[33] This prayer is in Ashmole's handwriting.
[34] This prayer is in Ashmole's handwriting.
[35] Not too much importance should be attached to the inclusion of these two transcriptions of Nostradamus' letters (which were available in print anyway) as it was common practice amongst collectors' bookbinders to sometimes bind completely unrelated material in the same volume.

The original folio numbers listed in this contents list have since been superseded by a Library renumbering. The renumbering however obscures the separateness of these items, which is clear here.

We know that Sloane MS 307 is the earlier manuscript, and that Sloane MS 3821 is a copy made by Elias Ashmole. The text of both is parallel till folio 158 of Sloane MS 3821. Therefore the material after this folio number was added later.

At this point Sloane MS 307 ends, but Sloane MS 3821 continues with further Operations for each of the four Angles of the Table (under the jurisdiction of Oriens, Paymon, Egin and Amaymon) and operations for the 7 days of the week running from Saturn to Venus in the traditional weekly order, which is not at all like the structure of the first part. Also as we have seen, although the modern folio sequence continues uninterrupted, an earlier folio numbering sequence begins at folio 1 with the Operations of the East Angle, confirmation of the separate nature of this item.

After this are bound in two prayers transcribed by Ashmole. These are addressed respectively to Almighty God and the prophet Enoch, and as they were obviously used by Ashmole in his own angel magic, so they have been here transcribed.

The Author of the Manuscript

The question then is who created Sloane MS 307, which is in effect an extensive expansion of the original Dee manuscript found in Dee's chest. Tentatively we would like to suggest that one strong candidate is Thomas Rudd.

In 1570, just one year after Dee took up invoking the angels, a certain 'T.R.' who may have been 'Thomas Rudd' was involved in the transcription and publishing of Johann Weyer's *Pseudomonarchia Daemonum*[36]. This book, a seminal magical text of the period, has the same roots as the *Goetia,* as it replicates fairly closely the list of the 72 spirits of the *Goetia.* It is also a source of some of the techniques of angel magic.

There were at least another two Thomas Rudds during this period, and because of the similarity between their interests it is likely they were father and son. At least one, and possibly both, knew Dee.

The first Thomas Rudd, who was a doctor, lived from 1583 to 1656. On 19th October 1605, just three years before Dee's death, Thomas

---

36 Johann Weyer (1515-1588) was a pupil of Henry Cornelius Agrippa.

Rudd wrote a letter to Dee about alchemical vitriol. It is conceivable that Dee also shared his work on angel magic as well as alchemy with the young Rudd. If so, then this Rudd may have made a copy of the *Book of Invocations or Calls* before Dee's death. Certainly Dr Thomas Rudd was heavily involved in angel magic. This suggests a creation date for Sloane MS 307 between 1605 and 1608.

In 1651, Thomas Rudd published an edition of Dee's *Mathematical Preface* to Euclid. It is tempting to think this is the son of the Thomas Rudd who knew Dee. This Thomas Rudd styles himself as 'Captain'. This would tie in with a considerable knowledge of navigation, which was another of Dee's well known areas of considerable expertise and interest. It can hardly be a coincidence that not only is the mathematical preface to this work written by Dee, but the book published by Rudd is an edition of Euclid.

Yet another book on geometry (this time the geometry of gunnery) was published by Captain Thomas Rudd in 1668. It is very likely that Captain Thomas Rudd was the son of Dr Thomas Rudd, and that both of them had a serious interest in the practice of angel magic.

Because of his association with Rudd, it is worth mentioning Peter Smart. Smart, who flourished around 1699-1714, was the copyist who transcribed some of Thomas Rudd's manuscripts[37] at the end of the 17th century, and who also claimed to have transcribed one of Dee's manuscripts.[38]

A second candidate for the authorship of Sloane MS 307 is Richard Napier, rector of Great Linford (a relative of John Napier, the inventor of logarithms) who was also definitely a practitioner of angel magic and who met Dee through their joint interest in mathematics. He dined with Dee on at least one occasion[39]. Napier was a pupil and colleague in astrology and magic of Simon Forman. As a result of this dinner with Napier, Dee and Forman also met and dined some 24 days later.

Dee's patron Queen Elizabeth I had died just the year before and Dee was feeling his mortality, and probably looking for someone to whom he could pass his work and precious manuscripts and books.

---

[37] Harley MSS 6481-6486.
[38] More likely to have been a manuscript *owned* by Dee, rather than written by him. This was later published under the very misleading title *The Rosicrucian Secrets of Dr John Dee*.
[39] 2nd July 1604.

So Napier might have had access to his precious *Book of Invocations or Calls* during this period.

This helps with the dating of Sloane MS 307 which was therefore probably expanded from Dee's manuscript either:

a) Between 1605 and before Dee's death in 1608, by someone like Rudd or Napier whom Dee saw as a potential collaborator, or

b) After the discovery of Dee's chest in 1662 but before Ashmole's death in 1692, by someone who had never met Dee.

Because of the topicality of the Du Bartas reference, the first of these two possibilities is definitely the most likely.

Aristocratic Angel Magic after the Sixteenth Century

After Dee's death in December 1608,[40] a number of his books and manuscripts were scattered (except the four key manuscripts hidden away in the chest). By 1626, Dee's library was pillaged, but the remainder was still unsold due to ongoing litigation. Some of Dee's books and manuscripts were finally acquired by Sir Robert Cotton, who, after his death in 1631, left them to his son Sir Thomas Cotton.[41] Amongst these was the manuscript of the later *Libri Mysteriorum* that was published by Casaubon as *A True & Faithful Relation...*[42].

Around this time, copies of grimoires such as the *Lemegeton*, the *Armadel* and the *Ars Notoria*[43] that had been known to Dee in manuscript form began circulating and even appearing in print, attesting to an increasing interest in angelic and demonic evocation. Robert Turner, who lived 1620 - 1665(?), and who should not be confused with the late 20th century Robert Turner who had the same interests, began translating and publishing a number of these grimoires. Several of them were published in 1655 as part of the *Fourth Book of Occult Philosophy*[44] which was attributed to Agrippa.

Elias Ashmole (1617-1692)

Ashmole is the man more than any other, who we can thank for the preservation of Dee's work, and who in his own right attempted a series of experiments in angel magic based on Dee's techniques. In 1646 Ashmole met the astrologer William Lilly (1602-1681) and they became firm friends, staying for long periods at each other's houses. They soon began to share their interests in both astrology and magic and were later to experiment together with some of the techniques of angel magic. Ashmole was eager to learn all he could about these techniques. Lilly knew, and may have introduced Ashmole, early in their relationship, to someone called William

---

[40] Edward Fenton suggests that Dee died instead on 26 February 1609 on the basis of John Pontoys' diary entry which shows a death's head and 'Jno Dee [shown as a triangle], hor[a] 3.a.m.' Pontoys was the beneficiary of Dee's library, and this entry is just as likely to have been the record of a post mortem appearance of Dee to Pontoys in a dream, especially considering the carelessness with which Pontoys appears to have treated Dee's library.

[41] Some 69 years later these were in turn left to the British Museum.

[42] First republished by Askin Publishers in 1973.

[43] Published 1657.

[44] Published in 1655 and reprinted in 1978 by Askin Publishers.

Hodges who regularly called the angels Raphael, Gabriel and Uriel[45].

Ashmole also received a number of Simon Forman's papers, after his death (probably including his detailed manuscript on angel magic) from the son of Sir Richard Napier, who inherited them from Richard Napier, the rector of Great Linford, who in turn was Forman's pupil and colleague.

Ever interested in practical results, on 27th September 1652 Ashmole writes "I came to Mr. Jo. Tompson, who dwelt near Dove Bridge; he used to call [i.e. summon spirits or angels], and had [angelic] responses in a soft voice".

In 1659 Meric Casaubon published *A True and Faithful Relation...* which consisted of Dee's later *Libri Mysteriorum*. Although he had been interested in angel magic for over 20 years it was strangely not till around 1670 that Ashmole borrowed some of Dee's original manuscripts from Sir Thomas Cotton.

The year after Meric Casaubon died in 1671 was the turning point for Ashmole. On 1st August 1672 his servant brought the 4 manuscripts hidden since 1608 in Dee's secret chest to Ashmole, as we have related above. He was staying with Lilly at the time. You can imagine how they eagerly devoured these manuscripts together. A few months after on 26th October 1672, Ashmole began to painstakingly transcribe Dee's early Spiritual Diaries, or *Libri Mysteriorum*. Simultaneously Ashmole began his own Actions with Spirits that he persisted with till at least 1676. The record of these experiments still exists and contains details of a number of interesting, and often very physical, poltergeist and other magical phenomena.

On 13th August 1674 Ashmole records triumphantly that he has completed his transcription of Dee's early *Libri Mysteriorum*. In the same year the British Museum, which was to be the final resting place of these manuscripts, was founded. The BM, as it has been affectionately called by generations of scholars had its origins in the collections of the Royal Society. It is amusing to note that this organisation, which is credited with the founding of experimental and scientific method in England, has also become the eventual custodian of the most important manuscripts and traditions of angel magic in England.

---

[45] see Lilly's *History,* 1774, pp. 49-50.

Baron Somers of Evesham (1651-1716)

John Somers (or Sommers) was Lord Chancellor of England. It is no surprise to discover that he was born near Worcester. He was the eldest son of John Somers, an attorney in a large practice in that town, who had formerly fought on the site of the Parliament. After being at school at Worcester he was entered as a 'gentleman commoner' at Trinity College, Oxford, and afterwards studied law under Sir Francis Winnington, and joined the Middle Temple. He was the author of a major reference book of the time, the *History of the Succession of the Crown of England, collected out of Records, &c.* His interest in the descent of the monarchy reflected Dee's interest in proving that Elizabeth I was heir to the titles of various lands other than England.

In May 1689 Somers was made Solicitor-General, and became King William III's most confidential adviser. He was soon after appointed Attorney-General, and in that capacity strongly opposed the bill for the regulation of trials in cases of high treason. On the 23rd of March 1693, Somers was appointed Lord-Keeper, with the then very significant pension of £2000 a year,[46] and at the same time was made a Privy Councillor. He had previously been knighted. Somers then became the most prominent member of the Junto, the small council that comprised the chief members of the Whig party. When William III left in 1695 to take command of the army in the Netherlands, Somers was made one of the seven lords-justices to whom the administration of the whole kingdom was entrusted during his absence.

In April 1697 Somers was made Lord Chancellor, and was created a peer with the title of Baron Somers of Evesham (a town very near Worcester). His connection with, and financing of, the notorious pirate Captain William Kidd adds an interesting dimension to his character, but caused a parliamentary vote of censure. The vote went in his favour. On the subject of the Irish forfeitures another parliamentary attack was made on him, with a motion being brought forward to request the king to remove Somers from his counsels and presence for ever; but this was also rejected by a large majority. However in consequence of the incessant agitation William finally requested Somers to resign; this he refused to do, but gave up his seals of office to William's messenger. In 1701 he was impeached by the Commons on account of the part he had taken in the negotiations relating to the Partition Treaty in 1698, but the

---

[46] Eighty pounds a year was considered a good income.

impeachment was voted upon, and later dismissed.

On the death of the king, Somers retired almost entirely into private life. From then on he devoted himself to his other passion, angel magic. In fact it is recorded in the catalogue entry for Sloane MS 3821, that he was one of the owners of the manuscript here transcribed. He took a totally scientific interest in many things including angel magic.

His scientific approach is confirmed by the fact that he was president of the Royal Society from 1699 to 1704. He was made president of the council of the Royal Society in 1708 upon the return of the Whigs to power, and retained the office until their downfall in 1710. He died on the 26th of April 1716. Somers was never married, but left two sisters, of whom the eldest, Mary, married Charles Cocks, whose grandson, became the second Lord Somers.

Sir Joseph Jekyll [1663 – 1738], Master of the Rolls

Somers' second sister married Sir Joseph Jekyll, who in turn inherited many of Somer's magical books and manuscripts, including Sloane MS 3821. He also lived in Worcestershire, and took up Somers' interest in angel magic. Jekyll was also an eminent lawyer, like Somers, and appointed Master of the Rolls. He owned a number of manuscripts by Dee and many others about angel magic, many of which he had inherited from Somers. On his death his huge library was sold by auction on 21 January 1740. You can appreciate its size from the fact that the auction lasted for sixteen days. One of the keenest bidders at this auction was Sir Hans Sloane.

Sir Hans Sloane [1660-1753]

The present manuscript Sloane MS 3821, plus almost all the other key angel magic manuscripts were bought by Sir Hans Sloane at Sir Joseph Jekyll's sale. Sloane was an ardent collector, but also fascinated by magic and scrying. He also knew Somers well, and shared his interest in angel magic, as is proved by the correspondence between them[47]. Sloane has always been looked upon as merely a collector, but in fact he was passionately interested in the magical techniques preserved in the manuscripts he collected.

---

[47] Sloane MS 4042 f.159 and Sloane MS 4061 ff. 27-33 consist of letters from John Sommers to Sir Hans Sloane dated 1710.

Goodwin Wharton [1653-1704]

One of the most important Whigs of the time was Goodwin Wharton who definitely knew Somers (and also probably knew Jekyll), and who rose, after many false starts, to eventually become Lord Admiral.

Wharton was described by Keith Thomas [48] as "continuously engaged in a treasure quest for which he enlisted sprits, fairies and the latest resources of contemporary technology". He is even credited with inventing diving gear to try and raise sunken treasure.

His kinsman, Richard Wharton, was not known to share Goodwin's talent for speaking to angels and disembodied spirits, but got involved with his many commercial and speculative ventures, especially searching for sunken treasure, and showed that he was equally zealous in looking for treasure and profit.

In 1683 a friend of Goodwin Wharton shared with him "a method, which he had found among his father's papers for conversing with good angels." Wharton does not say who this was in his Diaries, but it is an intriguing possibility, and some evidence, that it might have been William Lilly's son, thus connecting Wharton's first efforts at angel magic with our present manuscript. After this initial encounter, Wharton became more serious about angel magic, and learned his angel magic from a contact of Mary Paris, his long term companion, seer and bedfellow. His association with Mary Paris was a saga that in some respected reflected Dee's relationship with Kelly. Communication with other spiritual creatures, including the Queen of the fairies, was part of Wharton's passionate interests encouraged by Mary Paris. However such interests did not prevent him, and may even have helped, his final promotion to Lord Admiral of England.

Foundation of the British Museum

Sir Hans Sloane's angel magic manuscripts arrived in the British Museum in 1753, upon Sloane's death, forming the Sloane collection in what is now the British Library. At this point the passing on of these angel magic manuscripts from one scholar magician to another ceases. But a wider range of readers and scholar magicians now had access to these key manuscripts.

---

[48] Keith Thomas in *Religion and the Decline of Magic*, p. 281.

Resurgence of Magic: The Impact of the Golden Dawn

Magical practice resurfaced at the end of the Nineteenth century in the form of an organisation known as the Hermetic Order of the Golden Dawn, whose members numbered amongst them many well know names such W B Yeats, the poet, Florence Farr the actress, and Annie Horniman the tea heiress. To understand where the Golden Dawn sprung from we have to pick up the angel magic thread again.

Frederick Hockley (1808 – 1885)

In the nineteenth century, one of the most influential angel scryers was Frederick Hockley. He was part of the direct line of transmission of angel invocatory techniques, and owned and used Thomas Rudd's 18 Angelic Calls. His scrying generated 30 volumes of conversations with angelic beings. Hockley in turn influenced the late 19th century founders of the Golden Dawn. He was friends with both Kenneth Mackenzie and the Reverend W. A. Ayton, a colleague of Wynn Westcott within the SRIA (Societas Rosicruciana in Anglia).

Hockley is credited, in the History Lecture written by Westcott for members of the Hermetic Order of Golden Dawn, along with Mackenzie and Eliphas Levi, with being one of the adepts who influenced the founding of the Golden Dawn.

It is Hockley who effectively passed the traditions of angel magic to the founders of the Golden Dawn. From Hockley, who was working with both Dr Rudd's angel magic and the *Key of Solomon*, the material was bequeathed to Kenneth Mackenzie, a freemason and member of the SRIA. Mackenzie was also a close friend of the famed French occultist Eliphas Levi (Louis Alphonse Constant) and the Reverend Ayton. Ayton also worked with Mackenzie in the Society of Eight, an occult order founded by Mackenzie in 1883. Another member of the Society of Eight was Frederick Holland, who was also a member of SRIA, and interestingly gave Mathers his first instruction in the Kabbalah.

Reverend William Alexander Ayton (1816-1909)

Ayton was one of the early members of the Golden Dawn. He was 72 when he joined, and brought a wealth of knowledge and experience with him to the Order. Mathers introduced Ayton to W B Yeats, the poet, with the words "He unites us to the great adepts of the past", referring to his friendships with both Kenneth Mackenzie and Eliphas Levi.

Ayton was a strict vegetarian, being a member of the Vegetarian Society, which also required abstinence from alcohol and tobacco of its members. It was Ayton who actually married Mathers to Mina Bergson. Ayton had known Wynn Westcott for some years when he joined the Golden Dawn, and remained in touch with him after leaving in 1903. He was also one of the chiefs of the Stella Matutina from 1903 until his death in 1909.

Wynn Westcott (1848-1925)

Wynn Westcott was one of the three founders of the Golden Dawn. Many people have credited S.L. MacGregor Mathers with being the main creator of the rituals of the Golden Dawn, but in fact Westcott was probably just as active, certainly on a day to day basis.

The creation of the Golden Dawn has been well documented elsewhere[49] and does not need to be outlined here. Westcott was already well-established as an occultist by this time, having become a member of SRIA in 1880, and knowing such figures as Ayton and Kenneth Mackenzie from this period. In 1892 Westcott became the Supreme Magus of the SRIA, and this position brought him into contact with other major occult figures such as Theodor Reuss, head of the OTO, who sought to start a German branch of SRIA.

By profession Westcott was the coroner for Hoxton, and this eventually forced him to leave the Golden Dawn in 1900 due to the unsuitability of his membership of the Order in the eyes of the authorities, when knowledge of it became public. However Westcott remained involved in the Stella Matutina, and in touch with many of the members. It is clear that Westcott was very popular amongst the members of the Golden Dawn, and his role in the organisation has often been downplayed, with Mathers being given more prominence, possibly because of his better known published works, not to mention his colourful life style. There can be no doubt that Westcott was supremely important in the Golden Dawn, and its downfall may be seen as being as much due to his departure as to Mathers' erratic behaviour.

Sloane MS 307 was discovered in the British Museum by one of the above, and when its importance was recognised, a partial copy of it

---

[49] See for example, *Magicians of the Golden Dawn* by Ellic Howe, and *The Golden Dawn, Twilight of the Magicians*, by R.A. Gilbert.

was used by Alan Bennett, Wynn Westcott, Frederick Leigh Gardner, Ayton, and other higher grade members of the Hermetic Order of the Golden Dawn. However to simply say this, ignores the major line of descent of information through the prominent magicians of the nineteenth century which we have already detailed, who may well have also been aware of the manuscript.

Only a small part of Sloane MS 307 was transcribed as *Book H*, and the G.D. members who used this transcript did not seem to be aware at all of the rest of it. Nor were they aware of Sloane MS 3821, or indeed the sections of the text which we found in the 18th century Rawlinson MS D.1067 and Rawlinson MS D.1363 in the Bodleian Library.

We have included *all* of Alan Bennett's copy of Book H in the Appendix 3, in order to show how small a portion of the relevant material was actually used by the Golden Dawn.

Bennett also worked with Gardner, Florence Farr and Charles Rosher, in the inner working group of the Golden Dawn called the "Sphere". This group focused on areas like skrying the Enochian alphabet in the astral, which suggests that this group may have also been using *Book H*. If this were the case, then the latter two members would also have had access to copies of *Book H*. Whilst it is probable that other members of the Order had copies of *Book H*, we have only mentioned the individuals who we know definitely had access to it. The fact that it was considered an inner circle paper, and that its source was a closely guarded secret comes from the scrap of Golden Dawn cipher on Bennett's copy. The cipher simply said 'Sloane MS 307' with the numbers additionally protected from the eyes of the curious by being encoded in Hebrew.

Anyway *Book H* was lost to sight, or maybe suppressed, before the publication of the Golden Dawn papers by Israel Regardie in the 1940s. This suggests that this material may not have been passed on to members of the Stella Matutina. Subsequent work on the Golden Dawn has always used Regardie's text, and no attempt was made to restore this early Enochian paper.

Frederick Leigh Gardner (1857-1930)

Gardner did not join the Golden Dawn until March 1894, though he had been corresponding with Ayton for years prior to this, and was aware through this correspondence of the existence of the Order. He was also a member of the SRIA and the Theosophical Society.

By profession Gardner was a stockbroker, running his own small stockbroking firm.

Gardner rose quickly through the grades to the Second Order, but he left in September 1897 after quarrelling with various members of the group. By all accounts he was a very blunt individual. Apart from his friendship with Alan Bennett and membership of the Sphere group, his other main contributions to occultism are probably the detailed correspondence he kept, and the money he loaned Mathers to help ensure the publication of *The Sacred Magic of Abra-Melin the Mage*.

Alan Bennett (1872-1923)

Alan Bennett was an analytical chemist who suffered from chronic ill health. He was renowned through the Golden Dawn for his magical ability, and was one of the most respected (and possibly feared) members of the order. Bennett was one of the founder members of the "Sphere" group within the Golden Dawn, skrying the astral with other members like Florence Farr and Charles Rosher to learn more about the astral side of subjects like the Enochian alphabet. According to Aleister Crowley, Bennett was a "genius, a flawless genius."

In 1899 Bennett left England due to his health problems, travelling to the Buddhist monasteries of Ceylon. In 1908 he returned to England, and is credited with being the first Buddhist missionary to bring Buddhism to English shores.

The involvement of his most famous magical pupil, Aleister Crowley, with the Golden Dawn's version of Dee's angel magic is too well known to need any amplification here.

A Briefe Introduction vnfolding and explaining ye vse of the
foregoing Table or Tables of ye Earth, as it standeth divided into
fowr parts East. West. North. & South.

Man in his creation being made an Inocent, was also Authorized and
made partaker of ye power presence & Spirit of God, and a Speaker of
his mysteryes and ye society of his Blessed Angells. wherby he knew all
things vnder his Creation, naming them as they were, So that in
his Inocency he became holy in y^e Sight of God, vntill that mighty
devill Choronzon (for so is his true name) envying his felicity and
perceaving that y^e Substance of his Lesser part was fraile and Im=
perfect in respect of his pure Eßer, began to aßaile him and so pre=
vailed,

Then man thus offending became accursed in y^e Sight of God, and so lost
y^e garden of felicity [the true Judgm^t of his vnderstanding] but .
not vtterly y^e favour of God and was driven forth into y^e Earth w^{ch}
being accursed also for his Sake was covered with Bryars and
Brambles and such like, being little profitable to him for food,
vnless he daily Scratched and tore his Skin of his Back to thrust
through the Thicketts for a few plums, &c. or hazarding his Life
among ye devouring Tygers and other wild Beasts of prey, being
a measuring cast which of ye two (in a probable Sense) should
devour the other, but this Subject being learnedly handled by
Du Bartas in his divine workes w^e shall say noe more thereof.
now if Adam after his fall had continued in y^e garden of
Eden his wickedness would have altered y^e Inocency of y^e place
Therefore is paradise distinguished from y^e Earth in respect of
her purity, because the Earth is said and knowne to be corrupt=
ed in respect of mans Sinne. y^{et} although y^e Earth was accurs=
ed for Adams Sake by reason of his fall, The garden of Eden
was not therfore accursed too, for that remaineth still ---
while .

A sample folio from Sloane MS 307 showing the red ruling.

Part 2 - The Manuscripts

The two manuscripts transcribed in Part 3 of this book are Sloane MS 307 and Sloane MS 3821, both from the British Library. These were then checked against manuscripts in the Bodelian Library.

None of the manuscripts has a title page[50], although Elias Ashmole refers to one of the manuscripts as *A Book of Supplications and Invocations.'*[51]

Sloane MS 307 opens with the key Table (see page 58) before starting straight in on the text. Sloane MS 3821 opens at the same point, without the Table entitled '*Clavicula Tabularum Enochi'*. The title of the Table has sometimes been used as a title for the whole manuscript.

The text contains the actual invocations of the Kings, Seniors, Angels (including evil angels) and Spirits of the Table shown at the beginning of Sloane MS 307. None of this material has ever been published in full before. Sloane MS 307 probably was written between 1605 and 1608, whilst Sloane MS 3821 is a copy made from it in the second half of that century. Both are obviously a translation and a tenfold expansion of the Latin of the Dee manuscript which is the last item in Sloane MS 3191.

These manuscripts were both written with considerable care, indicating their value to the scribe. One of the most important features of these very beautifully written manuscripts is that they supply the correct invocations to use in conjunction with the Enochian Tablets, something that has hitherto been missing from the material published on John Dee's magic, the Golden Dawn, or Enochian Magic.

Joseph Peterson's recent excellent publication of John Dee's pre-Casaubon Spiritual Diaries, the early *Libri Mysteriorum,* gives the background, in the form of the diaries, to the original scrying that produced the Enochian system. This present manuscript *is* the working parts of the Enochian system, as used by angel magicians continuously without a break from the 17th to 20th centuries. The

---

[50] Sloane MS 307 has a misleading half-title page written in a latter hand that erroneously entitles it *Clavicula Salomonis,* which is one of the reasons it has not been noticed before.
[51] In Ashmole MS 1790 fol. 52r

system did not suddenly get rediscovered by Mathers after lying fallow for three hundred years, but had been used consistently!

Clay Holden suggests that:

"Sloane 3821 is partly in the hand of Elias Ashmole. I do not know who did Sloane 307. As has been pointed out more than once, neither Dee's MSS. nor Sloane MS. 307 give elemental attributions to the Tablet of the Earth (at least not directly), nor do they use the truncated pyramids found in *Book H* and the G.'.D.'. system."

During our research we also discovered material in the Bodleian Library which is clearly derived from Sloane MS 3821. This material is found within two manuscripts, being Rawlinson D.1067 and Rawlinson D.1363. Rawlinson D.1363 contains a variant of one of the prayers and this has been included to demonstrate textual differences. Rawlinson MS D.1067 contains a unique prayer and a set of invocations which are derivative of the two sets of invocations contained within the Sloane manuscripts, merged together to give "hybrid" invocations. We have included the prayer but not the invocations as they are clearly later and merely repeat the form already given at great length.

We have used Sloane MS 307 as our primary text, and footnoted any variant wording found in the others. However it is obvious that this manuscript has been written as a fair copy of the original draft.

The scribe who wrote Sloane MS 307 obviously got tired of the repetition of some of the formulae, and instead of inserting the correct functions, began to write the special knowledge and abilities of *every* angel as only one of two possibilities:

"the knitting together of natures, and also as well the destruction of nature and of things that may perish, as of conjoining and knitting them together" or

"the true knowledge of physick[52] in all its parts, and the curing of all diseases whatsoever: that are Incident to Humane bodyes".

Unfortunately these were just two of the eight possible functions of the angels. A later hand has gone through, underlining these incorrectly repeated phrases, and inserting in the margin the true functions of the angels concerned. Ashmole even inserted a table in his own hand to keep track of this.[53] We have indicated this change where it appears, which is more than 35 times.

---

[52] Medicine.
[53] See Appendix 1.

Notes on Style used in the Manuscript Transcription

Abbreviations

Some abbreviations have been expanded for convenience of reading. Where the abbreviation "E. W. N. & S." appears in the text it has been expanded to "East, West, North & South".

The abbreviation "C.S. or G.R." has been expanded to "Crystal Stone or Glass Receptacle". This expression is a common expression in many of the manuscripts of angel magic and can be seen fully expanded in for example the *Art Theurgia Goetia*[54] where is says "you may call these spirits into a Crystal stone or Glass Receptacle, [this] being an Ancient & usual way of Receiveing & binding of spirits, This Crystal Stone must be four Inches Diameter set on a Table of Art". Likewise "C.G." has been expanded to "Crystal Glass". This clearly also shows the influence of Goetic magic on Dee's Enochian system.

The term "Essce" has been expanded to its full form of "Essence". However "&", which is used frequently through the manuscript has been maintained, as has "&c" for "etcetera".

Style

Capitalisation and punctuation have been reproduced faithfully from the manuscripts, even where they seem curious. Paragraph structure has also been kept to the original form, resulting in some very long paragraphs that we decided to preserve to maintain the flavour of the original.

In general the spelling of the manuscript has been rationalised to modern English, without interfering with the meaning. For example words like "soe" and "doe" have been transcribed as "so" and "do", "cœlestial" as "celestial", and "Angell" as "Angel".

The grammar of the manuscript is reproduced faithfully, and no attempt has been made to render it into a modern English form, the text being sufficiently clear in its original form as not to warrant such alteration.

---

[54] See *The Lesser Key of Solomon*, edited by Joseph H. Peterson, p. 65.

The colouring of the original is likewise reproduced faithfully. All words printed in red ink are likewise written in red ink in the original manuscripts.

Footnotes

Where footnotes occur, the following is the standard we have adopted:

- 'Insert' or 'omit' indicates additional text or the removal of text.
- Struck-through text indicates that this occurs in addition to the text.
- A single word or phrase indicates a replacement for the word or phrase marked by the footnote.

Manuscript variants

The following abbreviation codes are used in the footnotes to distinguish between the different source manuscripts:

S1: for Sloane MS 307 (the primary text).

S2: for Sloane MS 3821.

R1: for Rawlinson MS D.1067.

R2: for Rawlinson MS D.1363.

G: for the F L Gardner copy of *Book H.*
     (which is a derivative rather than a source manuscript).

Part 3 – Tabula Bonorum Angelorum Invocationes

Clavicula Tabularum Enochi

Top-left quadrant

r	Z	i	l	a	f	A	u	t	l	p	a	
a	r	d	z	a	i	d	p	a	L	a	m	
c	Z	o	n	s	a	r	o	Y	a	u	b	
T	o	i	T	t	X	o	p	a	c	o	C	
S	i	g	a	s	o	m	r	b	Z	n	h	
f	m	o	n	d	a	T	d	i	a	r	i	
o	r	o	i	b	A	h	a	o	z	p	i	
C	n	a	b	r	V	i	X	g	a	z	d	
O	i	i	i	t	T	P	a	l	o	a	i	
A	b	a	m	o	o	o	a	c	V	c	a	
N	a	o	c	o	T	t	n	p	r	a	T	
O	c	a	n	m	a	g	o	t	r	o	i	
S	h	i	a	l	r	a	p	m	z	o	X	

Top-right quadrant

T	a	o	A	d	V	p	t	D	n	i	m	24
a	a	b	c	o	o	r	o	m	e	b	b	48
T	o	g	c	o	n	X	m	a	l	G	m	72
n	h	o	d	D	i	a	l	e	a	o	c	96
P	a	c	A	X	i	o	V	S	P	S	y	120
S	a	a	i	x	a	a	r	V	r	o	i	144
m	p	h	a	r	S	l	g	a	i	o	l	168
m	a	m	g	l	o	i	n	L	i	r	X	192
o	l	a	a	D	a	g	a	T	a	p	a	216
p	a	L	c	o	i	d	X	P	a	c	n	240
n	d	a	z	n	X	i	V	a	a	s	a	264
i	i	d	p	o	n	s	d	a	S	P	i	288
X	r	i	i	h	t	a	r	n	d	i	l	312

Central cross

e	x	a	r	p
h	c	o	m	a
n	a	n	t	a
b	i	t	o	m

Bottom-left quadrant

b	o	a	Z	a	R	o	P	h	a	R	a	
V	N	n	a	x	o	P	S	o	n	d	n	
a	i	g	r	a	n	o	o	m	a	g	g	
o	r	P	m	n	i	n	g	b	e	a	l	
r	S	O	n	i	Z	i	r	l	e	m	u	
i	Z	i	n	r	c	Z	i	a	M	h	l	
m	o	r	d	i	a	l	h	c	t	G	a	
A	o	c	a	n	c	h	i	a	S	o	m	
A	r	b	i	Z	m	i	i	l	p	i	Z	
o	p	a	n	a	l	a	m	s	m	a	L	
d	o	l	o	p	i	n	i	a	n	b	a	
r	X	p	a	o	c	s	i	Z	i	X	P	
a	x	t	i	r	V	a	s	t	r	i	m	

Bottom-right quadrant

d	o	n	p	a	T	d	a	n	V	a	a	336
O	l	o	a	G	e	o	o	b	a	V	i	360
o	P	a	m	n	o	O	G	m	d	n	m	384
a	p	l	s	T	e	d	e	c	a	o	P	408
S	c	m	i	o	o	n	A	m	l	o	X	432
V	a	r	s	G	d	L	b	r	i	a	P	456
O	i	P	t	e	a	a	P	d	o	c	e	480
P	s	V	a	c	n	r	Z	i	r	Z	a	504
S	i	o	d	a	o	i	n	r	z	f	m	528
d	a	l	t	T	d	n	a	d	i	r	e	552
d	i	X	o	m	o	n	s	i	o	s	P	576
O	o	D	P	Z	i	a	P	a	n	l	l	600
r	g	o	a	n	n	R	A	C	r	a	r	624

Clavicula Tabularum Enochi transcription[55]

r	Z	i	l	a	f	A	U	t	i	p	a			
a	r	d	z	a	i	d	p	a	L	a	m			
c	Z	o	n	s	a	r	O	Y	a	u	b			
T	o	i	T	t	X	o	p	a	c	o	C			
S	i	g	a	s	o	m	r	b	Z	n	h			
f	m	o	n	d	a	T	d	i	a	r	i			
o	r	o	i	b	A	h	a	o	z	p	i			
C	n	a	b	r	V	i	x	g	a	z	d			
O	i	i	i	t	T	p	a	l	O	a	i			
A	b	a	m	o	o	o	a	c	v	c	a			
N	a	o	c	o	T	t	n	p	r	a	T			
O	c	a	n	m	a	g	o	t	r	o	i			
S	h	i	a	l	r	a	P	m	z	o	X			

T	a	O	A	d	V	P	t	D	n	i	m	24
a	a	b	c	o	o	r	O	m	e	b	b	48
T	o	g	c	o	n	X	m	a	l	G	m	72
n	h	o	d	D	i	a	l	e	a	o	c	96
P	a	c	A	x	i	o	V	S	P	S	yl	120
S	a	a	i	x	a	a	r	v	r	o	i	144
m	p	h	a	r	s	l	g	a	I	O	l	168
m	a	m	g	l	o	i	n	L	i	r	x	192
o	l	a	a	D	a	g	a	T	a	P	a	216
p	a	L	c	o	i	d	X	P	a	c	n	240
n	d	a	z	n	X	i	V	a	a	s	a	264
l	i	d	p	o	n	s	d	a	S	P	i	288
X	r	i	i	h	t	a	r	n	d	I	l	312

e	x	a	r	p
h	c	o	m	a
n	a	n	t	a
b	i	t	o	m

b	o	a	Z	a	R	o	P	h	a	R	a			
V	N	n	a	x	o	P	S	o	n	d	n			
a	i	g	r	a	n	o	o	m	a	g	g			
o	r	P	m	n	i	n	g	b	e	a	l			
r	s	O	n	i	Z	i	r	l	e	m	u			
i	Z	i	n	r	c	Z	i	a	M	h	l			
m	o	r	d	i	a	l	h	C	t	G	a			
Æ	o	c	a	n	c	h	i	a	s	o	m			
A	r	b	i	Z	m	i	i	l	p	i	Z			
O	p	a	n	a	l	a	m	s	m	a	L			
d	O	l	o	P	i	n	i	a	n	b	a			
r	x	p	a	O	c	s	i	Z	i	X	P			
a	x	t	i	r	V	a	s	t	r	i	m			

d	o	n	p	a	T	d	a	n	V	a	a	336
O	l	o	a	G	e	o	o	b	a	v	i	360
o	p	a	m	n	o	O	G	m	d	n	m	384
a	p	l	s	T	e	d	e	c	a	o	p	408
s	c	m	i	o	o	n	A	m	l	o	X	432
v	a	r	s	G	d	L	b	r	i	a	P	456
o	i	p	t	e	a	a	P	d	o	C	e	480
P	s	v	a	c	n	r	Z	i	r	Z	a	504
S	i	o	d	a	o	i	n	r	z	f	m	528
d	a	l	t	T	d	n	a	d	i	r	e	552
d	i	x	o	m	o	n	s	i	o	S	P	576
O	o	D	P	Z	i	a	P	a	n	l	i	600
r	g	o	a	n	n	Q	A	C	r	a	r	624

[55] Literally the 'Key of the Tables of Enoch.' It has not always been possible to determine if the scribe intended capitals for letters like Z, X, O and P. Note the double letters at positions 120 and 481, and the interesting form at 312.

[A Brief Introduction to the Use of the Tables[56]]

A Brief Introduction unfolding and explaining the use of the foregoing Table or Tables of the Earth[57], as it standeth divided into four parts, East, West, North, &[58] South.

Man in his Creation being made an Innocent was also Authorized and made partaker of the power presence & Spirit of God, and a speaker of his mysteries and the society of his[59] Blessed Angels, whereby he knew all things under his Creation, naming them as they were so that in his Innocency he became holy in the sight of God, until that mighty Devil Choronzon[60] (for so is his true name) envying his felicity and perceiving that the substance of his lesser part was frail and imperfect in respect of his pure essence, began to assail him and so prevailed.

Then man, thus offending became accursed in the Sight of God, and so lost the garden of felicity [61] [the true judgement of his understanding] but not utterly the favour of God and was driven forth into the Earth, which being accursed also for his sake was covered with Briars and Brambles and such like[62], being little profitable to[63] him for food, unless he daily scratched and tore his[64] skin of his Back to thrust through the Thickets for a few plums, &c or hazarding his life among the devouring Tigers, and other wild Beasts of prey, being a measuring cast which of the two (in a probable[65] sense) should devour the other, But this subject being learnedly handled by Du Bartas[66] in his divine works we shall say no more thereof.

---

[56] Headings in [square brackets] have been inserted to clarify the structure. They are not in the original manuscript.

[57] It is interesting that although these Tables are usually referred to as Angelic Tables, here they are clearly referred to as Tables of Earth.

[58] Throughout the Gardner manuscript "&" is replaced by "and".

[59] G: "the".

[60] Choronzon appears in the guise of the original tempter in the Garden of Eden, guarding the Tree of Knowledge.

[61] The Garden of Eden.

[62] S2: Inserts "things".

[63] G: "unto".

[64] G: "the".

[65] G: Gives the word "profitable" here, but it has clearly been mis-transcribed.

[66] For information on Du Bartas see Part 1.

Now if Adam after his fall had continued in the garden of Eden his wickedness would have altered the Innocency of the place. Therefore is paradise distinguished from the Earth in respect of her[67] purity, because the Earth is said and known to be corrupted in respect of man's Sins, yet although the Earth was accursed for Adam's Sake by reason of his fall, The garden of Eden was not therefore accursed too, for that remaineth still where it was first erected & ordained by the [68] mighty Creator in the vale of Jehosaphat[69] wherein liveth Ely, Enoch[70], and John, who shall never die &c.

Adam for his Transgression being cast out of paradise, and driven a great distance from there into that depraved world, being there as dumb & not able to speak (for during the time of his being in Paradise) he spake the[71] Angelical and Celestial Language of which he also lost the benefit and was deprived of[72] in his fall, and was never since heard of or known to[73] any, but some such particular persons, whom God hath been pleased to permit the same to be revealed [74], by the converse society, and oft times familiar community between them and the Celestial Angels.

He began of necessity to speak the language which we call Hebrew (yet not the same Hebrew which is amongst us now). In which Language he declared and delivered to[75] his posterity the nearest Knowledge he had of God, his creatures, and other his manifold and bountiful mercies and Justice. And from his own self divided his speech into 3 parts viz. Twelve, Three, and Seven[76], the number whereof remaineth but the true forms & pronunciations are wanting, and therefore is not of that force and goodness that is was originally in its own dignity, much less to be compared with that Angelical & Celestial Language which Adam verily Spake during his Innocency, and wherein (by divine permission) great secrets and

---

[67] Note Eden is described as female.
[68] G: "that".
[69] Between Jerusalem and the mount of Olives is the vale of Jehosaphat, under the walls of the city
[70] Enoch is particularly significant, given that Enoch was supposed to be able to converse with angels.
[71] G: Omits "the".
[72] G: Omits "of".
[73] G: "unto".
[74] G: Inserts "unto".
[75] G: "unto".
[76] An obvious reference to the 12 Single, 3 Mother and 7 Double letters of the Hebrew Alphabet.

mysteries have been revealed to several holy, pious reserved, and studious men of old, but we in this latter Age being (in a manner) ever deprived of so great and inestimable a Benefit and Blessing as to converse with Celestial Angels, as not being worthy so to do, are left also as depraved in our Judgements and reasons &c. Thus when Adam offended he received punishment therefore that he was turned out into the Earth, for if he had been turned out to[77] a blessed place, then it could not be said that he was turned out, for he that is turned out goeth to[78] dishonour (for God Knowing he would offend knew also how to dishonour him). So from Innocency, through his fall, he was turned out to corruption into a prison prepared for him before: Adam being thus cast out and the Earth cursed for his Transgression, thereby bringing all misery and wretchedness into the World, which also befell all posterity and shall even so continue to[79] the end of time, for then did God suffer and permit the Spirit of malice to enter into, and have power in the world, and ever since is perfect love taken away from amongst men, who are always at variance, striving to weed & destroy one another, and so it must be, and will be to the End. And in the same instant that Adam was expelled and the Earth accursed for his sake, yet the infinite mercies of God were such, that he also put a restraint to the wicked spirits, that by their envy and malice they should not quite extinguish & destroy the admirable works of his Creation, neither by their subtle Temptations and Illusions, for lo[80], Then said the Lord of Hosts let the world have his[81] time; and let there be keepers, watchmen[82], and princes placed over her, for years months and days &c.

From hence it plainly appeareth that the world was not committed to their charge with their creation but afterwards in diverse times and offices both to God and man.

Now we are to understand that there are 4 Angels as overseers thereof, whom the Eternal God in his providence hath placed against the usurping Blasphemy, misuse, & stealth of the wicked

---

[77] S2, G: "into".
[78] G: "unto".
[79] G: "till".
[80] G: Omits these two words.
[81] S2: "its".
[82] The term "watchmen" clearly links to the watchtowers, and their occurrence in Enochian magic.

and great Enemy or[83] Tempter of man, the Devil, to the end, he being put out into the Earth, and permitted to Tempt and ensnare[84] the sons of man to all manner of wickedness and disobedience to Almighty God their Creator & Protector (yet this way as a Restriction), that his envious will might be bridled, The determinations of God fulfilled, and his creatures kept and preserved within the compass and measure of order, what the evil spirit doeth, the good Angels permit and what they wink at, the evil spirit wasteth, and mostly when they[85] think themselves assured then they feel the Bit[86], Thus doth[87] God and the good Angels put a snaffle[88] to the wicked. Each one of these 4 Angels is a mighty prince, a mighty Angel of the Lord, and are by him according to his divine order and decree as chief watchmen and overseers set over several & respective parts of the world, viz. East, West, North & South as (under the Almighty) their governor, protector & defender. And the Seals & Authority of whom are confirmed in the beginning of the world. And to every of[89] them belong 4 characters, being tokens of the presence of the Son of God, by whom all things were made in[90] creation, and are the natural marks of Holiness, and unto which belong 4 Angels severally, and before each one of those great Angelical Princes, is[91] borne 3 Banners wherein is[92] displayed 3 great names of God, comprehending 3, 4 & five[93], which in all are Twelve[94], and those Twelve[95] great names of God govern all creatures upon Earth both visible and invisible[96].

---

[83] G: "and".
[84] S2: "~~Ensnare~~".
[85] G: Inserts "(the Evil Ones)".
[86] "Bit" here refers to a horse-bit.
[87] G: "do".
[88] A snaffle is a type of horse-bit, so its use here is clearly in the context of control as when a horse is bridled.
[89] G: Omits "every of".
[90] G: Inserts "the".
[91] G: Corrects the grammer, replacing "is" with "are".
[92] Ibid.
[93] G: "5".
[94] Ibid.
[95] Ibid.
[96] A circular diagram showing these 12 banners appears in Sloane 3191 which was Dee's original of the current manuscript. The banners run from the East clockwise: Oro, Ibah, Aozpi, Mor, Dial, Hctga, Oip, Teaa, Pdoce, Mph, Arsl, Gaiol around a square marked 'Terra' emphasising again that these are Tables of Earth.

[The Hierarchy of Angels]

Each one of these 4 Great Angelical Princes hath 5 providential[97] Angels or guardian[98] princes attending him, under whom are Six[99] Angels called Seniors which St John remembereth[100] (who as their offices are &c)[101] judge the government of their mighty Angelical King, and fulfil the will of God as it is written &c.

Under which Seniors are 4 presidential good Angels, who are dispositors of the commands of those that are the Superior governors of the four principal Angles or Quarters, East, West, North and South, over the which they are severally and respectively constituted and set over[102] &c.

Under whom again are many and numberless of Aerial ministering Subservient Spirits of several offices both good and bad. All which shall be further explained in the opening & exemplifying[103] the following[104] Tables &c which is as followeth.

Here we have 4 Tables or Quadrangles, which are but one General Table, only divided into 4 Parts, East, West, North, & South, In the centre between these 4 Quadrangles is another little Table joined cornerly to them all, and[105] serveth to unite the[106] several parts of them together, according as they are to be diversely referred as shall be seen hereafter &c.[107]

Each Single Quadrangular Table containeth 12 Squares athwart and 13 downwards[108]. The Two middle lines downwards that are of

---

[97] S2: "Presidential".
[98] S2, G: Omits the "t" given in the original text, making the word "guardian".
[99] G: Gives the number "6" rather than writing it out in full.
[100] This is a reference to the book of *Revelations* chapter 4 verse 4 in The Bible.
[101] S2: "to".
[102] G: Records "attributed and set &c".
[103] G: Inserts "of".
[104] G: Adds "of" and omits "following". The Table appears at the beginning of the manuscript.
[105] G: Inserts "which".
[106] S2: Omits "the".
[107] The Table of Union.
[108] In short, there are four Elemental Tables, each of 12 by 13 squares. Each of these Tables is attributed to one of the four compass directions. Clockwise from the top left: East, South, West, North ???

black letters enclosed also within black Ruled lines, and the middle line going athwart that again composed also of black letters enclosed between two black Ruled lines and standing crosswise in the middle of the two perpendicular or upright lines make up the name of the mighty Angelical King, and the[109] 3 names of God displayed in the Regal Banners[110] borne before him, being the Arms of the Ensign[111], and the names of Six[112] Angelical Seniors, governing in that Angle or Quarter of the compass which they are set over.

In every Lesser Angle of every Quadrangular Table standeth also black letters enclosed within black Ruled lines crosswise in form of a crucifix thus ✝[113] out of which are collected the Names of God that call forth, and constraineth[114] those Angels & Spirits both good & bad, that are to be gathered out of that particular lesser Angle, belonging & serving to that Quarterly Angle or Table.

---

[109] G: Omits "the".
[110] S2: "Banner".
[111] In this context "Ensign" refers to an individual flag holder, not a design.
[112] G: "6".
[113] G: A drawing of a 5x6 square cross is given here in the text.
[114] G: "constrain".

[East Quadrangle]

The particular exemplification of all is as followeth viz As in the East Quadrangle or Quarterly Table,[115] which is the first Quadrangle, on the top towards the left hand, [116] The two middle upward or perpendicular black lines, the first of them from the top downward to the bottom hath these thirteen letters viz f, i, a, X, o, a, A, u[117], t[118], o, t[119], a, r. The second which is the next upright or perpendicular black[120] line to it from the top down to the bottom hath these thirteen letters, a[121], d, r, o, m, t[122], H[123], i, p[124], o, t, g, a. The middle black line standing crosswise athwart these two upright or perpendicular black lines hath these Twelve letters, o, r, o, i, b, A, H, a, o, z, p, i – being all added together, and set crosswise in order as they stand in the Quadrangular Table. Stand thus, as in the annexed form is represented and so make the similitude of a cross.

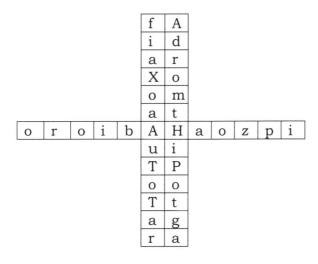

In the centre of this cross like example is contained the name of the

---

[60] G: Opens brackets here.
[61] G: Closes brackets here.
[117] G: Records this letter as "V".
[118] Note the table drawn in the text has a capital T but a small t is given in the text here. S2, G: records it as "T".
[119] Ibid.
[120] G: Omits this word.
[121] Note the table drawn in the text has a capital A but a small a is given in the text here. Again S2, G: records the capital "A".
[122] G: Records this letter as "T".
[123] G: Records this letter as "h".
[124] Again, small p in text, capital P in table.

great and mighty Angelical King set as a governor, overseer, or watchman over the East angle and is thus collected.

There is (B) the fifth letter in the middle black line athwart and (a)[125] the sixth letter in the perpendicular line accounting from the top downwards and (T) the sixth letter in the second perpendicular from the top downwards and (a)[126] the fifth letter from the Right hand to the left in the said middle over thwart[127] line and (i)[128] the sixth letter ascending from the lowermost part of
the second perpendicular line upwards and (v)[129] the sixth   A   T
letter ascending from the lowermost part of the first   B   A
upright line standing thus, unto which six letters bring   V   I
added together put the letter (a)[130] or (h)[131] which two letters are concentrated with the aforesaid six letters, either of them serveth, and these seven or eight letters make up the name BATAIVA or BATAIVH, or BATAIVAH, which letters set   A   T
together as they stand in the Table,   B A H A
& they stand heteromaces[132] or centrally therein thus.   V   I
And this is the true name of the mighty Angelical King, watchman[133] and overseer of the East Angle or Quarter of the world, &c, moreover divide the middle cross line into 3 parts from the left hand to[134] the Right, and divide it into 3, 4 or[135] five[136] letters and they will make up these 3[137] words Oro Ibah Aozpi, which are the 3 great names of God borne in the 3 Banners or the Arms of the Ensigns belonging to the great and mighty Angel BATAIVA, King and governor of the East Angle.

The names of the six Angelical Seniors ruling in the East Angle under this great prince BATAIVA[138] which[139] are thus collected. The

---

[125] S2, G: Records capital "A".
[126] Ibid.
[127] G: "athwart".
[128] G: Records as capital "I".
[129] Ibid.
[130] Ibid.
[131] Ibid.
[132] S2: Crossed out by Ashmole, and replaced by 'Hebecomaces'.
[133] S2: "~~watchtower~~".
[134] G: "unto".
[135] G: "and".
[136] G: Records the digit "5".
[137] G: "three".
[138] G: Spells this with the additional H, i.e. "BATAIVAH".
[139] G: Omits this word.

sixth letter of the middle transverse or cross line going athwart the two upright black lines is (A) and the letters from the right hand to the left following it as it were backwards are (b.i.o.r.o.) which maketh the name[140] Abioro, and it is the name of the first Angelical Senior made up of six letters, and if the letter (H) which followeth the letter (A) and is the seventh letter of the said transverse line, be added to[141] And set before the other six letters it maketh the name Habioro, and is the name of the said first Angelical Senior comprehended of seven letters.

Then take the aforesaid letter (A) again, (being the sixth letter in the middle transverse black line as aforesaid) and ascend upward from thence to the top or uppermost letter of the first upright black line and they are (A.a.o.X.a.i.f.) making the word Aaoxaif[142] which is the name of the second Angelical Senior.

Then again take the letter (H), which is the seventh letter, in the said middle transverse black[143] line, from the left to the Right and ascend from thence to the uppermost letter in the second perpendicular line and the letters are (H.t.m.o.r.d.a.) [144] which maketh the word Hetemorda, [145] and is the name of the Third Angelical Senior.

Then again take the letter (H) the seventh in the middle transverse line from the left to the Right, and the letters following it forwards and they are (H.a.o.z.p.i.) which maketh the word Haozpi, and is the name of the fourth Angelical Senior composed of the[146] six letters, and if the letter (A) that standeth just next before the letter (h)[147] be added thereto, and set before the other six letters then it maketh the name Ahaozpi, which is the name of the 4th[148] Angelical Senior composed of seven letters.

---

[140] S2: Inserts "of".
[141] S2: "too".
[142] S2: ", if".
[143] Ibid.
[144] G: "(H.T.M.o.r.d.A.)".
[145] G: "Hetomorda".
[146] S2, G: Omits this word.
[147] G: Capitalises, "H".
[148] G: "fourth".

Again take the said letter (H) the seventh letter of the middle transverse line, and descend from thence downwards to the bottom or last letter in the second perpendicular line and the letters are (H.i.p.o.t.g.a.) making the word Hipotga, which is the name of the fifth Angelical Senior.

And then again take the letter (A) being the sixth letter in the middle transverse line from the Left to the Right and from thence also descend downwards to the lowermost letter in the first upright line which are these (A.u.T.o.T.a.r.) which maketh the word Autotar, & this[149] is the name of the sixth & last Angelical Seniors ruling in the East Angle.

The name of this great Angelical and mighty Angel or King of the East BATAIVA, upon whom all the Angels and Spirits of the four[150] Lesser Angles in the Quadrangle of the East, attend and give obedience, calleth out the fore recited six Seniors whose offices are to give Scientiam Rerum Humanarum et Judicium[151], according to the nature of their parts, as in the East after one manner, In the West after another, and so of the rest according to their several gubernations[152].

Now for the sixteen Servient Angels next in order under the six Angelical Seniors in this Eastern Quadrangle their names are to be collected and composed out of each Lesser Angle attendant on the greater Angle thus. In the uppermost Lesser Angle on the left hand of this Quadrangular Table, there is a small crosslike form of black letters, whose perpendicular or upright line reacheth from the top of the said Lesser Angle to the middle black transverse line that goeth athwart that Quadrangle and containeth six letters from the top downwards which are (i.d.o.i.g.o.) making the name Idoigo, the which is one name of God, which is used to call forth the subservient good Angels, who are attendant next in order under those sixteen Angels next succeeding the Six Seniors according to their graduation.

---

[149] S2, G: Omits this word.
[150] G: "4".
[151] A knowledge of sciences, facts and laws. ??
[152] Governors.

The transverse line going athwart that upright line in this Lesser Angle, being the uppermost line but one, is of five letters, & these are[153] (A.r.d.z.a.)[154] making the name Ardza, which is another name of God; now as the Benevolent Angels serving in this said Lesser Angle, under the aforesaid sixteen[155] are ruled by and called forth by this name Idoigo, so by the name Ardza they do what they are commanded, all which shall be further explained in exemplification hereafter following in their proper places.

a	r	d	z	a
		i		
		o		
		i		
		g		
		o		

[156]This annexed Example is the form of the black letters as they stand crosswise in the uppermost lesser Angle of the Quadrangle over this lesser[157] transverse[158] are 4 red letters which are (r.z.l.a.)[159] setting a side or leaving out the black letter (i) standing in the middle between them, and it maketh

the name Vrzla,[160] and this is the substance of the[161] first of those sixteen Angels before spoken of, bearing rule next under the six seniors in the East[162] Quadrangle. Then take away the first of these Red letters which is (r) and make it the last and it maketh the name Zlar or Zodelar, (for z extended is to be pronounced zod) which maketh the name of the second of the aforesaid Sixteen[163] Angels. Again make the first letter of the second name which is[164] (z] the last

---

[153] G: Replaces "& these are" with "and they are these".
[154] G: Gives a small "a" for "ardza".
[155] S2: "and".
[156] G: Gives the top line as well thus:

r	Z	i	l	a
a	R	d	z	a
		o		
		i		
		g		
		o		

[157] G: Omits this word.
[158] G: Includes the phrase "upper black line".
[159] G: Gives a capital "Z".
[160] S2, G: Gives this name as "Urzla". In this period 'U' and 'V' were interchangeable letters.
[161] G: Inserts "name of the".
[162] G: "Eastern".
[163] S2: "Angles Angels".
[164] G: Replaces "which is" with "the".

of the third name and the letters will be Larz and it maketh[165] up the name Larzod which is the name of the third of the sixteen Angels aforesaid. Then again by making the first of those 4[166] letters of this last name, the last letter thereof, then will these letters be (a.r.z.l.) which makes the name Arzel, and is the fourth of the aforesaid sixteen Angels, and the[167] last are the four Superior Angels bearing rule under the Six Seniors in this first lesser Angle serving to the[168] greater[169] Eastern Quadrangle, and as to the names[170] of these 4 Angels, and governing in this Lesser Angle serving to the greater Quadrangle or East Quarter of the Table, and thus collected and gathered together, so are the names of the other Twelve Angels set as governors and Superiors over the 3 other Lesser Angles subservient to this Quadrangle.

As for example the second lesser succeeding Angle of this eastern Quadrangle[171] is that on the Right hand above next to this here above explained and hath in its upright or perpendicular black line these six letters (j.l.a.c.z.a.)[172] making the name Jlacza,[173] which is also a great name of God, The transverse black[174] line whereof hath these letters (p.a.l.a.m.) which being set together as they are in[175] the

---

[165] S2: "makes".
[166] G: "four".
[167] G: "these".
[168] S2: "lesser".
[169] S2: "Eastern".
[170] S2: "of".
[171] G: "Quarter".
[172] G: Replaces the "j" with an "I".
[173] And hence G: gives "Ilacza" instead of "Jlacza".
[174] G: Omits this word.
[175] G: Gives the table with the top line included, thus:

U	T	i	p	a
P	A	L	a	m
		a		
		c		
		z		
		a		

	j		
P a	L	a	m
	a		
	c		
	z		
	a		

Quadrangular Table, stand as in this annexed[176] exemplification is hereunto affixed[177].

The four Red letters over the black transverse line of this second lesser Angle of this Eastern Quadrangle are (V.t.p.a.) [178] making the name Vtepa, [179] which is the name of the fifth of the aforesaid sixteen Angels, and the first of the four Superior Angels set over the second Lesser Angle, and governing therein next under the six Seniors.

Then as before in the example of the first lesser Angle, take away the first letter of these four, and make it the last of the name then it will be Tepau, [180] which is the name of the sixth of the Sixteen Angels aforesaid, and the second of the great benevolent Angels governing in this second lesser Angle.

Again take away the first letter of the second name, and make it the last, then it will be Paut, which is the name of the seventh forementioned Angels and of the third[181] benevolent great Angels set over this second Lesser Angle.

Likewise take away the first letter of this last name, and make it the last then it will make the name Autep, which is the name of the Eight [182] of the four Recited Sixteen Angels, and of the 4th [183] governing Angel set over this second lesser Angle.

The other eight Angels names are to be collected after the same manner out of the other two[184] lesser Angles serving in the Eastern Quadrangle. That on the left hand underneath being the third Lesser Angle successively next following to the second, being that lesser Angle on the right hand above as is aforesaid, and that on the Right hand underneath is the fourth and last of the lesser Angles serving to[185] this Quarterly great Angle.

---

[176] G: Replaces "this annexed" with "the".
[177] G: Replaces "is hereunto affixed" with "above".
[178] G: Gives "U" rather than "V".
[179] Hence G: gives "Utepa" rather than "Vtepa".
[180] G: Gives this word as "Tpau".
[181] G: Inserts "of the".
[182] G: Adds an "h" to make the word "Eighth".
[183] G: "fourth".
[184] S2: "lesser".
[185] G: "unto".

73

Every of the aforesaid four Angels [186], whose names [187] are thus gathered out of every lesser Angle of the greater Quadrangle wherein they are contained are great and Benevolent Angels, and bear Rule and govern [188] over those several Angles [189] successively, under whom also are several Benevolent Angels, but far more Inferior in power, yet of the same nature, as their Superiors are, under whom again are many Angels and spirits of various and different nature [190], both good and bad, whose offices [191] are also manifold & various [192] gradually in their orders according as divine Authority hath directed [193] and appointed, both as to good and bad effects & purposes as for examples; those Benevolent Angels whose offices are of physick, as they by their temperance and benevolence cure diseases, and by their splendidness [194] and celestial irradiation [195] preserve the Elemental Vigour, and Radical humidity of things to the [196] prolongation of Life & health, according to the nature of their parts, &c. So the malevolent and Evil Spirits, whose names are collected out of the same lesser Angles [197] from whence the good Angels names are gathered of the aforesaid offices [198], are opposite in nature to them, as to their malignity and envy to [199] the prosperity of things, for instead of curing diseases they bring them in [200], and when permitted by the Superior powers do thereby mortify and destroy things, and by their more gross, Evil, Terrestrial and poisonous rays (being comparatively the same as their Aerial vapours of the Earth) weaken [201], In fact mortify and destroy the elemental vigour & radical moisture of things, so that if their envious will [202] were not bridled and restrained [203], nothing in this

---

[186] S2: "Angles", probably a copyist's error, substantiated by the following "~~whose names are thus gathered~~".

[187] S1: Repeats the phrase "whose names are thus gathered" in the text here.

[188] G: "governance".

[189] S2: "~~Severally~~".

[190] S2: "natures".

[191] S2: "~~also~~".

[192] G: Inserts "and".

[193] S2: "decreed".

[194] G: "splendour".

[195] S2: "irradiations".

[196] S2: "~~prolongation~~".

[197] S2: "angle".

[198] The Evil Spirits are derived from exactly the same place as the Good Spirits or angels. Dee is not as sanctimonious as he has been portrayed and knew full well that spiritual creatures of whatever hue were to be dealt with in the same way.

[199] G: "of".

[200] G: Replaces "bring them in" with "cause them".

[201] G: "would".

[202] G: Replaces "envious will" with "envy".

[203] G: Transposes this to "restrained and bridled".

World could be preserved, but of this matter, more shall be said &[204] explained in its proper place.

As for (example) the names of several Benevolent Angels Subservient to those Superior Angels set over & governing in each Lesser Angle in this Eastern Quadrangle they are to be collected out of each Lesser Angle as follows[205].

c	z	n	s
T	o	T	t
S	i	a	s
F	m	n	d

In the first Lesser Angle of this East Quadrangle, and under that black transverse line, are 4 lines of Red letters, and leaving out the black Letters in the middle upright line going between them, do stand[206] in the lesser Angle of the Quadrangle as in the[207] annexed example is represented the first lines whereof hath those 4 letters c.z.n.s. making the name cezodenes which is the name of one Inferior benevolent Angel serving in this first lesser Angle of the East Quadrangle.

Then next under that, the line hath these 4 letters T.o.t.t. making the name Totet, which is the[208] name of another subservient great Angel[209] serving in this said Lesser Angle.

The third line hath those four[210] letters s.i.a.s. making the name sias, which is the name of another good Angel subservient to this said Lesser Angle.

The fourth and last line of this Lesser hath these 4 letters F.m.n.d. making the name Efemende, which is the name of another benevolent Angel subservient to this aforesaid lesser Angle in the East Quadrangle.

The subservient good Angels[211] thereof are to be gathered out[212] in

---

[204] G: Omits "said and".
[205] S2: "followeth".
[206] G: Replaces "do stand" with "stands".
[207] G: Omits "the".
[208] S2: "a".
[209] S2: "great".
[210] G: "4".
[211] G: Inserts "of the 2nd Lesser Angle" here.
[212] G: Replaces "gathered out" with "selected".

the same manner as the former is[213] exemplified, as thus, under the black transverse line of this 2nd[214] Lesser Angle, are also 4 lines of red letters, and leaving out these[215] black letters that stand between them in the middle upright line, do[216] stand in this second Lesser Angle as in the exemplification hereunto annexed is set forth.[217]

o	Y	u	b
P	a	o	c
r	b	n	h
d	i	r	i

[218]The first line of which four red letters are these o.Y.u.b. making the name oYube, which is the name of one Inferior benevolent Angel, serving to this second[219] lesser Angle.

The next or second line hath these four letters P.a.o.c. which is another name of a subservient good Angel making the name Paoc.

The third line hath these four letters (r.b.n.h.)[220] making the name Vrbeneh,[221] which is the name of another Benevolent Angel serving to this Lesser Angle.

The fourth line hath these four letters (d.i.r.i.) making the name Diri, which is another name of a Benevolent Angel serving to[222] this second Lesser Angle.

The two other lesser Angles below those two here explained have also the like subservient good Angels attending them as these, whose names are also to be collected there out after the same manner as the former is, for their natures & offices and the[223] calling them forth to visible apparition and verbal community shall be showed hereafter, and likewise of the malignant, Evil, envious

---

[213] G: Replaces "the former is" with "before".
[214] G: "second".
[215] S2, G: "the".
[216] G: Omits "do".
[217] G: Replaces "in the exemplification hereunto annexed is set forth" with "is set forth in the annexed form".
[218] G: Gives the table thus, with the "v" in the third row replaced by an "n".

o	Y	u	b
p	A	o	c
n	B	n	h
d	I	r	i

[219] G: Omits "second".
[220] Because of the transcription error, G: gives "n.b.n.h" instead of "v.b.n.h.".
[221] Again, the error is continued with G: giving "Nebeneh".
[222] G: Omits "to".
[223] G: "for".

spirits whose names are also to be collected out of each particular, Inferior or Lesser Angle, as they are severally and respectively subject & serving to the greater Quadrangle, how to gather their names, and what their several offices are, &c, & the calling them forth &c, together with matters of concernment and some select consequences; and also what use is to be made of all, In like manner shall be set forth and explained hereafter, in their proper places, as shall follow in method.

[Table of Union]

First as to the little[224] Table, standing in the centre between the four greater Quadrangles & the use thereof, it is called the Table of Union, and showeth[225] to join such particular letters as are therein, to several particular names and letters in each of the Lesser Angles contained in every[226] of the greater[227] Angles of the Table in general for the collecting and making up of other peculiar[228] names for such proper, select, material & intricate purposes[229], as they are to be attributed and Referred to exemplification, whereof followeth.

The first line containeth these letters e.x.a.r.p. serveth[230] to bind the four lesser Angles of the East Quadrangle together.

The second line that[231] hath these letters h.c.o.m.a. serveth to bind the 4[232] lesser Angles of the second West Quadrangle together.

The third line hath these letters n.a.n.t.a. which serveth[233] to bind the four lesser Angles of the third or North Quadrangle together.

The fourth and last line have these letters b.i.t.o.m. serveth[234] also to bind the four lesser Angles of the fourth or South Quadrangle together, and note, the same that stretcheth from the left to the Right, must also stretch from the Right to the left[235]: observe also that the letters joining those names which may be put before the names of the four Angels set[236] over and governing in each one of every particular lesser Angle of these[237] four greater Quadrangles, as well from the Right as[238] the left, is the name of God whereby those Angels are called and do appear: as for example, The first letter of

---

[224] G: "small".
[225] S2, G: Inserts "how" here.
[226] G: "each".
[227] S2: "ater".
[228] G: Replaces "peculiar" with "particular" and omits "names".
[229] G: Gives singular "purpose".
[230] G: Replaces "serveth" with "and serve".
[231] S2: Omits "that".
[232] G: "four".
[233] G: "serve".
[234] G: Replaces "serveth" with "and serve".
[235] I.e. these names can be read forward or backwards.
[236] G: "sitting".
[237] S2, G: "the".
[238] S2: "to".

the first line of this little[239] Table of Union is (e), The name of the first Angel set[240] over the first lesser Angle of the East Quadrangle is Vrzla, take away the letter (v) being the first letter of[241] the name and put instead thereof, the said letter (e) and then the name[242] will be Erzla, which is the name of God which governeth and calleth forth the Angel Vrzla, and also the other three Angels that are set over the first lesser Angle of the East Quadrangle[243].

The name of the first Angel set[244] over the second lesser Angle is Vtepa,[245] Then by adding the aforesaid letter (e) thereto before it, the name will be Eutepa, which is the name of God governing those four Angels set[246] over the second lesser Angle of the East Quadrangle by which they are called forth and do appear.

The name of the first Angel set[247] over the third lesser Angle is cenbar, before which the aforesaid letter (e) being added maketh it Ecenbar which is the name of God governing those four Angels whereby they are called forth and do appear.

Then again the name of the first Angel set[248] over the fourth lesser Angle of this East Quadrangle is Xegezod, then by adding the said letter (e) thereunto[249] before it maketh it Exegezod, which is the name of God that governeth, & whereby these four Angels are called forth and do appear, and thus are gathered the four great names of God, governing those sixteen Angels bearing rule under the six Angelical Seniors in this Eastern Quadrangle, and whereby they are called forth and do appear as aforesaid.

---

[239] G: "small".
[240] G: "sitting".
[241] G: Inserts "pronouncing".
[242] S2: "is".
[243] An important formula for generating names of God.
[244] G: "sitting".
[245] G: Gives the name as "Utepa".
[246] G: "sitting".
[247] Ibid.
[248] Ibid.
[249] G: "thereto".

[Evil Angels in the Table of Union]

There are four letters left of the first line of this said Table of Union which are X.a.r.p. Every name sounding of 3[250] letters beginning out of the first line, and out of those four letters is[251] the name of a Devil or Evil Angel, as well from the right and from the left, Excepting the line containing the name of every[252] the four Angels set over, and governing in every lesser Angle in each one of the four greater Quadrangles[253] which are the sixteen[254] great benevolent Angels, mentioned next in power, under the six Seniors in each Quadrangle[255] severally and respectively, being the uppermost lines over every transverse black line of the lesser Angles. They are not to be made use of herein, for that[256] they have no participation with the Evil Spirits at all in the last[257], &c.

As for example thus. The four lines (that are under the transverse black line of the first Lesser Angle in the East Quadrangle)[258] the names of the good subservient Angels[259] are only to be[260] made use of herein.

The first letters are c.z. then take the letter (X) in the Table of Union, and add it before them, it will make up the name Xcez, which is one name of an evil Spirit. The two next letters against (c.z.) on the Right hand, the other side of the upright black line going between is[261] (n.s.) making the word[262] nes, or Enes, then by adding the said letter X thereto before it, it maketh[263] Xenes which is another name of an evil Spirit, and if the name Xcez be made backwards from the Right to the left then it will be zedocXe, which is another name of an Evil Spirit, so likewise if the name Xenes, be made backwards as aforesaid then it will be Exes which is the name also of a Devil.

---

[250] G: "three".
[251] G: "from".
[252] G: Inserts "one of".
[253] G: Inserts "(" here.
[254] G: "16".
[255] G: Inserts ")".
[256] G: Replaces "for that" with "because".
[257] G: Omits "at all in the last".
[258] G: Inserts "are".
[259] G: Inserts "and".
[260] S2: "made".
[261] G: "are".
[262] G: "name".
[263] S2: Inserts "it"; G: Omits the words "X thereto before it, it maketh".

The next two letters below c.z. is[264] T.o. and the next letter to the letter (X) in the Table of Union is (a) which being added to the two said letters T.o. from the left to the Right maketh the word ATo, but being added thereto from the Right to the left then it will be Aot, which are the names also of an Evil (Spirit) or Angels of an Infernal as well as of an Aerial nature: The two next letters against T.o. and the Right hand side of the upright black line &c[265] are T.t., the letter being added thereto, before from the left to the Right, maketh the name Atet, and being added thereto from the Right to the left as it happeneth maketh also the same name, The two first letters in the third line under the black transverse line of this first lesser Angle of the East Quadrangle is S.i. the third letter of the first line in the Table of Union (setting aside the letter (e) being the first letter of the line which belongeth only to the sixteen Angels, set as governors over these four Lesser Angles or rather of every the four lines of red letters over every of[266] the[267] four black transverse lines in each Lesser Angle of this East Quadrangle) and it is (r) but adding it to[268] the two letters (s.i.) before, from the left to the Right maketh the name Resi, but added thereto from the Right to the left, maketh the name Ries, which are the names likewise of two Evil Spirits.

The two letters against (s.i.) on the other side the black upright line are a.s., the letter (r) added thereto from the Right to the left maketh the name Resa, but being added thereto from the left to the Right, maketh the name Ras.[269] The first two letters in the last of the four lines under the over thwart, or[270] transverse lines aforesaid of this first Angle of the East Quadrangle are f.m. The last letter in this first line of the Table of Union is P which being added to the aforesaid two letters (f.m.) from the left to the Right maketh the name Pefem, but if it be added thereto from the Right to the left, then it maketh the name Pemef, which are also the names of 2 Evil Angels or Devils.

The other two letters against them on the other side of the black upright line are (n.d.) to which add the letter (P) before from the left to the Right, and it maketh the name Pend,[271] but if the said letter (P) be added thereto from the Right to the left, then it will make the

---

[264] G: "are".
[265] G: Omits "&c".
[266] S2: Omits "of".
[267] G: Omits the words "of the".
[268] G: Transposes "it to" making "to it".
[269] S2: "~~but being added thereto from the left to the right maketh the name~~".
[270] G: Omits the words "overthwart, or".
[271] G: Gives the name as "Pende".

name Peden, which are likewise the names of two Devils: And thus are gathered (the names) [272] of certain Evil Spirits, which are likewise (the names) collected after the same manner out of all the other Angels [273] respectively in the table saving [274] only to observe that the first line in the Table of Union belongeth to the first or East Quadrangle, The second line thereof to the second or west Quadrangle, The third line thereof belongeth to the third or North Quadrangle, and the fourth line serveth to the fourth or South Quadrangle, and the first letters of every line belong properly to the Red line set [275] over every [276] of the lesser transverse or cross black lines in every lesser Angle, and as there are four Quadrangular Tables in the general Table, so the first letter of every line of the Table of Union belongeth to the first line of every Lesser Angle of that Quadrangle unto which the line is referred, as is aforesaid in the explanation of the four Angels set [277] over the first lesser Angle of the East Quadrangle, The other four letters in each line of the Table of Union serveth to collect, join together and make up several names both of good and bad Angels out of the four Subservient lines, which are the red lines under the transverse black line of every Lesser Angle as hath been showed [278] in the foregoing Example; we will give you one Exemplification more, by which it will be sufficient to understand the whole Table, and that is thus [279]; As to the third or North Quadrangle the name of the first Angel set over and governing in the first Angle thereof is Boza, then taking the first letter of the third line in the Table of Union which is (n) and placing it before the name of the said Angel, then [280] it maketh the word Enboza, which is the great name of God, that governeth, and by which those four great and Benevolent Angels are to be called forth to visible appearance.

The name of the first Angel set [281] over the second lesser Angle serving to the third or north Quadrangle is Phra or Phara, then by adding the letter (n) thereto, before the said name then it will be Enphra, or Enphara, which is the great name of God that governeth

---

[272] S1: Repeats the phrase "(the names" here in the text.
[273] G: Changes "Angels" to "Angles", suggesting a mistake on the part of the original G.D. copyist.
[274] G: "having".
[275] G: "sitting".
[276] G: "each".
[277] G: "sitting".
[278] G: "shown".
[279] G: "as follows".
[280] G: Omits "then".
[281] G: "sitting".

those four Angels set[282] over the second lesser Angle, serving to the third or north Quadrangle, & by which they are called forth and do appear; The name of the first Angel set[283] over the third lesser Angle serving to[284] this north Quadrangle is Æoan, then add the said letter (n) before it, and make it Næoan, which is the great name of God that governeth those four Angels set[285] over that lesser Angle, and whereby they are called forth and do appear.

Then again the name of the first Angel set[286] over the fourth lesser Angle serving to[287] this north Quadrangle is Iaom,[288] then by adding the letter (n) before it, it[289] maketh the word Niaom,[290] which is the great name of God that governeth the four Angels set[291] over this fourth lesser Angle of the third or north Quadrangle and by which they are also called forth & do appear, & so it is of the rest.

The first letter[292] of the[293] line of the Table of Union added before the name of the first Angel set[294] over every[295] four lesser Angles serving to[296] the greater Quadrangle, wherein they are, maketh the name of God that governeth over every[297] of those said four Angels, set[298] over every said lesser Angle, unto which[299] Quadrangle, first, second, third, or fourth, Each[300] line of the Table of Union is properly formed[301], as aforesaid. The other four letters of each line of the Table of Union, serveth[302] to the four red lines of four letters

---

[282] Ibid.

[283] Ibid.

[284] G: Omits "to".

[285] G: "sitting".

[286] Ibid.

[287] G: Omits "to".

[288] G: Gives this name as "Taom" demonstrating another copying error.

[289] S2: Omits "it".

[290] See previous note, the name is given incorrectly as "Entaom", perpetuating the same mistake.

[291] G: "sitting".

[292] S2: Also "letter".

[293] G: Inserts "vertical".

[294] G: "sitting".

[295] G: "each".

[296] G: Omits this word.

[297] G: Replaces "over every" with "each".

[298] G: "sitting".

[299] G: Inserts "said".

[300] S2: Also "each".

[301] S2: "referred".

[302] G: "serve".

affixed[303] under the black cross or transverse lines of every Lesser Angle, and maketh up the names of several Evil Angels of a Terrestrial and[304] Infernal nature, that are composed and made up of 3 letters, by adding thereto, the first, second, third or fourth letter of the line of the Table of Union, being those four letters following the first. Every line of the Table containing five letters linear along, and four downwards, every first letter belonging properly to the line placed over, every black Transverse or Cross line in every lesser Angle, in each greater Quadrangle and the other four letters, to the four Red lines placed under the said transverse black line [305] successively as they are referred to be joined [306] one to another as[307] thus. The fourth line of the Table of Union belongeth to the fourth or South quadrangle.

The first letter thereof appertaineth to the first line thereof being (b) that is of the first lesser Angle; And likewise the first line of the second, and so the first line of the third and so to[308] the first line of the fourth lesser Angles, serving to this fourth or South Quadrangle, being those lines set[309] over the transverse black line[310] of each Lesser Angle. The four letters following which are I.T.O.M. belong to the four Red lines under the transverse black lines[311] thereof, the first of which four letters of union, (and the second from the first) is (i) and belongeth to the first red line under the transverse black line of this first Lesser Angle of the[312] fourth or South Quadrangle. The second letter (but the third from the first) is (T) the which appertaineth to the second line. The third letter (and fourth from the first) is (o), and this appertaineth to the third line. The fourth & last letter (but the fifth from the first) is (m) and appertaineth to the fourth and last red line, subservient in this lesser Angle (being the 1st of the four) serving to the fourth & South Quadrangle: The use thereof is[313] partly explained before.

Having briefly explained how to collect the name of the great and

---

[303] S2, G: "apiece".
[304] G: "or".
[305] G: Replaces "black line" with "lines".
[306] S2, G: Replaces "referred to be joined" with "to be referred and joined".
[307] S2, G: Omits "as".
[308] G: Omits "so to".
[309] G: "placed".
[310] G: "lines".
[311] G: "line".
[312] S2: "fourth".
[313] G: Replaces "is" with "has been already".

mighty Angelical King of the East Quadrangle, and of the three[314] great names of God borne in 3[315] Banners before him, and of the six Seniors, and of the sixteen Angels next under them, set[316] over every lesser Angle serving[317] to this greater East Quadrangle, and of some good Angels subservient to them, under whom again[318] are many benevolent Angels of inferior Orders. The collecting of whose names are omitted, being too tedious to exemplify, since this which hath been already said before, is sufficient, and also how to collect the names of several evil spirits of terrestrial & Infernal[319] natures, now shall be showed the method, how to invocate & call them forth to visible appearance.

---

[314] G: Inserts "or".
[315] G: "three".
[316] G: "placed".
[317] G: "subservient".
[318] G: Omits this word.
[319] S2: "infernal".

[Method to Invoke the Angels to Visible Appearance]

The three great names of God Oro. Ibah. Aozpi, governeth the King of the East Angle whose name is BATAIVA, and this name BATAIVA governeth the six seniors, and by which they are called forth and do appear. The name of God Erzla, governeth the four Angels set[320] over the first lesser Angle of this East Quadrangle.

The name of God Eutepa, governeth the four Angels set[321] over the second lesser Angle of this East Quadrangle.

The name of God Ecenbar governeth the four Angels set[322] over the third Lesser Angle of this East Quadrangle.

The name of God Exgezod governeth the four Angels set[323] over the fourth Lesser Angle of this East Quadrangle.

Then there is the middle black upright or perpendicular line, in this first lesser Angle serving[324] to the great Quadrangle of the East, the which hath these six letters from the top downward, to the black line that goeth cross [325] the Quadrangle i.d.o.i.g.o making the name[326] Idoigo, The transverse or cross black line, whereof hath those letters, a.r.d.z.a. making the name Ardeza, [327] The four subservient Angels that are under the transverse black line of this said first lesser Angle are ruled by the name Idoigo, and thereby are called forth and do appear, and by the name Ardza, they do what they are commanded: The like method is to be observed of the other 3[328] Lesser Angles of this East Quadrangle.

Then for the second or West Quadrangle of the Table, the three great names of God displayed in Banners, and borne before the great Angel and mighty King of this second or West Quadrangle is to be collected out of the middle transverse black line, that goeth crosswise athwart the Quadrangle, and to be composed of three,

---

[320] G: "placed".
[321] Ibid.
[322] Ibid.
[323] Ibid.
[324] G: "subservient".
[325] G: Changes this to "across".
[326] G: Inserts "of".
[327] G: Gives the name as "Ardza".
[328] S2, G: "three".

four and five letters after the same manner as is before taught in the first or East Quadrangle, and so likewise of the other two succeeding north and south Quadrangles.

The three great and powerful names of God governing the mighty & Angelical monarchy of the second or west Quadrangle whose name is RAAGIOS or RAAGIOSEL, are Empeh. Arsel. Gaiol, and the Royal high name RAAGIOSEL, governeth the six seniors, and by which they are called forth, & do appear.

The name of God HeTaad, governeth the four Angels set[329] over the[330] first Lesser Angle of the second or West Quadrangle.

The name of God HeTedim governeth the four Angels set[331] over the second Lesser Angle of this second or West quadrangle.

The name of God HeMagel, governeth the four Angels set[332] over the third or[333] Lesser Angle of this second or west Quadrangle.

The name of God Henlarex, governeth the four Angels set[334] over the fourth and last lesser Angle of the second and West Quadrangle of the Table, &[335] by which names they are called forth & do appear.

Then there is the name of God Obegoca, which are the six letters in the upright black line of the first Lesser Angle in this second and West Quadrangle, which name Ruleth and calleth forth, the four subservient Angels under the black Transverse line, by the power whereof they do appear.

Then in the transverse line there is the word Aabeco[336] by the efficacy whereof the said 4[337] subservient Angels do what they are commanded.

---

[329] G: "placed".
[330] S2: "first".
[331] Ibid.
[332] Ibid.
[333] G: Omits this word.
[334] G: "placed".
[335] S2: "and".
[336] S2: "Aabego".
[337] G: "four".

The name of God Nelapar, which are the six letters of the upright black line, Ruleth the four Angels subservient in this second lesser Angle and by the power whereof they are called forth and do appear.

And by the name of God Omebeb the five letters in the transverse line they do what they are commanded.

Then there is the name of God Maladi, in the upright line of the third Lesser Angle, by which the four subservient Angels herein are called forth and do appear.

Then there is the name of God Olaad in the transverse black line, whereby they do what they are commanded.

The name of God Jaasde,[338] which are the six letters in the upright line of the fourth lesser Angle of this second and West Quadrangle, calleth[339] forth the four subservient Angels in this Angle to visible apparition.

And the name of God ATAPA which are the five letters of the black transverse line, powerfully urgeth (and as it were) enforceth or constraineth them to do what[340] they are commanded.

After the same manner and method are the other names of God, peculiarly and particularly to be collected out of the subsequent north and south Quadrangles, by the virtue, power, and efficacy, and at the nominating and pronouncing whereof, all the ministering Angels of Light Celestially dignified both servient and subservient, even from the superior to the Inferior orders, under the great King or Supreme head, and governor[341] of every Respectively general or Quarterly greater Angle according to their degrees and offices, are called forth and moved to visible appearance and so accordingly to do what they are commanded as aforesaid. As for the Evil Spirits more of them hereafter.

---

[338] S2: "Iaaasdi".
[339] G: Shortens "calleth" to "call".
[340] G:" as".
[341] S2: Has "governeth or".

It is said before that the subservient Angels whose names are collected out of the four Red lines under the black transverse line, in every Lesser Angle of the Table are next in order (as servients) under the other Angels, whose names are collected out of the Red line above the black Transverse line in every lesser Angle of the Table, under which said servients, are many benevolent subservients inferior to them, and under whom again are many legions of assisting Angels more inferior to them in power and Authority; And likewise many legions of spirits more Inferior again to them[342] of several natures and offices both good and bad, as originally decreed by providence, who settled[343] all things both Celestial, Aerial, & Terrestrial, gradation to serve and execute his commands, according to their orders, offices, natures, government and degrees[344], wherein they are placed.

And hence it is affirmed, that Aerial & Elementary Spirits are of different and several natures, according as they[345] were constituted and appointed in their several and respective offices, places and orders, by the first and Supreme decree of the Highest, in the observing and fulfilling his decrees and commands according to his justice and mercy, and so often times are the executioners[346] of wrath and vengeance, yet nevertheless whom God is graciously[347] pleased to wink at, and pass by our wickedness and so[348] to show mercy, then they often times admonish, forewarn, and watch over us, and defend us from many dangers & perils and are benevolent and helpful unto us in any[349] respects, according to their offices, and are[350] as our necessity requireth.

---

[342] S2: "as".
[343] G: "setteth".
[344] G: Gives "decrees", but this is probably a copying error.
[345] S2: "are".
[346] G: "execution".
[347] G: Omits this word.
[348] G: Omits this word.
[349] G: "many".
[350] S2: "are".

[Of the Evil Malicious Spirits]

As to the evil malicious spirits before mentioned whose names are collected of the 3[351] letters, by joining thereunto, one letter of the Table of Union, as hath been before explained; They are thus to be called forth. Their names are collected out of those four Red lines under the black transverse line in every Lesser Angle of the Table, and by joining of one letter of the Table of Union[352], to two of those letters, in any line of those aforesaid lines of the Lesser Angle, either from the left to the Right, or from the Right to the left, they both serve, to one and the same purpose, being taken out and placed in such manner and order accordingly, as they are particularly referred to their proper places respectively, do make the name of a Devil, as hath been treated of, and showed by an Example elsewhere before &c.

The calling them forth is one[353] this wise, as for example In the first Lesser Angle of the East Quadrangle, the upright black line thereof from the top downwards, hath the name of God Idoigo, which God[354] calleth forth the subservient Angels of that Angle, in the black transverse line thereof is the name of God Ardza, by which they do what they are commanded: so by the name of God Idoigo, backwards and[355] the malignant spirits whose names are made of 3[356] letters out of[357] this 1st[358]Lesser Angle of the East Quadrangle to be called forth: And by the name of God Ardza backwards they do also what they are commanded, so that the names Ogiodi, causeth them to appear by the[359] order of Idoigo, And by the name Azdra backwards commandeth them by the like order &c.

In the second lesser Angle of this said East Quadrangle is in the middle upright line thereof the name of God Ilacza, which pronounced backwards is Azcali, which name calleth forth the malignant Spirits whose names are collected of 3[360] letters out of it, and by the name Palam,[361] which is the name Malap[362] backwards

[351] S2, G: Omits "the" and gives "three" spelled in full.
[352] G: Omits the section from "as hath been before explained ... Table of Union".
[353] G: "after".
[354] G: "name"
[355] G: "are".
[356] G: "three".
[357] S2: "the first".
[358] G: Omits this word.
[359] G: Omits this word.
[360] G: "three".
[361] G: Transposes this and the next name, giving this as "Malap".
[362] G: Transposes this and the previous name, giving this as "Palam".

they do what they are commanded.

The middle upright black line of the third Lesser Angle hath this name of God Aiaoai, which pronounced backwards is Iaoaia, and this calleth forth the Evil Spirits whose names are collected of the[363] 3[364] letters of this Angle, the transverse line whereof hath the name of God Oiiit, which being pronounced backwards maketh the name Tiiio, whereby they are constrained to obedience &c.

The upright black line of the fourth Lesser Angle of the[365] said Quadrangle hath this name of God Aovrrz, which backwards is Zrrvoa, and calleth forth those Evil Spirits, whose names are made of 3[366] letters thereout.

The transverse black line hereof[367], hath this name of God Aloai, which backward is Jaola, which constraineth them to do whatsoever they are commanded, &c.

The like Rule and method is to be observed in the other three Quadrangles of the general Table, Their offices shall be spoken of, by and by, so that for the calling forth of any Angel or Spirit[368] either good or bad, and for their yielding obedience to do what they are commanded, the repetition of those names of God, respectively unto which they are diversely and severally referred and by which they are governed is sufficient.

The names of God that call forth the subservient Angels of each Lesser Angle of the greater Quadrangle[369] call forth the Evil spirits whose names are made of 3[370] letters if[371] it be[372] pronounced backwards, for unto them so he is a God, &c.

---

[363] S2: Omits "the".
[364] G: "three".
[365] S2: "this".
[366] Ibid.
[367] G: "thereof".
[368] G: "spirits".
[369] S2: "Quadrangles".
[370] S2, G: "three".
[371] G: "of".
[372] G: "being".

[The General Use and Signification of the Tables]

Now as to the general use and signification of the Tables and the offices of the Angels &c & other Remarkable observations &c, these Tables (or Table) contain all human knowledge; they stretch to the Knowledge of Solomon, for out of it springeth physick, the knowledge, [373] finding and [374] use of metals, the virtues of them, the [375] congelations and virtues of stones (they are all of one matter),[376] the knowledge of all Elemental creatures amongst us, how many kinds there are, & for what use they are created[377].

Air
Those that live in the Water by themselves
Earth

The property of the fire, which is the secret Life of all things, but those more particularly.

The knitting together of natures, The moving from place to place as And also as well[378] the destruction of nature and of things that may perish as of the conjoining and knitting them together &c.
into this

country or that		First		East	
country at[379]	lieth in the	Second	Lesser	West	Great
pleasure. The	four Angels	Third	Angle	North	Quadrangle
Knowledge of	set[380] over	Fourth	of the	South	

all mechanical crafts whatsoever. The secrets of men knowing &c.

Likewise the offices of the subservient Angels in every of the Lesser Angles are as followeth.

---

[373] S2: Inserts "&".

[374] S2: "the".

[375] G: Omits "the".

[376] S2: The following section down to the words "4 Elements, Air, Water, Earth & Fire" is presented very differently and with some noticeable changes differently in this MSS, and is presented in Appendix 1 for convenience as **note 1**.

[377] The following pages effectively list the uses to which the spiritual creatures invoked can be put, and the categories of knowledge they give.

[378] G: Omits "as well".

[379] S2: Inserts "will &".

[380] G: "placed".

The knowledge of physick in all its parts, and the[381] curing of all diseases &c. The knowledge, finding and use of metals, the congelation of stones and the virtue of all stones.

Transformation,		First		East	
transplantation;	lieth in the	Second	Lesser	West	Greater
The knowledge	4 Angels	Third	Angle	North	Quadrangle
of all elemental	Serving to the	Fourth	of the	South	

creatures amongst us; how many kinds & their use in the creation as they are severally placed, in the 4 Elements, Air, Water, Earth & Fire.

By these Tables may be known the secret Treasures of the waters and the unknown caves of the Earth &c[382]. As for example, the subservient Angels in the second lesser Angle of every greater Quadrangle, and also all the ministering servient Angels under them give the knowledge, finding and[383] use of metals &c.

The Benevolent Angels of that order, will offer the passages of the Earth, unto the entrance of the senses[384] of man (chiefly of seeing[385]) so that the Earth lying opened unto their Eyes, by the benevolent assistance of the Angels of Light, they may plainly see and discover what Treasures are in the Earth, both as to the natural mines of the Earth, and all manner of Treasure Trove[386], and the Angels aforesaid[387] are ministers for this purpose.

Treasure Trove or such Treasures of the Earth that is Coin[388] and that hath been heretofore in man's possession is in the power of the Evil Spirits, whose names are made of three letters; And they can give the same to man &c.

---

[381] G: Omits "the".

[382] Using spirits and angels to find buried treasure was a common pre-occupation in the 16th and 17th century. A distinction was drawn between finding naturally occurring mineral wealth (through angels), and buried coinage or treasure trove (the latter often involving evil spirits).

[383] S2: Replaces "and" with "out the".

[384] G: "sons". Possibly a copyist's error

[385] G: "serving". Again possibly a copyist's error.

[386] S2: "treasures troves".

[387] S2: "and".

[388] G: Replaces "that is Coin" with "as is lying therein".

But as for the natural mines of the earth, they have nothing to do therewith, nor have any power over it at all, those treasures belong properly to the benevolent Subservient Angels, who are found in every second Lesser Angle of each Quadrangle, who (as I said before) can lay the caves of the Earth open to the Eyes of man &c, where he may see the Treasures of the Earth[389] as they are therein contained, in and according to their several and respective natures, and properties which being known to him, then hath he the benevolent assistance, both of the good and[390] bad Angels, to serve his necessities therewith, according to the nature[391] of their part[392] and offices, as to which they are concerned and[393] properly referred and have power over &c.

The natures and offices of the evil Spirits aforesaid are quite contrary to those of the good Angels, as thus, the good Angels belonging to physick, they[394] cure diseases, preserve the Elemental vigour, and humid Radicals[395] of things natural: on the contrary the Evil spirits maliciously bring in diseases, and seek to destroy the Elemental vigour, and strength of natural things &c. The practice of all shall be showed hereafter particularly in a Treatise by it self.

Having briefly showed by an example of the first and East Quadrangle of the Table, how to collect the names[396] of the great Angel thereof, or the mighty Angelical monarch, bearing Rule and governing the east part or point of the compass Angle or Quarter, both Celestially and Terrestrially, and of the six seniors and of many other, of[397] governing and subservient Angels, and their natures and offices, both good and bad together with the use of all &c.

The Right understanding whereof is a sufficient precedent[398] for unfolding the other three greater Angles or Quarters of the Table.

---

[389] S2: "open to the Eyes of man".
[390] S2: Inserts "the".
[391] G: Gives the plural form, "natures".
[392] S2: "parts".
[393] G: Inserts "are".
[394] G: "that".
[395] G: Gives "Radicate" here, which is clearly a copying error.
[396] S2: "name".
[397] S2: Inserts "the".
[398] G: Gives "evident" here, which seems likely to be another copying error.

The use of which severally are the same as in this, for the names of their princes, and the great names of God by which they are governed, and unto which they are subject and obedient, which are the Arms of the Ensigns or Banners borne before them.

The names of the Seniors and the Angels governing and set[399] over every Lesser Angle of each greater Quadrangle, and the names of God, governing, calling forth and commanding, and of the subservient benevolent Angels officiating again under them; and the names of God commanding, calling forth, and constraining them, and of many legions of others both good and bad, are to be gathered and collected thereout, after the self same method, as is showed in the Explaining[400] the East Quadrangle, and the offices also of all the Angels comprehended in the greater East Angle. Even from the superior monarch, to the most inferior subservient are the same as in this greater East Angle, so in the other 3[401] greater Angles Respectively. Viz, The offices and natures of the King and the Six Seniors are one and the same alike, in all the four Quadrangles of the Table, so also are the offices, and the natures of all the Angels both governing and subservient in all the lesser Angles, serving to each[402] Quadrangle. As the first lesser Angle of this East Quadrangle is of physick, and compriseth the whole body thereof in all its parts so doth the first lesser Angle in the second[403] Quadrangle the like. And the first lesser Angle of the third Quadrangle; And the first lesser angle of[404] the fourth Quadrangle the same likewise. So the Angels of the second lesser Angle of the East Quadrangle are of the same nature and offices, as are the other three lesser Angles serving to the three greater Quadrangles: and also the third and fourth lesser Angles of the west, north, and south Quadrangles are of the same nature and office[405], as the third and fourth Lesser Angles of the East Quadrangle, and every way hath the same signification, only they differ in this particular, that some are East, some west, some north, and some south. A due consideration therefore ought to be had and carefully taken in calling them, always observing to invocate from such a point of the

---

[399] G: "placed".
[400] G: Replaces "Explaining" with "Explanation of".
[401] G: "three".
[402] S2: "the East".
[403] G: Inserts" "(West)" here.
[404] G: "in".
[405] G: Transposes from "nature and office" to "offices and nature".

compass or Choir of heaven where their power and abode is &c[406].

And all other such concerns herein as is Requisite thereto, ought likewise to be directed to this, or that, or such and such a Quarter or Angle, East, West, North or South unto which they properly appertain and are properly referred &c. And with all is to be understood, that the other Letters of the Table thus to be collected (as aforesaid) should some hard to be pronounced for want of vowels to sound and make out each syllable, as to the pronouncing of a name proper, yet observing to pronounce every letter distinctly as if it had a vowel going before[407] or following it, then it sounds well enough. And the reason of this strange kind of difference in our common Orthography[408] is, that there is not a letter nor part of a letter, but is numbered and hath the same signification &c as for the practice it is[409] thus.

---

[406] An important point: invocation should be towards the correct direction, so that you do not inadvertently turn your back on the angel or spirit you are invoking. In the *Lemegeton* even more precise directions were given for the direction of invocation of each spirit.

[407] S2: "as".

[408] Way of writing and spelling.

[409] S2: Replaces "it is" with "of it".

[The Book and the Procedure]

Let the philosopher prepare a Book of very fine paper or parchment, and write very fairly therein, as shall be here directed &c and also a handsome convenient chamber or place for practice.

Which Book must consist first of the Invocations of the names of God, and secondly of the Angels by the names of God &c. As for example, In the black transverse line that goeth athwart the East Quadrangle, there are these three great names of God thus, Oro. Ibah. Aozpi, so likewise in the second or West Quadrangle thus Empeh. Arsel. Gaiol. In the third or north Quadrangle they are Emor. Dial. Hectega, and so in the 4th[410] or south Quadrangle Oip. Teaa. Pedoce. Four days after the Book is written the Magick Philosopher must only[411] call upon the names of God or rather on the God of Hosts, from the four Angles or Quarter[412] points of the compass, East, West, North, & South.

And fourteen days after he shall invocate the Angels by petition. And by the names of God to which they are obedient from the Angles[413] or mansions where they reside and dwell East, West, North, & South, as they are to be found in the Table &c.

The fifteenth day he shall cloth himself in a vesture made of white linen, and so have the Apparition, use and practice of the spiritual creatures, which when he hath attained to (as no doubt but he may) he may be so expert in the practical part hereof, that he need not make use of the linen vesture after[414], nor the book, nor to be confined to any such observations[415] and curiosities of places, or otherwise as was formerly commanded as to the entrance into the knowledge and practice of this Art in attaining to the society, converse, and use of the Spiritual creatures for if the philosopher can in his fifteen days Retirement & Reservation, but retain and remember the names of the Angels and the names of God, by which they are called forth, appear, and do what they are commanded, he may call upon them, converse with them, and make use of them (according to their natures and offices) without[416] either vestment or

---

[410] S2, G: "fourth".
[411] S2: 'Only' is crossed out.
[412] G: "Quaternary".
[413] S2: "in".
[414] G: Omits "after".
[415] G: "observances".
[416] S2: "Either".

Book or choice place, but whatsoever[417] or howsoever he will, or wheresoever he shall happen to be &c[418].

For the calls, Invocations, Invitations or petitions to be used herein, and that are to be curiously written in a select book to be made and provided for that purpose, according as is before expressed, is to be, but a short and brief speech *in verbis conceptis* as the mind shall prompt or dictate[419], observing the Angle or point of the Compass, wherever he shall be in respect of the poles, &c. And one thing a little extraordinary take notice of by the way, and that is thus, understand that the natures and offices of the subservient Angels of every second Lesser Angle of each greater Quadrangle of the Table, is the finding knowledge and use of[420] metals, to gather them together &c. This is meant as to the natural mines of the Earth, for they give no money coined[421] (which is such, as hath been in use amongst men, and by them despitefully hidden from posterity, and commonly termed Treasure Trove, or hidden Treasure &c) and also as[422] is said elsewhere before, will lay the passages of the Earth, and the secret caves of the hills open visibly to the sight of our Eyes, that we may see and know what is enclosed and contained in the bowels thereof, and to Instruct us in the use of metals in all their parts, and to serve our necessities with such of them as they have power over and can command, which are such as have not been (accomplished) amongst[423] men, nor corrupted by them &c.

On the contrary the Evil Angels which names consist of three letters, and that are collected out of the said Angels[424], have no[425] power over the natural mines of the Earth, nor have nothing[426] at all to do therewith, but they do[427] keep from the discovery and use of man all such Treasures of gold and silver &c As hath been formerly in use amongst them, and (as is said) most despitefully hidden and absconded from them, in the bowels of the Earth, and is called

---

[417] S2: "wheresoever".

[418] The objective of many systems of magic is to be able to command spiritual creatures in an ordinary setting, without the usual paraphernalia or preparation, however one that only a really skilled magician should aspire to.

[419] S2: "Direct ~~Dictate~~".

[420] G: Inserts "the".

[421] G: Changes this to "neither coined money" from "no money coined".

[422] G: Omits "as".

[423] G: "among".

[424] S2: Sidenotes "Angles".

[425] G: "neither".

[426] G: "anything".

[427] G: Omits "do".

Treasure Trove or hidden Treasures[428], and those sort of Treasures the good Angels have nothing to do withal, more than to lay them open to our sight, nor have no[429] power to serve our necessities otherwise than to discover them to us as aforesaid; but this kind of Treasure Trove are[430] wholly kept and possessed by the malignant Angels or Spirits aforesaid, who have sole power over them, and may be commanded, or constrained to serve our necessities with them.

The calling them forth, as well as the calling forth the good Angels and the moving them to visible appearance and to constrain them to do what they are commanded, is also showed before &c[431].

Understand also that when all this shall lay[432] open visibly to the sight of the philosopher, and that he perceiveth and well knoweth that it is kept by a malignant spirit, and that it may probably according to common apprehension prove hard or difficult to obtain, and the philosopher should be at a near place, or at a stand, how to encounter with[433], and discharge the Keeper thereof from it, so that he may peaceably and without molestation or interruption take away the same and enjoy it without any dread or fear of harm to him or any of his companions (if he hath any) or offence to God, or injurious[434] to the soul's health or in any way's prejudicial or contrary to Religion, the Christian faith, or a good conscience &c.

Let him consider his glorification and power in his Creation, and his souls dignification as man, and how near he is the great omnipotent Archetype, as he is the very Image and Idea thereof, and as he is monarch of the World, and commandeth all such malignant Spirits, to submission, subjection and obedience, and he shall absolutely & positively conclude that they are but inferior servants and vile slaves, and unto whom he shall say, Arise begone, Thou art of[435] hindrance, [436] destruction and of the places of darkness, these are provided for the use of man; Thou art vanquished, thy time is

---

[428] G: "Treasure".
[429] G: Omits "no".
[430] G: "is".
[431] G: Changes this phrase from "is also showed before &c" to "has also been shown before".
[432] S2: "laid"; G: "lie".
[433] G: Omits "with".
[434] G: "injury".
[435] G: "a".
[436] S2: "&".

shortened, and fully now expired, therefore I say depart to thy order Jeovah, Jeovaschah, and lo I seal[437] you to the end; Thus shall he use[438] the malignant spirits and Keepers of Treasure Trove, and not otherwise, and they will, nay must obey and immediately depart and thus briefly is laid open and explained the use and meaning of the Table containing the four Quadrangles East, West, North & South which is sufficient &c[439].

---

[437] G: Gives "fear" instead of "seal", but this is an unfortunate copyist's mistake, considering the context of the phrase.
[438] S2: "of".
[439] G: Omits "&c" and replaces it with "for this one purpose." Here ends the text of Document H of the Hermetic Order of the Golden Dawn.

The Practice of the East Table

The names of the four Kings governing the four Watch Towers set over the four Terrestrial Angles are
Bataiva King of the East.   Raagios King of the West.   Jezodhehca King of the North.   Edelperna, King of the South.

The Regal Invocation

O Thou great, mighty, and powerful Angel of the Immortal God Bataiva, who art by the primitive [440] design [441] of the Highest ordained, constituted and appointed, and set over the Terrestrial Angle of the East, as the only King, governor, overseer, principal Watchman, protector and Keeper thereof, from the malice, misuse, illusion, Temptation, wicked Encroachments and usurping Blasphemy of the great Enemy of God's glory and the welfare of mankind, the princes and spirits of darkness and art a snaffle to them to Restrain their wickedness, by the bit of God's boundless power and justice.

To the intent that (they being put out into the earth) their envious will might be bridled, the determinations of the heavenly God fulfilled, and his creatures kept within the compass and measure of order.

I the servant of the Highest do call upon you, O you mighty and Royal Angel Bataiva, most humbly and earnestly entreating you, In, and through these great names of the Infinite [442] and Incomprehensible God of Hosts Oro, Ibah, Aozpi, and by the virtue, power and efficacy thereof to assist and help me in these my present operations and affairs, and by the powerful permission and Authority to send and cause to come and appear unto me _____.

Residing under your Government in the Angle of the East whom I shall call forth by name, to instruct, direct & help me in all such matters or things, According to their offices, as I shall request and desire of them, both now and at all times also [443], whensoever necessity shall require their favourable aid and assistance and such

---

[440] S2: "~~primitive~~".
[441] S2: "decree".
[442] S2: "Immense".
[443] S2: "Else".

their good counsel and advertisements as shall be requisite and necessary for me, and herein I most ardently and incessantly Implore and Beseech you O Bataiva, humbly desiring your friendship, and to do for me as for the servant of the most high God of Hosts Oro, Ibah, Aozpi, the Almighty creator of Heaven and Earth, and disposer of all things both Celestial, Aerial, Terrestrial and Infernal.

Names of the Six Seniors and to call them forth
Habioro[1], Aaoxaif[2], Hetermorda[3], Ahaozpi[4], Hipotga[5], Autotar[6].

O You glorious and Beneficent [444] Angels Habioro, Aaoxaif, Hetermorda, Ahaozpi, Hipotga, Autotar who are the six Angelical Seniors serving before Bataiva the great honoured and Royal Angel of the high and Immortal God of Hosts in the Terrestrial Angle of the East, I most earnestly entreat, humbly request and powerfully adjure and call ye forth to visible apparition, In and through this mighty & Efficacious name of your King and Sovereign Lord of the East Angle of the world Bataiva, and by the Ineffable power and virtue thereof, preordinally decreed by the Highest to be most firmly and solidly effectual for the calling you forth; now therefore O you Benevolent Angels Habioro, Aaoxaif, Hetermorda, Ahaozpi, Hipotga, Autotar, I adjure and call you forth, in this true and most especial name of your King Bataiva, and by the Excellency thereof, urgently and potently entreating you to gird up and gather your selves together and by divine permission, move, descend, and appear visible and friendly unto me, in this Crystal Stone or Glass Receptacle [445] and In and through the same to transmit your Splendid Rays to my sight, and your Benevolent voices unto[446] my Ears; that I may plainly see and audibly hear you speak unto me, and to assist, direct, Instruct, Illuminate, and show forth what I shall humbly desire and request of you; O you servants of mercy Habioro, Aaoxaif, Hetermorda, Ahaozpi, Hipotga, Autotar, come away and appear visibly unto me (as aforesaid) to the honour and glory of the Omnipotent Creator and the praise of his great and holy

---

[444] S2: "Benevolent".
[445] In all the manuscripts this is abbreviated to "C.S. or G.R.", and is clearly a term derived from *The Art Theurgia Goetia*. See *The Lesser Key of Solomon*, edited by Joseph H. Peterson, p65 – "you may call these spirits into a Crystal Stone or Glass Receptacle, [this] being an Ancient & usual way or Receiving & binding of spirits, This Crystal Stone must be four Inches Diameter set on a Table of Art". This is a clear demonstration of the influence of Solomonic magic on Dee's Enochian system. Dee's stone was set on a 'Holy Table'.
[446] S2: "to".

name. For unto this remembrance is given power, and my strength waxeth strong in my comforter; Move therefore and show your selves, open to the mysteries of your creation: Be friendly unto me for I am a servant of the same your God, the true worshipper of the Highest.[447]

Names of the four Angels set over the first (Table) Lesser Angle of the East and to call them forth.

Vrzla[1], Zlar[2], Larzod[3], Arzel[4], divine name governing Erzla.

O You glorious and benevolent Angels Vrzla, Zlar, Larzod, Arzel, who are the four Angels set over the first lesser Angle of the greater Terrestrial Angle of the East, I invoke, adjure and call you forth to visible apparition, in and through this great, Signal, prevalent and divine name of the most high God Erzla, and by Ineffable and Efficacious virtue and power thereof, whereby you are governed and called forth, it being therefore absolutely necessary, preordained (and appointed) and decreed[448] to be most solidly effectual; now therefore I do most earnestly entreat and powerfully adjure you, O you benign Angels Vrzla, Zlar, Larzod, Arzel in this potent name of your God Erzla, to move, descend, appear and visibly show your selves to me, in this Crystal Stone or Glass Receptacle here before me, and in, and through the same to transmit your Rays to my sight, and your voices to my Ears, that I may audibly hear you speak unto me, and plainly see you[449] and conclude me as a Receiver of your mysteries, wherefore I do urgently request and adjure you, O you luminous and amicable Angels Vrzla, Zlar, Larzod, Arzel, in this most excellent name of your God Erzla, and I (as the servant of the Highest) do thereby efficaciously move you in power and presence to appear now presently visible to me as aforesaid; O you Servants of mercy, move, Descend, personally show forth, and apply your selves friendly unto me as unto the partaker of his secret wisdom in your Creation, for why our Lord & master is all one.

---

[447] Compare this with Dee's invocation 'Sex Seniorvm Orientalium Invitatio' in Sloane 3191, from which it is derived.
[448] S2: "directed".
[449] The intention is very plainly to have sight of the angels or spiritual creature in the crystal or glass receptacle.

Names of the 4 Angels serving to the first Lesser Angle of the East Table and to call them forth.

Cezodenes, Totet, Sias, Efermende, Divine names governing, calling forth Idoigo, & constraining Ardza.

O You Benevolent Angels of Light Cezodenes, Totet, Sias, Efermende[450], who are the four servient Angels serving in the first Lesser Angle of the greater Terrestrial Angle of the East; I invoke, adjure, command, and powerfully call you forth from your orders and mansion to visible apparition, in and through this great, prevalent, signal, and divine name of God Idoigo, and by the Efficacy, virtue, and power thereof most firmly and solidly effectual, for the calling you forth, commanding you to transmit your Rays visibly to my sight,[451] your voices to my Ears, in and through this Crystal Stone or Glass Receptacle or otherwise to appear out here before me that I may plainly see you and audibly hear you speak unto me; Move therefore O you Benign Servient Angels of Light Cezodenes, Totet, Sias, Efermende, and in the potent name of God Idoigo, and by the Imperial dignity thereof, Descend and by divine permission, visibly show yourselves as pleasant deliverers, that you may praise him amongst the sons of men. O you servants of mercy Cezodenes, Totet, Sias, Efermende, come away and in this Ineffable and most excellent name of your God Idoigo, visibly and personally appear to the admiration of the Earth, and to my comfort, come away open the mysteries of your creation be friendly unto me, for I am a servant of the same your God the true worshipper of the Highest[452].

When the servient Angels of this order appeareth and are known, then receive them as followeth.

---

[450] This is an example where the author of this manuscript has applied the rules and filled out and improved upon Dee's original which lists the four angels unpronounceably as 'CZNS sive CZONS, TOTT sive TOITT, SIAS sive SIGAS, FMND sive FMOND'. 'Sive' simply indicates alternatives, as if Dee was not sure of the orthography even when he reached the final fair copy of the invocations.

[451] S2: Inserts "&".

[452] The last 26 words are recognisably derived from the first Call of Dee's earlier system of Enochian Calls as recorded in 'The 48 Angelic Keys' or *48 Claves Angelicae*, bound in Sloane 3191. There they are translated into Enochian as 'Odo cicle Qaa Zorge, Lap zirdo Noco MAD Hoath Iaida'

Welcome be the Light of the Highest whose name be glorified for his mercies endureth for ever; And O you servants of mercy and benign Angels of Light Cezodenes, Totet, Sias, Efermende, you are to me sincerely welcome, And I do in this Inestimable and divine name of your Eternal God Ardza, and by the absolute virtue, Efficacy, and force thereof, most firmly solidly, and also effectually binding, constraining you to speak Audibly unto me, and to fulfil my earnest petitions and requests, for which I am now at this time very much necessitated to call you forth, desiring your benevolent Aid & assistance in these my Temporal and Terrestrial undertakings and affairs, constraining you in this Imperial name of your Omnipotent God Ardza, and the dignity thereof, to be friendly unto me, and to do for me, as for the servant of the Highest wherein your office is apparently manifest and Efficient.

Names of the four Angels set over the second Lesser Angle of the East Table, and to call them forth.
Vtepa[1], Tepau[2], Paute[3], Autep[4], divine name governing is Eutepa.

O You glorious and benevolent Angels Vtepa, Tepau, Paute, Autep, who art the four Angels set over the second Lesser Angle of the greater Terrestrial Angle of the East, I invoke, adjure, & call you forth to visible apparition, In and through this great, signal and divine name of your[453] most high God Eutepa, and by the Ineffable and Efficacious virtue and power thereof whereby you are governed and called forth, it being therefore absolutely preordained and decreed to be most solidly effectual; now therefore I do most earnestly entreat and powerfully adjure you, O you Benign Angels Vtepa, Tepau, Paute, Autep, in this potent name of your God Eutepa, to move, descend, appear and visibly show your selves in this Crystal Stone or Glass Receptacle here before me, and in, and through the same to transmit your Rays to my sight and your voices to my ears; that I may plainly see you and audibly hear you speak unto me, and conclude and receive[454] of your mysteries, wherefore I do earnestly request and adjure you, O you Luminous and amicable Angels Vtepa, Tepau, Paute, Autep, in this most excellent name of your God Eutepa, and I (as a servant of the Highest) do thereby efficaciously move you in power & presence to appear now presently visible unto me as aforesaid; O you servants of mercy, move,

---

[453] S2: "the".
[454] S2: Replaces "and receive" with "as receivers".

descend, personally show forth and appear[455] your selves friendly unto me, as unto the partaker of his Great Wisdom in your Creation for why our Lord & master is all one.

Names of the four Angels serving in the second Lesser Angle of the East Angle and to call them forth OYube[1], Paoc[2], Vrbeneh[3], Diri[4], divine names governing, calling forth Haeza, & constraining Palam.[456]

O You Benevolent Angels of Light OYube, Paoc, Vrbeneh, Diri, who are the four servient Angels serving in the second Lesser Angle of the greater Terrestrial Angle of the East, I invocate, adjure, command, and powerfully call you forth from your orders and mansion to visible apparition [457], In and through this great, prevalent, signal and divine name of your God Haeza, and by the efficacy, power and virtue thereof; most firmly and solidly, effectual for the calling you forth, commanding you to transmit your Rays visibly to my sight and your voices to my ears, In and through this Crystal Stone or Glass Receptacle or otherwise to appear thereout, here before me, That I may plainly see you and Audibly hear you speak unto me: move therefore O you Benign Servient Angels of Light OYube, Paoc, Vrbeneh, Diri, and in the potent name of your God Haeza And by the imperial dignity thereof, Descend & visibly show your selves as pleasant deliverers that you may praise him amongst the sons of men. O you servants of mercy OYube, Paoc, Vrbeneh, Diri, Come away and in this Ineffable and most excellent name of your God Haeza, visibly and personally appear to the admiration of the Earth and to my comfort, come away open the mysteries of your Creation, be friendly unto me, for I am a servant of the same your God the true worshipper of the Highest.

When there is apparition then receive it, and constrain as followeth saying

Welcome to[458] the Light of the Highest, whose holy name be glorified for his mercies endure for ever, And O you Benign Angels of Light OYube, Paoc, Vrbeneh, Diri, you are to me sincerely welcome, and I

---

[455] S2: "apply".
[456] S2: "Haeza, Palam".
[457] S2: "app earance arition".
[458] S2: "be".

do in and through this Inestimable and divine name of your Eternal God Palam, and by the absolute virtue, efficacy and force thereof, most firmly solidly and effectually binding constraining you to speak Audibly unto[459] me, and to fulfil my earnest petitions and requests, for which I am now at this time very much necessitated to call you forth, requesting your Benevolent instructions, aid, and assistance, in[460] these my Temporal and Terrestrial undertakings and affairs urgently constraining you in this Imperial name of your omnipotent God Palam, and the dignity thereof to be friendly unto me, and to do for me as for the servant of the Highest who in your office is apparently manifest and efficient.

Names of the four Angels set over the Third Lesser Angle of the East Table and to call them forth Cenbar[1], Enbarc[2], Barcen[3], Vrcenbre, - divine name governing is Ecenbar.

O You glorious and Benevolent Angels Cenbar, Enbarc, Barcen, Vrcenbre, who are the four Angels set over the Third Lesser Angle of the greater Terrestrial Angle of the East, I invoke adjure, and call you forth to visible apparition, in and through this great signal prevalent and divine name of your most high God Ecenbar, and in the Ineffable and Efficacious virtue and power thereof, who by[461] you are governed and called forth, it being therefore absolutely preordained and decreed to be most solidly effectual: now therefore I do most earnestly entreat, and powerfully adjure you, O you Benign Angels Cenbar, Enbarc, Barcen, Vrcenbre, in this potent name of your God Ecenbar, to move, descend, appear and visibly show yourselves in this Crystal Stone or Glass Receptacle here before me, and in and through the same to transmit your Rays unto my sight and your voices unto my Ears, that I may plainly see you and audibly hear you speak unto me, and conclude as a receiver of your mysteries, wherefore I do most urgently request and (desire) or adjure you, O you Luminous and amicable Angels Cenbar, Enbarc, Barcen, Vrcenbre, in this most excellent name of your God Ecenbar, and I (as a servant of the Highest) do thereby efficaciously move you in power and presence to appear now presently visible unto me as aforesaid; O you servants of mercy, Descend, (appear) and by divine permission, personally show forth and apply your selves friendly unto me as unto the partaker of his secret wisdom in your Creation,

---

[459] S2: "to".
[460] S2: "~~thy~~".
[461] S2: "whereof".

for why Our Lord and master is all one.

Names of the four Angels serving in the Third Lesser Angle of the East Table and to call them forth, Abemo, Naco, Ocenem, Shael, divine names governing, calling forth Aiaoai, & constraining Oiiit.

O You Benevolent Angels of Light Abemo, Naco, Ocenem, Shael, who are the four servient Angels serving in the Third Lesser Angle of the greater Terrestrial Angle of the East; I invocate, adjure, command, and powerfully call you forth from your orders and mansion to visible apparition In and through this great, prevalent, signal and divine name of your God Aiaoai, and by the efficacy power and virtue thereof, most firmly and solidly effectual for the calling you forth, commanding you to transmit your Rays visibly unto my sight, and your voices to my ears, in and through Crystal Stone or Glass Receptacle or otherwise to appear thereout here before me, that I may plainly see you and audibly hear you speak unto me move therefore O you Benign Servient Angels Abemo, Naco, Ocenem, Shael, in the potent name of your God Aiaoai, and by the Imperial Dignity thereof, descend and by divine permission visibly show your selves as pleasant deliverers, that you may praise him among[462] the sons of men; O you servants of mercy Abemo, Naco, Ocenem, Shael, come away open the mysteries of your Creation, be friendly unto me, and in this Ineffable and most excellent name of your God Aiaoai, visibly and personally appear to the admiration of the earth and to my comfort, for I am a servant of the same your God: The true worshipper of the Highest.

When there is apparition[463] then receive it, & constrain as followeth saying

---

Welcome to the Light of the Highest whose name be glorified for his mercy endureth for ever; And O you Benign Angels of Light Abemo, Naco, Ocenem, Shael, you are to me sincerely welcome, and I do in and through this Inestimable and divine name of your Eternal God Oiiit, and by the absolute virtue, efficacy and force thereof, most firmly solidly and effectually binding and constraining you to speak

---

[462] S2: "amongst".
[463] S2: "is there".

108

Audibly unto me, and to fulfil my earnest petitions and requests, for which I am now at this time very much necessitated to call you forth, Requesting your Benevolent Assistance, aid, and Instructions, in these my Temporal and Terrestrial undertakings and affairs, urgently [464] constraining you in this Imperial name of your omnipotent God Oiiit and the dignity thereof to be friendly unto me and by divine permission to do for me as for the servant of the Highest, wherein your office is apparently manifest and efficient.

Names of the four Angels set over the fourth Lesser Angle of the East Table & to call them forth Exgezod, Gezodex, Zodexge, Dexgezod – divine name governing Eexgezod.

O You glorious and Benevolent Angels Exgezod, Gezodex, Zodexge, Dexgezod, who are the four Angels set over the fourth Lesser Angle of the greater Terrestrial Angle of the East, I invoke adjure, and call you forth to visible apparition, In and through this great signal prevalent and divine name of your most high God Eexgezod, and by the Ineffable and efficacious virtue and power thereof whereby you are governed and called forth, it being therefore absolutely preordained and decreed to be most solidly effectual, now therefore I do most earnestly entreat, and powerfully adjure you O you Benign Angels Exgezod, Gezodex, Zodexge, Dexgezod, in this potent name of your God Eexgezod, to move, descend, appear and visibly show your selves in this Crystal Stone or Glass Receptacle here before me, and in and through the same to transmit your Rays unto my sight and your voices unto my ears, that I may plainly see you, and Audibly hear you speak unto me, and conclude me as a receiver of your mysteries; wherefore I do urgently request & adjure you, O you Luminous and Amicable Angels Exgezod, Gezodex, Zodexge, Dexgezod, in this most excellent name of your God Eexgezod, and I (as a servant of the Highest) do thereby efficaciously move you in power and presence to appear now presently visible unto me, as aforesaid: O you servants of mercy, move, Descend, and by divine permission personally show forth and apply your selves friendly unto me, as unto the partaker of his secret wisdom in your creation: for why, Our Lord and master is all one.

---

[464] S2: "~~constraining~~".

Names of the four Angels serving in the fourth Lesser Angle of the East Table and to call them forth Acca[1], Enpeat[2], Otoi[3], Pemox[4], divine names governing, calling forth Aovararzod, and constraining Moar.

O You Benevolent Angels of Light Acca, Enpeat, Otoi, Pemox, who are the four servient Angels serving in the fourth Lesser Angle of the greater Terrestrial Angle of the East, I invocate, adjure, command, and powerfully call you forth from your orders and mansion to visible apparition, In and through this great prevalent, signal and divine name of your God Aovararzod, and by the Efficacy power and virtue thereof, most firmly & solidly effectual for the calling you forth, commanding you to transmit your Rays visibly to my sight and your voices to my Ears, in and through this Crystal Stone or Glass Receptacle or otherwise to appear thereout here before me, That I may plainly see you and audibly hear you speak unto me move therefore; O you Benign Servient Angels of Light Acca, Enpeat, Otoi, Pemox, and in the potent name of your God Aovararzod, and by the Imperial dignity thereof, Descend and visibly show your selves as pleasant deliverers, that you may praise him among the sons of men; O you servants of mercy Acca, Enpeat, Otoi, Pemox, and in this Ineffable and most excellent name of your God Aovararzod, visibly & personally appear to the admiration of the Earth and to my comfort, come away open the mysteries of your creation be friendly unto me for I am a servant of the same your God the true worshipper of the Highest.

When there is apparition, then receive it, & constrain as followeth saying

---

Welcome to the Light of the Highest, whose holy name be glorified for his mercies endure for ever; And O you Benign Angels of Light Acca, Enpeat, Otoi, Pemox, you are to me sincerely welcome, and I do in and through this inestimable name of your Eternal God Moar, and by the absolute virtue and power, Efficacy and force thereof, most firmly solidly and effectually binding constrain you to speak audibly unto me and to fulfil my earnest petitions and requests, for which I am now at this time very much necessitated to call you forth, Requesting your Benevolent Instructions Aid and Assistance in these my Temporal and Terrestrial undertakings and affairs, urgently constraining you in this Imperial name of your Omnipotent

God Moar and the dignity thereof to be friendly unto me and by divine permission to do for me as for the servant of the Highest wherein your office is apparently manifest and efficient.

The Practice of the West Table[465]

The Regal Invocation

O Thou great, powerful, and mighty Angel of the Immortal God Raagios, who art ordained, constituted, and appointed, & set over the Terrestrial Angle of the West, by and according to the original and divine decree of the (Highest) omnipotent God of Hosts Empeh, Arsel, Gaiol, and under whom art the only King, governor, overseer, principal Watchman, protector and Keeper thereof, from the malice, misuse, Illusion, Temptation wicked encroachments and usurping Blasphemy of the great Enemy of God's glory and the welfare of mankind, the Devil and spirits of darkness and art a snaffle to them to restrain their wickedness by the bit of God's boundless power and justice; To the intent that (they being put out into the earth) their envious will might be bridled, the determinations of the heavenly God fulfilled, and his creatures kept within the compass and measure of order.

I the servant of the Highest do call upon you, O you mighty and Royal Angel Raagios, most humbly & earnestly entreating you, in and through these great names of the Infinite and Incomprehensible God of Hosts Empeh, Arsel, Gaiol, and by the virtue, power and efficacy thereof, to assist and help me in these my present operations and affairs, and by your[466] powerful permission and Authority to send and cause to come and appear unto me (N).

Residing under[467] your Government in the Angle of the West, whom I shall call forth by name, to Instruct, direct, and serve me in all such matters and things according to their offices, as I shall request and desire of them, both now and at all times also, whensoever necessity shall require their favourable Aid and Assistance, and such their good counsel and advertisements, as shall be requisite and fit for me, And herein I most ardently and Incessantly implore and beseech you; O Raagios, humbly desiring your friendship, and to do for me as for the servant of the most High, and Heavenly God of Hosts Empeh, Arsel, Gaiol, the Almighty creator and disposer of all things both Celestial, Aerial, Terrestrial and Infernal.

---

[465] S2: Has "Tab: 2" underneath the heading.
[466] S2: "the".
[467] S2: "the".

Names of the six Angelical Seniors and to call them forth
Lefarahpem[1], Saiinou[2], Laoaxarp[3], Selgaiol[4], Ligdisa[5], Soaixente[6].

O You glorious and Beneficent Angels Lefarahpem, Saiinou, Laoaxarp, Selgaiol, Ligdisa, Soaixente, who are the six Angelical Seniors serving before Raagios, the great honoured and Royal Angel of the high and Immortal God of Hosts in the Terrestrial Angle of the West, I most earnestly entreat, humbly request, and powerfully adjure and call you forth to visible apparition, in and through this mighty and Efficacious name of your King and Sovereign Lord of the West Angle of the Earth Raagios, and by the Ineffable virtue and power thereof, preordinally decreed by the Highest to be most firmly and solidly effectual for the calling you forth, now therefore O you Benevolent Angels Lefarahpem, Saiinou, Laoaxarp, Selgaiol, Ligdisa, Soaixente, I adjure and call you forth, in this true and most especial name of your King Raagios, and by the excellency thereof, urgently and potently entreating you to gird up and gather your selves together and by divine permission, move, Descend, and appear visibly and friendly unto me in this Crystal Stone or Glass Receptacle and in and through the same to transmit your Rays to my sight, and your Benevolent voices to my Ears, that I may plainly see you, and Audibly hear you speak unto me, and to assist, direct, Instruct, Illuminate, and show forth, what I shall humbly desire and request of you; O you servants of mercy Lefarahpem, Saiinou, Laoaxarp, Selgaiol, Ligdisa, Soaixente, come away and appear visibly unto me (as aforesaid) to the honour and glory of the omnipotent Creator, and the praise of his great and holy name, for unto this Remembrance is given power, and my strength waxeth strong in my comforter; Move therefore and show your selves, open the mysteries of your Creation, Be friendly unto me for I am a servant of the same your God the true worshipper of the Highest.

Names of the four Angels set over the first Lesser Angle of the West Table and to call them forth. Taad[1], Aadet[2], Adeta[3], Detaa[4], divine name governing Hetaad.

O You glorious and Benevolent Angels Taad, Aadet, Adeta, Detaa, who are the four Angels set over the first Lesser Angle of the greater Terrestrial Angle of the West, I invoke, adjure and call you forth to visible apparition, in and through this great, signal prevalent[468] and divine name of your most high God Hetaad, and by your Ineffable and Efficacious virtue and power thereof, whereby you are governed and called forth, it being therefore absolutely preordained and decreed to be most solidly effectual; now therefore I do most earnestly entreat, and powerfully adjure you, O you Benign Angels Taad, Aadet, Adeta, Detaa, in this potent name of your God Hetaad, to move, Descend, appear, and visibly show your selves to me, in this Crystal Stone or Glass Receptacle here before me, and in and through the same to transmit your Rays to my sight and your voices to my Ears, that I may plainly see you and audibly hear you speak unto me and conclude me as a Receiver of your mysteries; wherefore I do urgently request and adjure you: O you Luminous and amicable Angels Taad, Aadet, Adeta, Detaa, in this most Excellent name of your God Hetaad, and I (as the servant of the Highest) do thereby efficaciously move you in power and presence to appear now presently visible to me as aforesaid; O you Servants of mercy, move, Descend, personally show forth, and apply your selves friendly unto me as unto the partaker of his secret wisdom in your creation, for why; our Lord & master is all one.

Names of the four Angels serving to the first Lesser Angle of the west Table and to call them forth [469] Paax[3], Toco[1], Enheded[2], Saix[4], [470] divine names governing, calling forth Obegoca, & constraining Aabeco.

O You Benevolent Angels of Light Toco, Enheded, Paax, Saix, who are the four Servient Angels, serving in the first Lesser Angle of the greater Terrestrial Angle of the West; I invoke, adjure, command, and powerfully call you forth, from your orders and mansion to visible apparition, In and through this great, prevalent, signal, and divine name of God Obegoca, and by the efficacy, virtue, and power thereof, most firmly and solidly effectual for the calling you forth, commanding you to transmit your Rays visibly to my sight, and your voices to my Ears, in and through this Crystal Stone or Glass Receptacle or otherwise to appear thereout here before me, that I may plainly see you, and audibly hear you speak unto me; move therefore O you Benign Servient Angels of Light Toco, Enheded, Paax, Saix, and in the potent name of your God Obegoca, and by

[468] S2: "name being the".
[469] S2: "Paax, calling forth Obegoca".
[470] S2: "Divine name governing & constraining Aabeco".

the Imperial dignity thereof, Descend, and by divine permission, show yourselves as pleasant deliverers that you may praise him amongst the sons of men; O you servants of mercy Toco, Enheded, Paax, Saix, come away, and in this Ineffable and most excellent name of your God Obegoca, visibly and personally appear to the admiration of the Earth and to my comfort, come away, open the mysteries of your creation, be friendly unto me, for I am a servant of the same your God, the true worshipper of the Highest.

When the servient Angels of this order appeareth and is known, then receive them as followeth.

Welcome be the Light of the Highest whose name be glorified for his mercies endureth for ever. And O you servants of mercy and benign Angels of Light Toco, Enheded, Paax, Saix, you are to me sincerely welcome, and I do in this inestimable and Divine name of your Eternal God Aabeco, and by the absolute virtue and power, Efficacy & force thereof, most firmly solidly, and also effectually binding, constrain[471] you to speak Audibly unto me, and to fulfil my earnest petitions and requests, for which I am now at this time very much necessitated to call you forth, desiring your Benevolent Aid and Assistance in these my Temporal and Terrestrial undertakings and affairs, constraining you in this [472] Imperial name of your Omnipotent God Aabeco, and the dignity thereof, to be friendly unto me, and to do for me as for the servant of the Highest wherein your office is apparently manifest and Efficient.

Names of the four Angels set over the Second Lesser Angle of the West Table, and to call them forth Tedim, Dimet, Imted, Emtedi, divine name governing Hetedim.

O You glorious and Benevolent Angels Tedim, Dimet, Imted, Emtedi, who art the four Angels set over the second Lesser Angle of the greater Terrestrial Angle of the West, I invoke, adjure, and call you forth to visible apparition, in and through, this great, Signal, prevalent and divine name of your most high God Hetedim, and by the Ineffable and Efficacious virtue and power thereof whereby you are governed and called forth, it being therefore absolutely

---

[471] S2: "constraining".
[472] S2: "the".

preordained and decreed to be most solidly effectual; now therefore I do most earnestly entreat and powerfully adjure you, O you Benign Angels Tedim, Dimet, Imted, Emtedi, in this potent name of your God Hetedim, to move, descend, appear, and visibly show your selves in this Crystal Stone or Glass Receptacle here before me, and in and through the same to transmit your Rays to my sight and your voices to my Ears that I may plainly see you and Audibly hear you speak unto me, and conclude me a receiver of your mysteries, wherefore I do earnestly request and adjure you, O you Luminous and Amicable Angels Tedim, Dimet, Imted, Emtedi, in this most excellent name of your God Hetedim, And I (as a servant of the Highest) do thereby Efficaciously move you in power and presence to appear now presently visible unto me as aforesaid, O you Servants of mercy, move, descend, personally show forth and apply your selves friendly unto me as unto the partaker of his[473] Secret Wisdom in your Creation, for why, our Lord and master is all one.

Names of the four Angels serving in the second Lesser Angle of the West Table & to call them forth Magem[1], Leoc[2], Vsyl[3], Vrvoi[4], divine names governing, calling forth Nelapar, & constraining Omebeb.

O You Benevolent Angels of Light Magem, Leoc, Vsyl, Vrvoi, who are the four servient Angels serving in the second Lesser Angle of the greater Terrestrial Angle of the West, I invoke, adjure, command, and powerfully call you forth from your orders and mansion to visible apparition, in and through this great, prevalent, signal & divine name of your God Nelapar, and by your[474] efficacy, power and virtue thereof, most firmly and solidly effectual for the calling you forth, commanding you to transmit your Rays visibly to my sight and your voices to my Ears in and through this Crystal Stone or Glass Receptacle or otherwise to appear thereout here before me, that I may plainly see you, and Audibly hear you speak unto me; move therefore O you Benign Servient Angels of Light Magem, Leoc, Vsyl, Vrvoi, and in the name of your God Nelapar, And by the imperial Dignity thereof, Descend, and visibly show your selves as pleasant deliverers that you may praise[475] among the sons of men; O you servants of mercy Magem, Leoc, Vsyl, Vrvoi, come away and in this Ineffable and most excellent name of your God Nelapar, visibly and personally appear to the admiration of the Earth and to

---

[473] S2: "this".
[474] S2: "the".
[475] S2: "be praised".

my comfort; come away open the mysteries of your Creation, be friendly unto me, for I am a servant of the same your God the true worshipper of the Highest.

When the Servient Angels of this order appeareth and are known then receive them as followeth saying

Welcome be the Light of the Highest, whose holy name be glorified for his mercies endure for ever: And O you Benign Angels of Light Magem, Leoc, Vsyl, Vrvoi, you are to me sincerely welcome, and I do in and through this inestimable and divine name of your Eternal God Omebeb, and by the absolute virtue, Efficacy and force most firmly, solidly and effectually binding, constrain you to speak Audibly unto me, and to fulfil my earnest petitions and requests, for which I am now at this time very much necessitated to call you forth, Requesting your Benevolent Instructions, Aid, and Assistance, in these my Temporal and Terrestrial undertakings and affairs, urgently constraining you, in this Imperial name of your omnipotent God Omebeb, and the dignity thereof to be friendly unto me and by divine permission to do for me as for the servant of the Highest, wherein your office is apparently manifest and efficient.

Names of the four Angels set over the Third Lesser Angle of the West Table and to call them forth Magel[1], Agelem[2], Gelema[3], Lemage[4], - divine name governing is Hemagel.

O You glorious and Benevolent Angels Magel, Agelem, Gelema, Lemage, who are the four Angels set over the Third Lesser Angle of the greater Terrestrial Angle of West Table, I invoke adjure and call you forth to visible apparition, In and through this great, signal, prevalent and divine name of your most high God Hemagel, and by the Ineffable and Efficacious virtue and power thereof whereby you are governed and called forth, it being therefore absolutely preordained & decreed to be most solidly effectual: Now therefore I do most earnestly entreat, & powerfully adjure you; O you Benign Angels Magel, Agelem, Gelema, Lemage, in this potent name of your God Hemagel, to move, Descend, appear, and visibly show yourselves in this Crystal Stone or Glass Receptacle here before me, and in and through the same to transmit your Rays unto my Sight and your Voices unto[476] my ears, that I may plainly see you, and Audibly hear you speak unto me, and conclude me as a Receiver of your mysteries, wherefore I do most[477] urgently request & adjure you, O you Luminous and Amicable Angels Magel, Agelem, Gelema, Lemage, in this most excellent name of your God Hemagel, And I (as a servant of the Highest) do thereby efficaciously move you in power and presence to appear now presently visible unto me as aforesaid, O you servants of mercy, move, Descend, personally show forth and apply your selves friendly unto me, as unto the Secret wisdom in your Creation, for why Our Lord & master is all one.

Names of the four Angels serving in the Third Lesser Angle of the West Table and to call them forth, Paco[1], Endezen[2], [478] Fipo[3], Exarih[4], divine names governing, calling forth Maladi, and constraining Olaad.

O You glorious and Benevolent Angels Paco, Endezen, Fipo, Exarih, who are the four Servient Angels serving in the Third Lesser Angle of the greater Terrestrial Angle of the West; I invocate, adjure, command, and powerfully call you forth from your orders and mansion to visible apparition, in and through this great, prevalent, signal and divine name of your God Maladi, and by the efficacy power and virtue thereof, most firmly and solidly effectual for the calling you forth, commanding you to Transmit your Rays visibly unto my sight, and your voices to my ears, in and through this Crystal Stone or Glass Receptacle or otherwise to appear thereout here before me, that I may plainly see you, & Audibly hear you speak unto me: Move therefore O you Benign servient Angels of Light Paco, Endezen, Fipo, Exarih, in the potent name of your God Maladi, and by the Imperial Dignity thereof, Descend, and by the divine permission of the Highest visibly show your selves as pleasant deliverers, that you may praise him amongst the Sons of men. O you Servants of mercy Paco, Endezen, Fipo, Exarih, come away, open the mysteries of your creation, be friendly unto me, and in this Ineffable and most Excellent name of your God Maladi, visibly and personally appear to the admiration of the Earth and to my comfort, for I am a servant of the same your God, The true Worshipper of the Highest.

---

[476] S2: "to".
[477] S2: Omits "most".
[478] S2: "~~calling forth Maladi constraining Olaad~~".

When there is apparition, then receive it &[479] constrain as followeth saying

---

Welcome to the Light of thy countenance, whose holy name is[480] glorified for his mercies endure for ever, And O you Benign Angels of Light Paco, Endezen, Fipo, Exarih, you are to me sincerely welcome, and I do in and through the Inestimable and divine name of your Eternal God Olaad, and by the absolute virtue, Efficacy and force thereof, mostly firmly solidly and effectually binding, constrain[481] you to speak Audibly unto me, and to fulfil my earnest petitions and Requests for which I am now at this time very much necessitated to call you forth, Requesting your Benevolent Instructions, Aid, and Assistance in these my Temporal and Terrestrial undertakings and affairs, urgently constraining you in this Imperial name of your Omnipotent God Olaad, and the dignity therein to be friendly unto me, and by divine permission of the Highest to do for me as for his servant, wherein your office is apparently manifest and efficient.

Names of the four Angels set over the fourth Lesser Angle of the West Table & to call them forth Enlarex[1], Larexen[2], Rexenel[3], Xenelar[4], divine name governing is Henlarex.

O You glorious and Benevolent Angels Enlarex, Larexen, Rexenel, Xenelar, who are the four Angels set over the fourth Lesser Angle of the greater Terrestrial Angle of the West, I invoke adjure, and call you forth to visible apparition, in and through this great, Signal, prevalent and divine name of your most high God Henlarex, and by the Ineffable and Efficacious virtue and power thereof whereby you are governed and called forth, it being therefore absolutely preordained & decreed to be most solidly effectual: now therefore I do most earnestly entreat and powerfully adjure you. O you Benign Angels Enlarex, Larexen, Rexenel, Xenelar, in this potent name of your God Henlarex, to move, descend, appear and visibly show your selves in this Crystal Stone or Glass Receptacle here before me, and in and through the same to transmit your Rays to my sight and your voices to my Ears, that I may plainly see you and Audibly hear you speak unto me, and conclude me as a Receiver of your

---

[479] S2: "~~confine~~".
[480] S2: "be".
[481] S2: "and constraining".

mysteries; wherefore I do urgently request and adjure you, O you Luminous & amicable Angels Enlarex, Larexen, Rexenel, Xenelar, in this most excellent name of your God Henlarex, And I (as a servant of the Highest) do thereby efficaciously move you in power and presence to appear now presently visible unto me, as aforesaid: O you servants of mercy, move, Descend, and by divine permission personally show forth and apply your selves friendly unto me, as unto the partaker of his Secret wisdom in your Creation; as[482] for why, Our Lord and Master is all one.

Names of the four Angels serving in[483] the fourth Lesser Angle of the West Table Expeceh[1], Vasa[2], Dapi[3], Reniel[4], divine names governing, calling forth Jaaasde, and constraining Atapa.

O You Benevolent Angels of Light Expeceh, Vasa, Dapi, Reniel, who are the four servient Angels serving in the fourth Lesser Angle of the greater Terrestrial Angle of the West, I invocate, adjure, command, & powerfully call you forth, from your orders and mansion to visible apparition, in and through this great prevalent, signal and divine name of your God Jaaasde, and by the efficacy virtue and power thereof, most firmly and solidly effectual for the calling you forth, commanding you to transmit your Rays visibly to my Sight and your voices to my Ears, in and through this Crystal Stone or Glass Receptacle or otherwise to appear thereout here before me, that I may plainly see you and Audibly hear you speak unto me: move therefore, O you Benign Servient Angels of Light Expeceh, Vasa, Dapi, Reniel, and in the potent name of your God Jaaasde, and by the Imperial Dignity thereof, descend and by divine permission visibly show your selves as pleasant deliverers, that you may praise him among the sons of men; O you servants of mercy Expeceh, Vasa, Dapi, Reniel, come away and in this Ineffable and most excellent name of your God Jaaasde, visibly and personally appear to the admiration of the Earth and to my comfort; Come away open the mysteries of your Creation, be friendly unto me for I am a servant of the same your God the true worshipper of the Highest.

When the Servient Angels of this order appeareth and are known then receive them as followeth saying

---

[482] S2: Omits "as".
[483] S2: "to".

Welcome to[484] the Light of the Highest, whose holy name be glorified for his mercies endure for ever; And O you Benign Angels of Light Expeceh, Vasa, Dapi, Reniel, you are to me sincerely welcome, and I do in and through this inestimable & divine name of your Eternal God Atapa, and by the absolute virtue efficacy and force, most firmly, solidly and effectually binding, constrain[485] you to speak Audibly unto me and to fulfil my earnest petitions and requests, for which I am now at this time very much necessitated to call you forth, Requesting your Benevolent Instructions Aid and Assistance in these my Temporal and Terrestrial undertakings & affairs, urgently constraining you in this Imperial name of your Omnipotent God Atapa and the dignity thereof, to be friendly unto me and (by the[486] Divine permission of the Highest) to do for me as for the servant of the most high God wherein your office is apparently manifest and Efficient.

---

[484] S2: "be".
[485] S2: "& constraining".
[486] S2: Omits "the".

The Practice of the North Table

The Regal Invocation

O Thou great powerful, and mighty Angel of the Immortal God Jezodhehca, who art ordained constituted & appointed, and set over the Terrestrial Angle of the North, by and according to the original and divine decree of the Omnipotent God of Hosts Emor, Dial, Hectega, and under whom art the only King, governor, overseer, principal watchman, protector and Keeper thereof, from the malice, misuse, Illusion, Temptation, wicked encroachments and usurping Blasphemy of the great Enemy of God's glory and the welfare of mankind, the Devil and Spirits of darkness and art a snaffle to them to restrain their wickedness by the bit of God's boundless power and justice; To the intent that (they being put out into the Earth) their envious will might be bridled, the determinations of the heavenly God fulfilled and his creatures kept within the compass and measure of order.

I the servant of the Highest do call upon you, O you (Servient) mighty and Royal Angel[487] Jezodhehca, most humbly and earnestly entreating you, in and through these great names of the Infinite[488] and Incomprehensible God of Hosts Emor, Dial, Hectega, and by the virtue, power, and efficacy thereof, to assist and help in these my present operations and affairs, and by the powerful permission and Authority to send and cause to come and appear unto me [Name].

Residing under your government in the Angle of the North, whom I shall call forth by name to Instruct, direct, and serve me in all such matters and things according to their offices, as I shall request and desire of them both now and at all times also, Whensoever necessity shall require their favourable Aid and Assistance, and such their good counsel and advertisements, as shall be requisite and fit for me, And herein I most ardently and Incessantly implore and beseech you O Jezodhehca, humbly desiring your friendship, and to do for me as for the servant of the most high and heavenly God of Hosts Emor, Dial, Hectega, the Almighty creator and Disposer of all

---

[487] S2: Replaces "and Royal Angel" with "Angel Royally called".
[488] S2: "Immense".

Names of the six Angelical Seniors and to call them forth
Laidrom[1], Aczinor[2], (or Aczodinor), Elzinopo[3], Alhectega[4], Elhiansa[5], Acemliceve[6].

O You glorious and Beneficent Angels Laidrom, Aczinor, Elzinopo, Alhectega, Elhiansa, Acemliceve, who are the six Angelical Seniors serving before Jezodhehca, the great, honoured and Royal Angel of the high and Immortal God of Hosts in the Terrestrial Angle of the North, I most earnestly request, humbly entreat and powerfully adjure and call you forth to visible apparition, in and through this mighty and efficacious name of your King and Sovereign Lord of the North Angle of the Earth Jezodhehca, and by the Ineffable virtue and power thereof, preordinally decreed by the Highest to be most firmly and solidly effectual [489], for the calling you forth; Now therefore O you Benevolent Angels Laidrom, Aczinor, Elzinopo, Alhectega, Elhiansa, Acemliceve, I adjure and call you forth in this true and most especial name of your King Jezodhehca, and by the excellency thereof, urgently and potently entreating you, to gird up and gather your selves together and by divine permission, move, Descend, and appear visibly and friendly unto me in this Crystal Stone or Glass Receptacle and in and through the same, to transmit your Rays to my Sight, and your Benevolent voices to my ears, that I may plainly see you, and Audibly hear you speak unto me, and to assist, direct, Instruct, Illuminate and show forth what I shall humbly request and desire of you: O you servants of mercy Laidrom, Aczinor, Elzinopo, Alhectega, Elhiansa, Acemliceve, come away and appear visibly unto me as aforesaid to the honour and glory of the omnipotent Creator and the praise of his great and holy name: for unto this Remembrance is given power, and my strength waxeth strong in my comforter, Move therefore and show your selves, open the mysteries of your Creation, Be friendly unto me for I am a servant of the same your God, the true worshipper of the Highest.

Names of the four Angels set over the first Lesser Angle of the North Table and to call them forth Boza, Ozab, Zabo, Aboz,
The divine name governing is Enboza.

O You glorious and Benevolent Angels Boza, Ozab, Zabo, Aboz, who

---

[489] S2: "effectually".

are the four Angels set over the first Lesser Angle of the greater Terrestrial Angle of the North: I invoke, adjure, and call you forth to visible apparition, in and through this great, signal, prevalent and divine name of your most high God Enboza, and by the Ineffable and Efficacious virtue and power thereof, whereby you are governed and called forth, it being therefore absolutely preordained and decreed to be most solidly effectual: now therefore I do most earnestly entreat, and powerfully adjure you, O you Benign Angels Boza, Ozab, Zabo, Aboz, in this potent name of your God Enboza, to move, Descend, appear and visibly show your selves to me in this Crystal Stone or Glass Receptacle here before me, and in and through the same to transmit your Rays to my sight and your voices to my Ears, that I may plainly see you and Audibly hear you speak unto me and conclude me as a receiver of your mysteries wherefore I do urgently request and adjure you: O you Luminous and Amicable Angels Boza, Ozab, Zabo, Aboz, in this most Excellent name of your God Enboza, and I (as the servant of the Highest) do thereby efficaciously move you in power and presence to appear now presently visible to me as aforesaid; O you servants of mercy, move, Descend, personally show forth, and apply your selves friendly unto me, as unto the partaker of his secret wisdom in your creation, For why, Our Lord and master is all one.

Names of the four Angels serving to the first Lesser Angle of the north Table and to call them forth Aira[1], Ormen[2], Reseni[3], Jzodenar[4], divine names governing, calling forth Angepoi, [490] & constraining Vnenax.

O You Benevolent Angels of Light Aira, Ormen, Reseni, Jzodenar, who are the four Servient Angels, serving in the first Lesser Angle of the greater Terrestrial Angle of the north, I invoke, adjure command, and powerfully call you forth, from your mansions and orders to visible apparition, In and through this great, prevalent Signal and divine name of your God Angepoi, and by the Efficacy, virtue, and power thereof, most firmly and solidly effectual for the calling you forth, commanding you to transmit your Rays to my sight, and your voices to my ears in and through this Crystal Stone or Glass Receptacle or otherwise to appear thereout here before me, that I may plainly see you, and Audibly hear you speak unto me, move therefore O you Benign Servient Angels of Light Aira, Ormen, Reseni, Jzodenar, And in the potent name of your God Angepoi, and

---

[490] S2: "Angepoi Unenax, constr".

by the Imperial Dignity thereof, Descend and visibly show yourselves as pleasant deliverers that you may praise him amongst the sons of men; O you servants of mercy Aira, Ormen, Reseni, Jzodenar, come away and in this Ineffable and most excellent name of your God Angepoi,[491] and personally appear to the admiration of the Earth and to my comfort, come away open the mysteries of your creation, be friendly unto me, for I am a servant of the same your God; The true worshipper of the Highest.

When there is apparition, then say as followeth.

Welcome be the Light of the Highest whose name be glorified for his mercies endureth for ever, And O you servants of mercy and benign Angels of Light Aira, Ormen, Reseni, Jzodenar, you are to me sincerely welcome, and I do in and through this Inestimable and divine name of your Eternal God Vnenax, and by the absolute virtue, Efficacy & force, most firmly, solidly & effectually binding, constrain[492] you to speak audibly unto me, and to fulfil my earnest petitions and requests, for which I am now at this time very much necessitated to call you forth desiring your benevolent Aid and assistance in these my Temporal and Terrestrial undertakings and affairs, constraining you in this Imperial name of your Omnipotent God Vnenax, and the dignity thereof, to be friendly unto me, and to do for me, as for the servant of the Highest wherein your office is apparently manifest and Efficient.

Names of the four Angels set over the Second Lesser Angle, and to call them forth Phra[1] (or Phara), Harap[2], Rapeh[3], Aphar[4], divine name governing[493] Enphra.

O You glorious and benevolent Angels Phra, Harap, Rapeh, Aphar, who art the four Servient Angels set over the second Lesser Angle of the greater Terrestrial Angle of the north; I invoke, adjure, and call you forth to visible apparition, in and through, this great, Signal, prevalent and divine name of the most high God Enphra, and by the ineffable and efficacious virtue and power thereof whereby you are governed and called forth, it being therefore absolutely preordained and decreed to be most solidly effectual; now therefore I do most

---

[491] S2: Inserts "visibly".
[492] S2: "& constraining".
[493] S2: Inserts "is".

earnestly entreat and powerfully adjure you, O you benign Angels Phra, Harap, Rapeh, Aphar, in this potent name of your God Enphra, to move, descend, appear and visibly show your selves in this Crystal Stone or Glass Receptacle here before me, and in and through the same to transmit your Rays to my sight and your voices to my Ears that I may plainly see you and Audibly hear you speak unto me, and conclude me as a receiver of your mysteries, wherefore I do earnestly request and adjure you, O you Luminous and Amicable Angels Phra, Harap, Rapeh, Aphar, [in this most excellent name of your God Enphra,][494] and I (as a servant of the Highest) do thereby Efficaciously move you in power and presence to appear now presently visible unto me [as aforesaid: O you servants of mercy, move, Descend, personally show forth and apply your selves friendly unto me,][495] as unto the partakers of his Secret Wisdom in your Creation; For why our Lord and master is all one.

Names of the four Angels serving to the Second Lesser Angle of the north Angle and to call them forth Omgege[1], Gebal[2], Relemu[3], Jahel[4], divine names governing, calling forth Anacem, & constraining Sonden.

O Ye Benevolent Angels of Light Omgege, Gebal, Relemu, Jahel, who are the four Servient Angels serving in the second Lesser Angle of the greater Terrestrial Angle of the north, I invocate, adjure, command, and powerfully call you forth from your orders and mansion to visible apparition, in and through this great, prevalent, Signal and divine name of your God Anacem, and by the efficacy virtue and power thereof most firmly and solidly effectual for the calling you forth, commanding you to transmit your Rays visibly to my sight, and your voices to my Ears in and through this Crystal Stone or Glass Receptacle or otherwise to appear out of the same here before me, that I may plainly see you &[496] audibly hear you speak unto me. Move therefore. O you Benign Servient Angels of Light Omgege, Gebal, Relemu, Jahel, and in the potent name of your God Anacem and by the Imperial dignity thereof, descend and visibly show your selves, as pleasant deliverers, that you may praise him among the sons of men; O you servants of mercy Omgege[1],

---

[494] This phrase is omitted here, but is consistently present elsewhere in Sloane 301, so this may be a copyist's error.

[495] As for the previous note, also absent in Sloane 301 but consistently present elsewhere in the manuscript.

[496] S2: "Audibly".

Gebal[2], Relemu[3], Jahel[4], and in this potent name of your God Anacem and by the Imperial dignity thereof, descend and visibly show your selves, as pleasant deliverers, that you may praise him among the sons of men; O you servants of mercy Omgege[1], Gebal[2], Relemu[3], Jahel[4], come away and in this ineffable and most excellent name of your God Anacem, visibly and personally appear to the admiration of the Earth and to my comfort, come away open the mysteries of your Creation, be friendly unto me for I am a servant of the same your God the true worshipper of the Highest.

When there is apparition, then receive it, and constrain as followeth saying

---

Welcome to[497] the Light of the Highest, whose holy name be glorified for his mercies endure for ever; And O you Benign Angels of Light Omgege, Gebal, Relemu, Jahel, you are to me sincerely welcome, and I do in and through this inestimable and divine name of your Eternal God Sonden, and by the absolute virtue Efficacy and force thereof, most firmly solidly and effectually binding, constrain[498] you to speak Audibly unto me, and to fulfil my earnest petitions and requests for which I am now at this time very much necessitated to call you forth, requesting your benevolent instructions, aid and assistance, in these my Temporal and Terrestrial undertakings and affairs, urgently constraining you, in this Imperial name of your Omnipotent God Sonden, and the dignity thereof to be friendly unto me, and by divine permission to do for me, as for the servant of the Highest wherein your office is apparently manifest & efficient.

Names of the four Angels set over the Third Lesser Angle of the East Table and to call them forth Æoan[1], Oanæ[2], Anæo[3], Næoa[4], divine name governing is[499] NÆOAN.

O Ye glorious and benevolent Angels, who are the four Angels set over the Third Lesser Angle of the greater Terrestrial Angle of the north, I invoke, adjure and call you forth to visible apparition, in and through this great, Signal, prevalent and divine name of your

---

[497] S2: "be".
[498] S2: "& constraining".
[499] S2: Omits "is".

most high God Næoan, and by the ineffable and efficacious virtue and power thereof, whereby you are governed and called forth; it being therefore absolutely preordained and decreed to be most solidly effectual: now therefore I do most earnestly entreat and powerfully adjure you; O you Benign Angels of Light Æoan, Oanæ, Anæo, Næoa, in this potent name of your God Næoan, to move, descend, appear, and visibly show yourselves in this Crystal Stone or Glass Receptacle here before me, and in and through the same to transmit your Rays unto my Sight and your voices unto[500] my Ears, that I may plainly see you and Audibly hear you speak unto me and conclude me as a receiver of your mysteries, wherefore I do urgently request and adjure you; O you Luminous and Amicable Angels Æoan, Oanæ, Anæo, Næoa, in this most excellent name of your God Næoan, and I (as a servant of the Highest) do there by efficaciously move you in power and presence to appear now presently visible unto me as aforesaid, O you servants of mercy move, descend, and by divine permission; personally show forth, and apply your selves friendly unto me as unto the partaker of his Secret wisdom in your Creation, for why; Our Lord & master is all one.

Names of the four Angels serving in the Third Lesser Angle of the north Table and to call them forth, Opena[1], Dopa[2], Rexao[3], Axir[4], divine names governing, calling forth Cebalpet, & constraining Arbizod.[501]

O Ye Benevolent Angels of Light Opena, Dopa, Rexao, Axir, who are the four Servient Angels, serving in the Third Lesser Angle of the greater Terrestrial Angle of the North, I invocate, adjure, command and powerfully call you forth, from your orders and mansion to visible apparition, in and through this great, prevalent, signal and divine name of your God Cebalpet, and by the Efficacy power and virtue thereof, most firmly and solidly effectual for the calling you forth, commanding you to Transmit your Rays visibly unto my sight, and your voices to my ears, in and through this Crystal Stone or Glass Receptacle or otherwise to appear thereout here before me, that I may plainly see you and Audibly hear you speak unto me; move therefore O you Benign Angels of Light Opena, Dopa, Rexao, Axir, in the potent name of your God Cebalpet, and by the Imperial dignity thereof, descend, and by the divine permission of the Highest visibly show your selves as pleasant deliverers that you

---

[500] S2: "to".
[501] S2: "~~Cebalpet * Arbizod~~".

may praise him amongst the Sons of men; O you servants of mercy Opena, Dopa, Rexao, Axir, come away, open the mysteries of your Creation, be friendly unto me, and in this Ineffable[502] and most Excellent name of your God Cebalpet, visibly and personally appear to the admiration of the Earth and to my comfort, for I am a servant of the same your God, The true Worshipper of the Highest.

When there is apparition, then receive it, & constrain as followeth saying

---

Welcome be the Light of the Highest, whose holy name is[503] glorified for his mercies endure for ever, And O you Benign Angels of Light Opena, Dopa, Rexao, Axir, you are to me sincerely welcome, and I do in and through the Inestimable and divine name of your Eternal God Arbizod, and by the absolute virtue, Efficacy and force thereof, mostly firmly solidly and effectually binding, constrain you to speak Audibly unto me, and to fulfil my earnest petitions and requests, for which I am now at this time very much necessitated to call you forth, requesting your benevolent instructions, aid and assistance in these my Temporal & Terrestrial undertakings and affairs, urgently constraining you in this Imperial name of your Omnipotent God Arbizod, and the dignity thereof, to be friendly unto me, and by divine permission to do for me as for the servant of the Highest wherein your office is apparently manifest and Efficient.

Names of the four Angels set over the Fourth Lesser Angle of the north Table and to call them forth Iaom[1], Aomi[2], Omia[3], Miao[4] divine name governing is Niaom.

O Ye glorious and Benevolent Angels Iaom, Aomi, Omia, Miao, who are the four Angels set over the Fourth Lesser Angle of the greater Terrestrial Angle of the north, I invoke adjure and call you forth to visible apparition, in and through this great, Signal, prevalent and divine name of your most high God Niaom, and by the Ineffable and Efficacious virtue and power thereof whereby you are governed and called forth, it being therefore absolutely preordained and decreed, to be most solidly effectual: now therefore I do most earnestly

---

[502] S2: "Inestimable".
[503] S2: "be".

entreat and powerfully adjure you; O you Benign Angels Iaom, Aomi, Omia, Miao, in this potent name of your God Niaom, to move, descend, appear and visibly show your selves in this Crystal Stone or Glass Receptacle here before me, and in and through the same to transmit your Rays unto my sight and your voices unto my Ears, that I may plainly see you and Audibly hear you speak unto me and conclude me as a receiver of your mysteries, wherefore I do urgently request and adjure you; O you Luminous and amicable Angels Iaom, Aomi, Omia, Miao, in this most excellent name of your God Niaom, and I (as a servant of the Highest) do thereby efficaciously move you, in power and presence to appear now presently visible unto me as aforesaid, O you Servants of mercy, move, descend, and by divine permission personally show forth, and apply your selves friendly unto me as unto the partaker of his Secret wisdom in your Creation For why, Our Lord and master is all one.

Names of the four Angels serving in the Fourth Lesser Angle of the north Table Mesael[1], Jaba[2], Jezexpe[3], Estim[4], divine names governing, calling forth Espemenir, and constraining Hpizol.

O You[504] Benevolent Angels of Light Mesael, Jaba, Jezexpe, Estim, who are the four Servient Angels serving in the [fourth][505] Lesser Angle of the greater Terrestrial[506] Angle of the North, I invocate, adjure, command you, and powerfully call forth from your orders and mansion to visible apparition, in and through this great, prevalent, Signal and divine name of your God Espemenir, and by the efficacy power and virtue thereof, most firmly and solidly effectual for the calling you forth, commanding to transmit your rays visibly unto my sight, and your voices to my Ears, in and through this Crystal Stone or Glass Receptacle or otherwise to appear thereout here before me that I may plainly see you, and Audibly hear you speak unto me; move therefore; O you benign Servient Angels of Light Mesael, Jaba, Jezexpe, Estim, and in the potent name of your God Espemenir, and by the Imperial dignity thereof, descend and by the divine permission of the Highest, visibly show your selves as pleasant deliverers, that you may praise him among the sons of men; O you servants of mercy Mesael, Jaba, Jezexpe, Estim, come away open the mysteries of your Creation, be

---

[504] S2: "Yee".

[505] S1: Has a copying error, giving "Third" here instead of fourth. One suspects the copyist was tired and errors crept in.

[506] S2: "~~tiall~~".

friendly unto me and in this ineffable and most excellent name of your God Espemenir, visibly and personally appear to the admiration of the Earth and to my comfort, for I am a servant of the same your God, The true worshipper of the Highest.

When there is apparition, then receive it, & constrain as followeth, Welcome be the Light of the Highest, whose holy name be glorified for his mercies endure for ever. And O you Benign Angels of Light Mesael, Jaba, Jezexpe, Estim, you are to me sincerely welcome, and I do in and through this inestimable and divine name of your Eternal God Hpizod, and by the absolute virtue, power and efficacy thereof, most firmly and solidly & effectually binding constrain[507] you to speak Audibly unto me, and to fulfil my earnest petitions and requests, for which I am now at this time very much necessitated to call you forth, requesting your benevolent instructions, aid and assistance, in these my Temporal and Terrestrial undertakings and affairs, urgently constraining you, in this Imperial name of your Omnipotent God Hpizod, and the dignity thereof, to be friendly unto me, and by divine permission to do for me as for the servant of the Highest, wherein your office is apparently manifest and Efficient.

---

[507] S2: "solidly binding & effectually constraining".

The Practice of the South Table

O Thou great powerful, and mighty Angel of the Immortal God Edelperna, who art ordained constituted[508] and appointed and set over the Terrestrial Angle of the South: by and according to the original and divine decree of the omnipotent God of Hosts Oip, Teaa, Pedoce, and under whom art the only King, governor, overseer, principal Watchman, protector & Keeper thereof, from the malice, misuse, Illusion Temptation, wicked encroachments and usurping Blasphemy of the great Enemy of God's glory and the welfare of mankind, the Devil and spirits of darkness, and art a snaffle to them to restrain their wickedness, by the bit of god's boundless power and justice; To the intent that (they being put out into the Earth) their envious will might be bridled, the determinations of the heavenly God fulfilled and his creatures kept within the compass and measure of order.

I the servant of the Highest do call upon you, O you mighty and Royal Angel Edelperna, most humbly and earnestly entreating you, in and through these great names of the Immense and Incomprehensible God of Hosts Oip, Teaa, Pedoce, and by the virtue power and efficacy thereof, to assist and help me, in these my present operations and affairs, and by the powerful permission and Authority to send and cause to come, and appear unto me, [Name] residing under your Government in the Angle of the South, whom I shall call[509] forth by name, to instruct, direct and serve me in all such matters and things according to their offices, as I shall request and desire of them, both now and at all times also, whensoever necessity shall require their favourable aid, and assistance and such their good counsel and advertisements as shall be requisite and fit for me, and herein I most ardently and incessantly Implore and beseech you O Edelperna, humbly desiring your friendship and to do for me as for the servant of the most high and heavenly God of Hosts Oip, Teaa, Pedoce, the Almighty Creator and disposer of all things both Celestial, Aerial, Terrestrial & Infernal.

Names of the six Angelical Seniors and to call them forth Aaetpio[1],

---

[508] S1, S2: Has "(~~constituted~~)" inserted here after "constituted".
[509] S2: Inserts "by name" here so it occurs before and after "forth".

Adoeoet[2], Alendood[3], Aapedoce[4], Arinnaquu[5], Anodoin[6].

O Ye glorious and beneficent[510] Angels Aaetpio, Adoeoet, Alendood, Aapedoce, Arinnaquu, Anodoin, who are the six Angelical Seniors serving before Edelperna, the great honoured and Royal Angel of the high and Immortal God of Hosts in the Terrestrial Angle of the South, I most earnestly entreat, humbly request and powerfully adjure and call you forth to visible apparition, In and through this mighty and Efficacious name of your King Edelperna, Sovereign Lord of the South Angle of the world, and by the Ineffable virtue and power thereof preordinally decreed by the Highest to be most firmly and solidly Effectual for the calling you forth now therefore O you Benevolent Angels Aaetpio, Adoeoet, Alendood, Aapedoce, Arinnaquu, Anodoin, I adjure and call you forth in this true and most especial name of your King Edelperna, and by the excellency thereof, urgently and potently entreating you to gird up and gather your selves together and by divine permission, move, descend, and appear visibly and friendly unto me in this Crystal Stone or Glass Receptacle and in and through the same to transmit your splendid Rays to my Sight and your Benevolent voices to my Ears, that I may plainly see you and Audibly hear you speak unto me and to assist, direct, instruct, illuminate and show forth what I shall humbly desire & request of you, O you servants of mercy Aaetpio, Adoeoet, Alendood, Aapedoce, Arinnaquu, Anodoin, come away & appear visibly unto me (as aforesaid) to the honour and glory of the Omnipotent Creator, and the praise of his great and holy name, for unto this Remembrance is given power, and my strength waxeth strong in my comforter; move therefore and show your selves, open[511] the mysteries of your Creation; Be friendly unto me, for I am a servant of the same your God The true worshipper of the Highest.

Names of the four Angels set over the first Lesser Angle of the South Table, and to call them forth Dopa[1], Opad[2], Pado[3], Adop[4], divine name governing is[512] Bedopa.

O Ye glorious and benevolent Angels Dopa, Opad, Pado, Adop, who are the four Angels set over the first Lesser Angle of the greater Terrestrial Angle of the South, I invoke, adjure, and call you forth

---

[510] S2: "Benevolent".
[511] S2: "to".
[512] S2: Omits "is".

to visible apparition, in and through this great, Signal, prevalent and divine name of your most high God Bedopa, and by the Ineffable and Efficacious virtue and power thereof, whereby you are governed and called forth, it being therefore absolutely preordained and decreed to be most solidly effectual: now therefore I do most earnestly entreat and powerfully adjure you, O you Benign Angels Dopa, Opad, Pado, Adop, in this potent name of your God Bedopa, to move, descend, appear and visibly show your selves to me, in this Crystal Stone or Glass Receptacle here before me, and in and through the same to transmit your Rays to my sight and your voices to my Ears, that I may plainly see you and Audibly hear you speak unto me and conclude me as a Receiver of your mysteries, wherefore I do urgently request and adjure you; O you Luminous and Amicable Angels Dopa, Opad, Pado, Adop, in this Excellent name of your God Bedopa, and I (as the servant of the Highest) do thereby efficaciously move you in power and presence to appear now presently visible to me (as aforesaid) O you Servants of mercy, move, descend, personally show forth and apply your selves friendly unto me, as unto the partaker of his secret wisdom in your Creation, For why Our Lord and master is all one.

Names of the four Angels serving to the first Lesser Angle of the South Table and to call them forth Opemen[1], Apeste[2], Scio[3], Vasge[4], divine names governing, calling forth Noalmar, & constraining Oloag.

O Ye Benevolent Angels of Light Opemen, Apeste, Scio, Vasge, who are the four Servient Angels serving in the first Lesser Angle of the South; I invoke, adjure, command, and powerfully call you forth, from your orders and mansion to visible apparition, in and through this great, prevalent, signal and divine name of God Noalmar, and by the Efficacy virtue and power thereof most firmly and solidly effectual for the calling you forth, commanding you to transmit your Rays visibly to my sight and your voices to my Ears, in and through this Crystal Stone or Glass Receptacle or otherwise to appear thereout here before me, that I may plainly see you, and audibly hear you speak unto me; Move therefore O you Benign Servient Angels of Light Opemen, Apeste, Scio, Vasge, and in the potent name of your God Noalmar, and by the Imperial dignity thereof, descend & visibly show your selves as pleasant deliverers, that you may praise him amongst the sons of men; O you servants of mercy Opemen, Apeste, Scio, Vasge, come away, and in this Ineffable and most excellent name of your God Noalmar, visibly and personally appear to the admiration of the Earth and to my comfort, come away open the mysteries of your Creation, be friendly unto me, for I am a servant of the same your God; The true worshipper of the Highest.

When there is apparition, then receive it, & constrain as followeth [513]saying

---

Welcome be the Light of the Highest whose holy name be glorified for his mercies endure for ever, And O you servants of mercy Opemen, Apeste, Scio, Vasge, (and benign Angels of Light) you are to me sincerely welcome, and I do in this inestimable and divine name of your Eternal God Oloag, and by the absolute virtue, efficacy and force thereof, most firmly solidly, and also effectually binding, constrain[514] you to speak audibly unto me, and to fulfil my Earnest petitions and requests, for which I am now at this time very much necessitated to call you forth, desiring your benevolent aid & assistance in these my Temporal & Terrestrial undertakings and affairs, constraining you in this Imperial name of your Omnipotent God Oloag, and the dignity thereof, to be friendly unto me, & to do for me, as for the servant of the Highest, wherein your office is apparently manifest & efficient.

Names of the four Angels set over the Second Lesser Angle of the South Table, and to call them forth Anaa[1], Naaa[2], Aaan[3], Aana[4], divine name governing is Banaa.

O Ye glorious and benevolent Angels Anaa, Naaa, Aaan, Aana, who are the four Angels set over the Second Lesser Angle of the greater Terrestrial Angle of the South, I invoke, adjure, and call you forth to visible apparition, in and through this great, signal, prevalent and divine name of the most high God Banaa, and by the ineffable[515] and efficacious virtue and power thereof whereby you are governed and called forth, it being therefore absolutely preordained and decreed to be most solidly effectual now therefore I

---

[513] S2: "~~saying~~".
[514] S2: "and Constraining".
[515] S2: "Inestimable".

do most earnestly entreat and powerfully adjure you, O you Benign Angels Anaa, Naaa, Aaan, Aana, in this potent name of your God Banaa, to move, descend, appear, and visibly show your selves to me[516], in this Crystal Stone or Glass Receptacle here before me, and in and through the same to transmit your Rays to my sight, and your voices to my Ears, that I may plainly see you and Audibly hear you speak unto me, and conclude me as a Receiver of your mysteries; wherefore I do urgently request and adjure you, O ye Luminous and amicable Angels Anaa, Naaa, Aaan, Aana, in this most excellent name of your God Banaa, and I (as the servant of the Highest) do thereby efficaciously move you in power and presence to appear now presently unto to me as aforesaid, O you Servants of mercy, move, descend, personally show forth, and apply your selves friendly unto me, as unto the partaker[517] of his secret wisdom in your creation; For why, Our Lord and master is all one.

Names of the four Angels set over the Second Lesser Angle of the South Angle, and to call them forth Gemenem[1], Ecope[2], Amox[3], Berape[4], divine names governing, calling forth Vadali, and constraining[518] Obavi.

O Ye Benevolent Angels[519] Gemenem, Ecope, Amox, Berape, who art the four Servient Angels serving[520] the second Lesser Angle of the greater Terrestrial Angle of the south; I invocate, adjure, command, and powerfully call you forth, from your orders and mansion, to visible apparition, in and through this great prevalent, signal and divine name of your God Vadali, and by the Efficacy, power and virtue thereof, most firmly & solidly effectual for the calling you forth, commanding you to transmit your Rays visibly to my Sight, and your voices to my ears, in and through this Crystal Stone or Glass Receptacle or otherwise to appear thereout here before me, that I may plainly see you, and Audibly hear you speak unto me, move therefore O you Benign Servient Angels of Light Gemenem, Ecope, Amox, Berape, and in the potent name of your God Vadali, and by the Imperial dignity thereof, descend and visibly show your selves as pleasant deliverers, that you may praise him among the sons of men.   O ye servants of mercy Gemenem, Ecope, Amox,

---

[516] S2: Omits "to me".
[517] S2: "~~partaker~~".
[518] S2: "~~divine names governing~~".
[519] S2: Inserts "of Light".
[520] S2: Inserts "in".

Berape, come away, and in this ineffable and most excellent name of your God Vadali, visibly and personally appear to the admiration of the Earth and to my comfort; come away open the mysteries of your creation, be friendly unto me for I am a servant of the same your God, The true worshipper of the Highest.

When there is apparition, then receive it, & constrain as followeth saying.

Welcome be the Light of the Highest, whose holy name be glorified for his mercies endure for ever, and O ye Benign Angels of Light Gemenem, Ecope, Amox, Berape, you are to me sincerely welcome, and I do, in and through this inestimable and divine name of your Eternal God Obavi, and by the absolute virtue, efficacy and force thereof, most firmly, solidly and effectually binding, constrain[521] you to speak audibly unto me, and to fulfil my earnest petitions and requests, for which I am now at this time very much necessitated to call you forth, requesting your benevolent instructions, aid & assistance, in these my Temporal and Terrestrial undertakings and affairs, urgently constraining you, in this Imperial name of your Omnipotent God Obavi, and the dignity thereof to be friendly unto me, and by divine permission to do for me as for the servant of the Highest, wherein your office is apparently manifest & efficient.

Names of the four Angels set over the Third Lesser Angle of the South Angle, and to call them forth Pesac[1], Sacepe[2], Acepes[3], Cepesa[4], divine name governing Bepesac.

O Ye glorious and benevolent Angels, Pesac, Sacepe, Acepes, Cepesa, who are the four Angels set over the Third Lesser Angle of the greater Terrestrial Angle of the South, I invoke adjure and call you forth, to visible apparition, in and through this great signal, prevalent and divine name of your most high God Bepesac, and by the ineffable, and efficacious virtue and power thereof, whereby you are governed and called forth, it being therefore absolutely preordained and appointed to be most solidly effectual: now therefore I do most earnestly entreat and powerfully adjure you, O you Benign Angels of Light Pesac, Sacepe, Acepes, Cepesa, in this

---

[521] S2: "& constraining".

potent name of your God Bepesac, to move, descend, appear, and visibly show yourselves in this Crystal Stone or Glass Receptacle here before me, and in and through the same to transmit your Rays unto my Sight, and your voices to my Ears, that I may plainly see you and Audibly hear you speak unto me, and conclude me as a Receiver of your mysteries, wherefore I do urgently request, and adjure you, O you Luminous and amicable Angels Pesac, Sacepe, Acepes, Cepesa, in this most excellent name of your God Bepesac, and I (as a servant of the Highest) do there by efficaciously move you in power and presence to appear now presently visible unto me as aforesaid; O you servants of mercy move, descend, and (by divine permission) personally show forth and apply your selves friendly unto me, as unto the partaker of his secret wisdom in your Creation; For why; Our Lord and master is all one.

Names of the four Angels serving in the 3rd[522] Lesser Angle of the South Table and to call them[523] Datete[1], Diom[2], Oopezod[3], Vrgan[4], divine names governing, calling forth Volexdo, and constraining Sioda.

O Ye Benevolent Angels of Light Datete, Diom, Oopezod, Vrgan, who are the four servient Angels serving in the Third Lesser Angle of the greater Terrestrial Angle of the South, I invocate, adjure command and powerfully call you forth, from your orders and mansion to visible apparition, in and through, this great prevalent, signal and divine name of your God Volexdo, and by the Efficacy, power and virtue thereof, most firmly and solidly Effectual, for the calling you forth, commanding you to transmit your Rays visibly unto my sight, and your voices to my ears, in and through this Crystal Stone or Glass Receptacle or otherwise to appear thereout, here before me, that I may plainly see you and audibly hear you speak unto me, move therefore O you [524] Benign Angels of Light Datete, Diom, Oopezod, Vrgan, in the potent name of your God Volexdo, and by the Imperial dignity thereof, descend, and by the divine permission of the Highest, visibly show your selves, as pleasant deliverers, that you may praise him among the sons of men, O you servants of mercy Datete, Diom, Oopezod, Vrgan, come away open the mysteries of your Creation, be friendly unto me, and in this ineffable and most Excellent name of your God Volexdo, visibly and

---

[522] S2: "third".
[523] S2: Inserts "forth".
[524] S2: "ye".

personally appear to the admiration of the Earth and to my comfort, for I am a servant of the same your God, The true worshipper of the Highest.

When the apparition appears, say as followeth

Welcome be the Light of the Highest whose holy name be glorified for his mercies endure for ever, And O you[525] Benign Angels of Light Datete, Diom, Oopezod, Vrgan, you are to me sincerely welcome, and I do in and through the Inestimable and divine name of your Eternal God Sioda, and by the absolute virtue, efficacy and force thereof, mostly firmly and solidly & effectually binding, constrain[526] you to speak audibly unto me and to fulfil my earnest petitions and requests, for which I am now at this time very much necessitated to call you forth, requesting your benevolent instructions, aid and assistance in these my Temporal and Terrestrial undertakings and affairs, urgently constraining you, in this Imperial name of your Omnipotent God Sioda, and the dignity thereof, to be friendly unto me and by divine permission to do for me as for the servant of the Highest, wherein your office is apparently manifest and efficient.

Names of the four Angels set over the fourth Lesser Angle of the South Table and to call them forth Ziza[1], Jzaz[2], Zazi[3], Aziz[4], divine name governing is BEZIZA.

O Ye glorious and benevolent Angels Ziza, Jzazod, Zazi, Azizod, who are the four Angels set over the Fourth Lesser Angle of the greater Terrestrial Angle of the South, I invoke adjure, and call you forth to visible apparition, in and through this great Signal, prevalent and divine name of your most high God Beziza, and by the Ineffable and Efficacious virtue and power thereof, whereby you are governed and called forth, it being therefore absolutely preordained and appointed to be most solidly effectual; now therefore I do most earnestly entreat and powerfully adjure you, O you[527] Benign Angels Ziza, Jzazod, Zazi, Azizod, in this potent name of your God Beziza, to move, descend, appear and visibly show your selves in this Crystal

---

[525] S2: "ye".
[526] S2: "and Constraining".
[527] S2: "ye".

Stone or Glass Receptacle here before me, and in and through the same to transmit your Rays unto my sight, and your voices to my ears, that I may plainly see you and Audibly hear you speak unto me, and conclude me as a Receiver of your mysteries; wherefore I do urgently request and adjure you, O you Luminous & amicable Angels Ziza, Jzazod, Zazi, Azizod, in this potent name of your God Beziza, and I (as a servant of the Highest) do thereby Efficaciously move you in power and presence to appear now presently visible unto me as aforesaid, O ye Servants of mercy, move descend, appear and by divine permission personally show forth and apply your selves friendly unto me as unto the partaker of his Secret wisdom in your Creation, for why; Our Lord & master is all one.

Names of the four Angels serving in the Fourth Lesser Angle of the South Table and to call them forth Adre[1], Sispe[2], Pali[3], Acar[4], divine names governing [528], calling forth Arzodionar, & constraining Narzefem.

O Ye Benevolent Angels of Light Adre, Sispe, Pali, Acar, who are the four Servient Angels serving in the Fourth Lesser Angle of the greater Terrestrial Angle of the South, I invocate, adjure, command, and powerfully call you forth from your orders and mansion to visible apparition in and through this great prevalent, signal and divine name of your God Arzodionar, and by the efficacy power and virtue thereof, most firmly and solidly effectual for the calling you forth, commanding you to transmit your Rays visibly unto my Sight, and your voices to my Ears, in and through this Crystal Stone or Glass Receptacle or otherwise to appear thereout here before me, that I may plainly see you and audibly hear you speak unto me; move therefore O you Benign Servient Angels of Light Adre, Sispe, Pali, Acar, in the potent name of your God Arzodionar, and by the Imperial dignity thereof, descend and by the divine permission of the Highest, visibly show your selves as pleasant deliverers, that you may praise him among the sons of men; O you servants of mercy Adre, Sispe, Pali, Acar, come away open the mysteries of your Creation be friendly unto me, and in this ineffable and most excellent name of your God Arzodionar, visibly and personally appear to the admiration of the Earth and to my comfort, for I am a servant of the same your God, The true worshipper of the Highest.

---

[528] S2: "~~calling forth constraining~~".

When there is apparition, then receive it, & constrain as followeth,

---

Welcome be the Light of the Highest, whose holy name be glorified for his mercies endure for ever, And O you Benign Angels of Light Adre, Sispe, Pali, Acar, you are to me sincerely welcome, and I do in & through this Inestimable and divine name of your Eternal God Narzefem, and by the absolute virtue efficacy and force thereof, most firmly solidly and effectually binding constrain[529] you to speak audibly unto me and to fulfil my earnest petitions and requests for which I am now at this time very much necessitated to call you forth, requesting your Benevolent instructions, [530] aid, and assistance, in these my Temporal and Terrestrial undertakings & affairs, urgently constraining you in this Imperial name of your Omnipotent God Narzefem and the dignity thereof, to be friendly unto me, and by divine permission to do for me as for the servant of the Highest, wherein your [office is] [531] apparently manifest and Efficient.

---

[529] S2: "and constraining".
[530] S2: "your Benevolent Instructions".
[531] S2 gives these words, which are omitted in S1, yet by the context and form of the manuscript should clearly be present.

The Title of the Following Prayer [before Invocation][532]

An Humble supplication to Almighty God by these his great, powerful, and sacred names, governing every particular and each Several[533] Respective Terrestrial Angle East, West, North, South. This prayer being properly Referred to the East Angle, and by changing the other names Governing the other 3 Angles in like manner and form, The same prayer serveth accordingly, (being so distinguished) for the whole &c. The which is to be said before Invocation is made for the moving and calling forth the spiritual powers of those natures orders and offices, as in the foregoing Introduction hereunto, is[534] specified and showed forth.

The 3 sacred names of God[535] over the East[536] Oro, Ibah, Aozpi,
Those 3 over the West[537] Empeh, Arsel, Gaiol,
Those 3 names over the North[538] Emor, Dial, Hectega,
Those 3 names over the South[539] Oip, Teaa, Pedoce,

O Thou Omnipotent, Incomprehensible, Immortal, and Eternal God of Hosts Oro, Ibah, Aozpi, who amongst the most great and wonderful works of thy creation, hast[540] in thy boundless & Infinite wisdom distributed the earth into four angles or Quarters, East, West, North & South And hast by thy Divine Institution[541] placed a most[542] mighty Regal Angel over each particular Terrestrial Angle, as King, governor, and principal Watchman there over, to protect

---

[532] R2: This prayer is also found in Rawlinson D1363, ff38-40, although it is not with any other material from these MSS, but rather prior to material on the Demon Princes and Olympic Spirits which will be covered in Volume 2 of this series.
[533] R2: "severally".
[534] R2: "are".
[535] S2: Omits the word "God".
[536] R2: "The three great, mighty & sacred names of God, Governing the Terrestrial Angle of the East".
[537] R2: "The three great, mighty & sacred names of God, governing the Terrestrial Angle of the West".
[538] R2: "The three great, mighty & sacred names of God, Governing the Terrestrial Angle of the North".
[539] R2: "The three great, mighty & sacred names of God Governing the Terrestrial Angle of the South".
[540] R2: "hath".
[541] R2: "Instruction".
[542] R2: Omits "most".

and defend thy servants from the usurping Blasphemy, misuse, malice, and Temptation of the wicked and great Enemy of thy glory and the welfare of mankind, the Devil and Spirits of darkness, and who again in thy Omniscience hast constituted under each particular mighty king six great Benevolent Angels called Seniors or senators to judge the government of each Terrestrial Angle and the King thereof, who are mentioned by thy servant S[t] John, in his Sacred Treatise of his Revelations And under whom again In thine Infinite wisdom hast placed sixteen Benevolent Angels to be dispositers of the Will of their superiors, and under whom again thou hast appointed many others, ever[543] numberless[544] spiritual creatures, according to thy primitive decrees, do make[545] to govern over, and to[546] teach, Instruct, direct and show forth unto the sons of men, all Arts, Sciences, mysteries, mechanical crafts and all things whatsoever that are[547] upon the Earth, and all the secret enclosures therein, who are all Aerial Spirits by thee set over this[548] Terrestrial Fabric whereon we live, and not by these restricted[549] but dignified, whom thou hast in thine Infinite gracious and paternal mercy preordained to give obedience to the will of man, when he sayeth[550] them all[551] words[552], names, orders, offices and mansions are to be found in four certain Tables, notes or mystical figures; The which were Received to the knowledge of thy servants and restored to them, and brought to Light out of darkness and oblivion by the ministry of thy[553] celestial Angel AUE and by him declared to be the knowledge of thy servant ENOCH[554], unto whom it was delivered by the Revelation of thy holy Angel[555]: now therefore O[556] most gracious and merciful Lord god of Hosts Oro Ibah Aozpi, the only creator of Heaven and Earth, who by thy word alone hast[557] most wonderfully and admirably made all creatures out of nothing and placed all things comprehended in the marvellous work of thy

---

[543] S2: "Even".

[544] S2: Inserts "of".

[545] S2, R2: Replaces "do make" with "determinate".

[546] R2: Omits "to".

[547] S2: Inserts "all".

[548] R2: "thy".

[549] S2, R2: Replaces "these restricted" with "thee rejected".

[550] S2, R2: "seeth".

[551] S2, R2: Inserts "whose".

[552] S2: Omits "words".

[553] R2: "the".

[554] R2: Gives the name Enoch in grey ink throughout the prayer.

[555] R2: "Angels".

[556] R2: Inserts "thou".

[557] R2: "hath".

creation according to thine[558] unspeakable wisdom in their several and Respective orders and offices to glorify and[559] extol thy holy name & fulfil thy divine[560] will. O Thou who art the true fountain of Light and wisdom, I thy humble servant here reverently and obediently prostrate in thy holy sight[561] in all contrition of heart and meekness of spirit do humbly beg such thus of thine[562] Infinite goodness and clemency to have mercy and compassion upon me, and to dignify me with the power of thy holy spirit[563], to forgive me my sins and to pardon all my Iniquities,[564] graciously to grant that all those Benevolent Angels or dignified Spiritual creatures whom thou hast set over the four Angles of the Earth[565] East, West, North, South, and[566] preordained to govern over all Arts, mysteries and sciences, mechanical crafts and all creatures there upon, and all things whatsoever that are contained therein, may show forth the same, and the true service and Right understanding[567] both of the natures and secret properties thereof unto me thy humble servant whensoever I shall call them forth and Invocate them thereunto whose names and orders are contained and to be found in the foresaid Tables or mystical Figures which were Revealed and Rendered[568] out of oblivion and lately restored again to Light unto thy servants by the ministry of thy celestial Angel AVE, and by him certainly verified to be the same which[569] was delivered to thy servant ENOCH, Immediately from thy self by the Revelation of thy holy Angel[570], by whom thou didst[571] converse with, and appeared unto him and opened his Eyes that he might see and judge the Earth, which thou permittest not unto his parents by reason of their fall wherein the holy Trinity determined, saying Let us show unto ENOCH, the[572] use of the Earth and for[573] Enoch, was become wise and full of the spirit of wisdom, And he humbly prayed unto

---

[558] S2: "thy".

[559] R2: Omits "and".

[560] S2: "~~and holy~~".

[561] S2, R2: "fear".

[562] S2, R2: Replaces "beg such thus of thine" with "beseech thee of".

[563] R2: Moves the phrase "and to dignify me with the power of thy holy spirit" to behind "all my iniquities".

[564] S2: Inserts "and".

[565] R2: Inserts "(viz)".

[566] R2: Omits "and".

[567] S2: "true uses & right understanding"; R2: "true uses & right understandings".

[568] R2: "sent".

[569] R2: "that".

[570] R2: "Angels".

[571] R2: "did".

[572] S2: "~~use~~".

[573] R2: "lo".

thee saying, O Lord let there be Remembrance of this thy mercy and let those that love Thee enjoy this Benefit as for[574] me; O let not thy mercies be forgotten, and behold thou were graciously pleased. Now therefore O most Bountiful and heavenly god of wisdom and[575] mercy Oro Ibah Aozpi, as the true knowledge of the Earth and the creatures thereof and the secret properties thereof[576] all things therein, even to the unknown depth[577] of the Sea, and the most private Infernal and obscure caves of the Earth, was by the foresaid[578] Tables, notes or mystical figures and the use of their[579] presence, thy gift delivered to thy servant Enoch, both Immediate from thy Self, and also by the ministry of thy[580] sacred Celestial Angel[581]. And at his humble request to thee, the uses[582] and Benefit thereof permitted to continue amongst the sons of men succeeding him on Earth in after Ages, that should[583] love, fear and obey thee, which they enjoyed till they rebelled against thee And became proud, wicked, Ingrateful [584], Ambitious and presumptuous, wherefore they[585] were as Justly by thee deprived again of that Inestimable Jewel and divine gift, The knowledge[586] whereof and benefits then wearing away and ceasing to be any more amongst men, and so remaining wholly unknown to them till lately (by thy gracious permission) it was again Revived and mercifully restored to Light by the ministry of thy holy[587] Angel AVE, unto thy servants. Now I beseech thee O Thou Almighty Father of mercy Oro Ibah Aozpi, let not thy promises made unto, nor the memory of thy servant Enoch, nor the use and benefit of[588] the knowledge thou gavest unto him be again washed away becoming[589] void and extinguished, but graciously be pleased to grant unto me thy humble servant the true knowledge and use of the Earth & the secret property[590] thereof and enclosures therein, by the ministry,

---

[574] R2: Replaces "as for" with "after".

[575] R2: Omits "wisdom and".

[576] S2, R2: "of".

[577] R2: "depths".

[578] R2: "aforesaid".

[579] S2: "~~presence~~".

[580] R2: "the".

[581] S2, R2: "Angels".

[582] S2, R2: "use".

[583] R2: "shall".

[584] R2: "ungrateful".

[585] S2: "~~are~~".

[586] R2: Transposes "and benefit"" before "whereof".

[587] R2: Omits "holy".

[588] S1: Repeats the word "of" here.

[589] R2: "become".

[590] S2, R2: "properties".

Assistance, Instruction [591] of those spiritual creatures governing over, and Subservient in the [592] Tables, notes, or mystical figures [593], whom I shall by name call [594] even from the Superior to the Inferior orders and degrees; And [595] humbly beg of thee, O Heavenly God of all consolation & compassion Oro Ibah Aozpi, to dignify me with thy Celestial dignity, open my eyes and give me sight, open my ears and give me hearing, open my understanding and give me knowledge, show me the Light of (thy) countenance and endow me with thy holy spirit, that by the virtue [596] , power of my Invocations being composed according to the Instructions of the Angel AUE, I [597] may effectually call forth all those Terrestrial dignified spiritual powers of Light, both of the Superior and Inferior orders and degrees, governing and subservient in the Terrestrial Angle of the East, and all creatures, Arts, Sciences, [598] mysteries thereof and the secret properties and enclosures [599] . And (by) [600] the utterance and repetition of thy infallible and secret names here specified [601] unto which they are severally and Respectively obedient and whereby [602] (according to thy primitive decree [603]) they are powerfully governed they may forthwith Immediately move, Descend and appear visibly unto me, at all times and in all places whensoever and wheresoever I shall call them forth according as necessity shall require their favourable and familiar society, community and Assistance, That it may be [604] one witness of thy promise for ENOCHs sake unto thy humble and obedient servant. [605]

---

[591] S2: "instructions"; R2: "& instructions".

[592] S2: "four".

[593] R2: Replaces "Tables, notes, or mystical figures" with "four Angles thereof, whose names are comprised, in the said four Tables, notes, or mystical figures".

[594] R2: Inserts "forth".

[595] S2, R2: Inserts "I".

[596] S2, R2: Inserts "&".

[597] R2: Omits "I".

[598] S2: Inserts "and".

[599] R2: Inserts "therein".

[600] S2, R2: "at".

[601] S2, R2: Replaces this with "sacred names therein specified".

[602] R2: "thereby".

[603] R2: "Decrees".

[604] S2: "one".

[605] R2: Inserts "Amen".

[Invocation of the Kings, Seniors, Angels and Spirits of the East]

Invocation by way of humble supplication & petition to the King and all the dignified Angels or Angelical powers of Light whose names, natures, mansions, orders and offices with other mysteries there unto properly appertaining are comprehended and to be found in and collected out of the foregoing Terrestrial Table or Tables according as in the Isagogical[606] preface or Introduction to the use thereof is before mentioned.

Humble supplication and petition made to the great King BATAIVA principal governor and Celestial Angelical watchman set over the Watch Tower or Terrestrial Table of the East, by the three mighty names of God ORO, IBAH, AOZPI.

O THOU Royal[607], great, mighty and powerful Angel of the most high, Immense, Immortal, and Incomprehensible God of Hosts BATAIVA who in the beginning of time by the divine decree and appointment of the Highest in the unity of the Blessed Trinity were set over the Terrestrial Angle of the East, as the only King, governor, overseer, principal watchman, protector and Keeper thereof, from the malice, misuse, Illusion, Temptation, Assault, Surprisal, Theft or other wicked Encroachments, usurping[608] Blasphemy of the great Enemy of God's glory and the welfare of mankind the Devil and spirits of darkness: And as a snaffle to restrain their wickedness by the Bit of God's boundless power and Justice, to the intent that (they being put on into the Earth) their Envious will may be bridled the determinations of the most high God fulfilled, and his creatures Kept within the compass and measure of order, We humbly Invocate, Entreat and Beseech you; O you Royal Angel BATAIUA, in by and through these potent, mighty, and great names of your God ORO, IBAH, AOZPI to preserve, defend, keep, and protect us, from the wicked Illusions, envious[609] Temptations, violent Assaults, or any other destructive surprisals of all evil spirits, or Inferior powers of darkness, whatsoever, And that we may not be thereby dismayed, vanquished or overcome, and that by the virtue, power, and efficacy

---

[606] An old term meaning Introductory.
[607] S2: "Regal".
[608] S2: "user".
[609] S2: "Temptations".

of those Tables, Seals or character of your Creation[610], and by these Banners, Ensigns or Trophies of Honour and glory, borne or standing before you,[611] both divine, Celestial, Angelical, natural and Royal Tokens and Testimonies of Monarchy, majesty and Imperial Authority given and confirmed unto you in the beginning of the world and by the Influence, Efficacy, force, and virtue thereof, we most earnestly entreat and humbly beseech you, to be gracious & friendly to[612] us herein; And furthermore likewise to help, Aid, and assist us, in all these, and such our Temporal and Terrestrial operations[613], affairs and concerns, as wherein you may or can by the Supreme powers of that your Kingly office, under Authority given you of the Highest, for the protection, preservation, care, conduct, effort[614], support, Benefit, Assistance, and use of mankind living on Earth; And amongst the rest, we also again humbly entreat and earnestly beseech you that all those six great Angels called Angelical Seniors, and all other governing or Superior Angelical and Elemental powers of Light Celestially dignified, and also that all other dignified servient and subservient Spirits or Benevolent Aerial powers who are by nature and office, friendly and good, and ordained (by divine appointment in the Unity of the Blessed Trinity) for the use, Benefit and service of Mankind of all degrees and offices from the Superior to the Inferior, in the orders and mansion serving the most high God under your Imperial and Sovereign power, Authority, command, subjection, service, and obedience, properly referred or appropriated to the East Angle of the Air, Respecting also the like point of the Compass, Quarter, Angle, or division of the Earth, may by the force and power of our Invocations be moved, to descend and appear visibly unto us, in this Crystal Glass [615] or otherwise out of the same, as either convenience or necessity of the occasion shall require, and that they may at the reading and repetition of our Invocations or calls on that Account by us made unto them, move, Descend, appear, visibly to the sight of our Eyes, and to speak Audibly unto us, as that we may plainly and perfectly both see and hear them and friendly to converse with us fulfilling our desires and requests in all things,

---

[610] S2: Replaces "Tables, Seals or character of your Creation" with "those three said mighty names of God ORO, IBAH, AOZPI, O you great, potent and Royal Angel BATAIVA, and by the true Seal and Character of your Creation".

[611] S2: Inserts "as".

[612] S2: "unto".

[613] S2: Inserts "and".

[614] S2: "comfort".

[615] The abbreviation C.G. or Crystal Glass used henceforth in the text is probably a contraction of "C.S. or G.R.". However to distinguish clearly we have replaced it with the term "Crystal Glass".

according to their several and Respective offices and to serve us therein, and also do for us as for the servants of the most high God, whensoever and wheresoever and whereunto we shall at any time and place move them both in power and presence whose works herein shall be a song of Honour to the glory & praise of the most high God both in your & their Creation Amen.

Invocation by way of humble supplication & petition made to the six Angels or Angelical Seniors Habioro[1], Aaoxaif[2], Hetemorda[3], Ahaozpi[4], Hipotga[5], & Autotar[6], by the great and mighty name of their Imperial King BATAIUA.

O You great Angels or Angelical Seniors Habioro, Aaoxaif, Hetemorda, Ahaozpi, Hipotga, & Autotar, serving the (mighty &) most high God Oro, Ibah, Aozpi, before the mighty Angelical monarch King BATAIVA, In the Angle, Region, or Division of the East, who are dignified with celestial power and Authority therein, and by office Judging the government of the Angelical King, thereby fulfilling the divine will & pleasure of the Highest, in all things appointed and committed to your charge, and placed in superior orders under the said Angelical King, and governing over all others both Superior, servient and subservient Angels or Angelical powers, Celestially dignified, and also all others [616] Elemental spirits whatsoever that in any wise hath power, mansion Residence, orders, office, place or being, in the East part, Region or Angle of the Air, with like Respect also from thence to be had to the East point of the compass, Angle, part or division of the Earth. We the servants of the most high God and reverently here present[617] in his holy fear, do humbly beseech and earnestly entreat you all: O ye Angelical Seniors Habioro, Aaoxaif, Hetemorda, Ahaozpi, Hipotga, Autotar, In by and through this Imperial mighty and powerful name BATAIUA, That all or some one, or any of you, Jointly and severally, Every and each one, in general and particular, for and by itself Respectively, would be favourable and friendly unto us, as that whensoever or wheresoever, we shall Invocate, move, or call you forth unto visible appearance and our Assistance, you then would be thereby moved, to descend and appear visibly unto us in this Crystal Stone or Glass Receptacle set here before us for that purpose, or otherwise personally to appear out of it, visibly here before us, and so as that we may plainly see you and Audibly here you speak unto us, and by

---

[616] S2: "other".
[617] S2: "present here".

such[618] your friendly and verbal converse with us, to Illuminate, Instruct, direct, help, aid, and assist us in all things whatsoever we shall humbly desire beseech and request of you, wherein by nature & office given you of the Highest you may or can; Hear us therefore, O ye Blessed Angels or Angelical seniors Habioro, Aaoxaif, Hetemorda, Ahaozpi, Hipotga, Autotar, And in the mighty name BATAIUA, and by the virtue, power, Influence, Efficacy and force thereof, we earnestly entreat and humbly beseech you to grant these our Supplications & petitions that all or any of you, which we shall at any time hereafter, Invocate, move or call[619] forth to visible appearance, would then be favourably and friendly placed in Celestial charity and Benevolence, forthwith and Immediately at such our Invocations and earnest requests accordingly of us made. Be thereby moved, and also to move, descend, visibly appear and speak Audibly unto us, either in this Crystal Glass[620] or otherwise out of the same as it shall please God, and you his Angelical ministers or Celestial messengers of divine grace, and Light, and shall be most beneficial and best befitting and convenient for us therein, and to administer unto us the bountiful gifts of all Earthly benefits and also endow us, with the gift of true Science and Sapience, and such like other gifts of human Accomplishments and enjoyments as may or shall be fit for us, and so beneficial unto us, that we may thereby live happy with comfort during our continuance in this our mortal being, all which we humbly beseech and earnestly entreat of all and every one of you Sacred Angels or Angelical Seniors in the name of your God and King, wherein these your friendly and Benevolent works (thus graciously communicated and given to us) shall be a song of Honour and the praise of your God in your Creation Amen

---

Invocation by way of humble supplication and petition made to the four Benevolent Angels or Angelical powers of Light placed in orders and set over the first Lesser Angle or division of the great Quadrangle or Table of the East Vrzela, Zlar, Larz, & Arzel, by the great and powerful name of God Erzela.

O You great and glorious Angels or Angelical powers of Light Vrzela, Zlar, Larz, Arzel, governing & set over the first Lesser Angle, division, or Quarter of the great Quadrangle of the East part of the Air, Respecting the like part or point of the compass appropriated to

[618] S2: "~~your~~".
[619] S2: "~~you~~".
[620] S2: "Crystal Stone or glass Receptacle".

150

the Earth, serving your most high God Erzela, in orders and office accordingly as you (by Celestial dignification) are in place and power more Aerially Superior, unto which[621] is also given of the Highest by nature and office the true knowledge of the knitting together of natures, and also as well the destruction of nature and of things that may perish, as of conjoining and knitting them together and to reveal, show forth and communicate the same (by your Angelical ministry) unto mankind living on Earth, whensoever you shall be Invocated or moved thereunto: we the servants of the Highest (and[622] the same your God) and Reverently here present in his holy fear, do earnestly entreat, humbly beseech and move you, O you Angels or Angelical powers of Light, or Celestially dignified spirits of the Air, governing in orders degree, mansion (as aforesaid) Vrzela, Zlar, Larz, & Arzel, Jointly and severally, Every and each one, for and by it self Respectively, in by & through this mighty and powerful name of your God Erzela, that you (at these our humble requests and Addresses) would be so favourable and friendly unto us, as that whensoever or wheresoever we shall invocate, move, or call you forth to visible appearance, and our Assistance, you would be thereby moved, to descend, & appear (out of the same) visibly here before us in this Crystal Stone or Glass Receptacle and so as that we may plainly see you and Audibly hear you speak unto us, and by Such your friendly and verbal converse with us to make us partakers of that undefiled knowledge and true sapience which by nature and office (given you of the Highest) may by such your Angelical ministry be revealed, given, or administered unto us; Hear us therefore O you[623] sacred Angelical powers of Light, or Celestially dignified spirits of the Air, by degree and orders superior and governing (as aforesaid) Vrzela, Zlar, Larz, Arzel, We do yet further in this great name of your God Erzela, and by the force, power and efficacy thereof, Earnestly Entreat and humbly beseech you, to grant these our Supplications and petitions, and that all or any of you, that we shall at any time hereafter, Invocate, move, or call forth to visible appearance, would readily and forthwith move, Descend, and visibly appear unto us, whensoever we shall Invocate, call forth, or move you thereunto in this Crystal Glass standing here before us or otherwise out of it, as it shall please God and you his ministers of divine grace, and as best befitted or shall be most convenient or beneficial for us, or unto us, in these our Actions and operations, speaking Audibly unto us, and also thereby directing and instructing us in the true knowledge of that your Angelical

---

[621] S2: "whom".
[622] S2: "of".
[623] S2: "ye".

sapience and science, given you of the Highest; And wherein also who hath accordingly by orders & office ordained and appointed you and this your Angelical Benevolence in Celestial grace & charity thus given & granted unto us, and also in the accomplishments & fulfilling of all these our humble desires and requests and whatsoever also shall be requisite and fit for us to know shall be a song of Honour and the praise of your God in your Creation Amen.

Invocation by way of humble supplication and petition made to the four Servient Angels or dignified Spirits of the Air, placed in orders and serving in the first Lesser Angle or division of the great Quadrangle or Table of the East Cezodenes[1], Totet[2], Sias[3], Efemende[4], who are moved and called forth, by the great and powerful name of God Idoigo, and constrained to do what they are commanded, according to their office by the great name of God Ardeza.

O You Angelical powers of Light or dignified spirits of the Air Cezodenes, Totet, Sias, Efemende, serving in orders under Superior powers your most high & omnipotent God Idoigo, Respecting the like part or point of the compass appropriated to the Earth in the first Lesser Angle or division of the great Quadrangle or East part of the Air, accordingly as you therein are placed more Inferior and Subservient, and unto whom is given of the Highest by nature and office the true knowledge of physick in all its parts and the curing of all diseases whatsoever are incident to human bodies, and to Reveal, show forth and giving the same unto mankind living on Earth, whensoever you shall be moved and called forth, and by the great name of your God Ardeza commanded thereunto: we the servants of the Highest and the same your God and Reverently here present in his holy fear, do earnestly entreat, call upon and move you all, O you Benevolent Angels,[624] dignified powers of the Air serving in orders, degree & mansion as aforesaid Cezodenes, Totet, Sias, Efemende, Jointly and severally, every and each one, for and by it self respectively in by and through this mighty and powerful name of your God Idoigo, that you (at these our Earnest Addresses) would be so truly willing and friendly unto us, that whensoever & wheresoever we shall Invocate, move, or call you forth unto visible appearance and our Assistance you then would readily & Immediately forthwith at our Invocations, move, descend, appear, and show your selves corporally visible unto us in this Crystal

---

[624] S2: "or".

152

Glass standing here before us, or otherwise personally to appear out of the same visibly here before us, and so as that we may plainly see you and Audibly hear you speak unto us, and by such your Spiritual Revelations unto us, to make us partakers of that true knowledge and sapience which by nature and office (given you of the Highest) may by such your visible appearance and verbal converse & show forth and given to us, And furthermore also that in by and through this great and powerful name of your God Ardeza and the force and virtue thereof; we do likewise, earnestly entreat, and Invocate you, to do accomplish and fulfil whatsoever (accordingly and[625] is by nature and office given you of the Highest) we shall request and command you: Hear us therefore O you Benevolent Servient Angels or dignified Spiritual powers of the Air serving in orders, office, degree and mansion and by nature as aforesaid Cezodenes, Totet, Sias, Efemende, you do yet further in this great name of your God Idoigo, and by the virtue and efficacy thereof, Earnestly Invocate and entreat you to yield up, and give unto us your assuredly firm, free, full and obliged consent herein, that all or any of you which we shall at any time hereafter Invocate, move, or call forth to visible appearance would certainly without any tarrying or delay, Immediately move, descend, and visibly appear unto[626] us, in this Crystal Glass standing here before us, or otherwise out of it, as it shall please God to give unto you, and thereby most beneficial convenient and fit for us, in these both our present and other our future Actions and operations, and to speak plainly unto us, so as that we may sensibly hear you and understand you directing and Instructing us in the true knowledge and judgement of that your spiritual sapience and science given to you of the Highest. And in this undoubted true and great name of your God Ardeza, and by the virtue and power thereof, whereby we also earnestly Invocate and entreat you not only to reveal, declare, show forth, and make known unto us the true and apprehensive knowledge[627] of all such occult & mystical Arcanaes in physick and of whatsoever else relates thereunto, as are unknown of mankind but also do whatsoever we shall further command, request or desire to be done for us relating to the said sciences, & our benefits therein, as you by office of the Highest accordingly preordained & appointed All which your obedience readily & willingly fulfilling and exemplifying[628] unto us, as here we have in the powerful and true names of your God Earnestly entreated and besought you,

---

[625] S2: "as".
[626] S2: "to".
[627] S2: "~~which apprehensive~~".
[628] S2: "accomplishing".

shall be a song of Honour, & the praise of your God in your Creation Amen

---

Invocation by way of humble supplication & petition made to the four Benevolent Angels or Angelical powers of Light placed in orders, and set over the Second Lesser Angle or division[629] of the great Quadrangle or Table of the East, Vtepa[1], Tepau[2], Paute[3], Autep[4], by the great and powerful name of God EUTEPA.

O Ye great and glorious Angels or Angelical powers of Light Vtepa, Tepau, Paute, Autep, governing or set over the Second Lesser Angle, division or Quarter of the great Quadrangle of the East part of the Air, Respecting the like part or point of the Compass appropriated to the Earth, serving[630] your most high God Eutepa, in orders and offices accordingly as you (by celestial dignification) are in place and power more Aerially superior, and to whom is also given of the Highest by nature and office (* moving from place to place) the true Knowledge of the Knitting together of natures and also as well the destruction of nature, and of things that may perish as of conjoining and knitting them together, and to reveal, show forth & communicate the same (by your Angelical ministry) unto mankind living on Earth, whensoever you shall be (called,) Invocated or moved thereunto; We the servants of the Highest (and the same your God) and Reverently here present in his holy fear, do earnestly entreat, humbly beseech and move you all, O you Angels or Angelical powers of Light or Celestially dignified spirits of the Air, governing in orders, degree, mansion as aforesaid Vtepa, Tepau, Paute, Autep, Jointly and severally, every and each, of for and by it self Respectively, in by and through this mighty and powerful name of your God Eutepa, that you (by these humble requests and Addresses) would be favourably friendly unto us, as that whensoever or wheresoever we shall Invocate, move, or call you forth to visible appearance and[631] Assistance, you would be thereby moved to descend & appear visibly unto us in this Crystal Stone or Glass Receptacle which stand here before us, or otherwise personally to appear out of the same visibly here before us, and so, as that we may plainly see you and Audibly hear you speak unto us, and by such your friendly and verbal converse with us to make us partakers of that undefiled knowledge and true sapience, which

---

[629] S2: "Divisions".
[630] S2: "~~the~~".
[631] S2: Inserts "our".

by nature and office (given you of the Highest) may by such your Angelical ministry be revealed given or administered unto us: Hear us therefore O ye Sacred Angelical powers of Light or Celestial dignified spirits of the Air, by degree, and order, Superior and governing (as aforesaid) Vtepa, Tepau, Paute, Autep, We do yet further in this great name of your God Eutepa and by the force power, and Efficacy thereof, earnestly entreat and humbly beseech you to grant these our Supplications and petitions and that all or any of you that we shall at any time hereafter, Invocate, move, or call forth to visible appearance would [632] readily and forthwith, move, descend, and visibly appear unto us, whensoever we shall Invocate, move, (or) call forth, or move you thereunto in this Crystal Glass standing here before is, or otherwise out of it, as shall please God and you his ministers of divine grace and as best befitted or shall be most convenient or beneficial for us, or unto us in these our Actions and operations, speaking Audibly unto us, and also thereby directing and Instructing us, in the true knowledge of that your Angelical Sapience and Science given of you of the Highest, and wherein also, he hath accordingly by orders and office ordained and appointed you, & also in the accomplishment and fulfilling of all these our humble desires and requests and this your Angelical benevolence in celestial grace and charity thus given and granted unto us, and whatsoever also shall be requisite and fit for us to know, shall be a song of Honour and the praise of your God in your Creation Amen.

Invocation by way of humble supplication and petition made to the four Servient Angels or dignified spirits of the Air placed in orders and serving in the Second Lesser Angle or division of the great Quadrangle or Table of the East Oyoube[1], Paoc[2], Vrbeneh[3], Diri[4], who are moved and called forth by the great and powerful name of God Hacza, and constrained to do what they are commanded according to their office, by the great name of God Palam.

O Ye Angelical powers of Light or dignified spirits of the Air O Yube, Paoc, Vrbeneh, Diri, serving in orders under Superior powers your most high and omnipotent God Hacza, in the Second Lesser Angle or division of the great Quadrangle or East part of the Air Respecting the like part or point of the compass appropriated to the Earth accordingly as you therein are placed more inferior and subservient; And unto whom is given of the Highest by nature and

---

[632] S2: "~~readly~~".

office the true knowledge of (* finding & use of metals, of Congelation of Stones & the virtues of all stones whatsoever,)[633] physick in all its parts and the curing of all diseases whatsoever that are incident to human bodies, and to Reveal, show forth, and give the same unto[634] mankind living on Earth, whensoever you shall be moved and called forth; And by the great name of your God Palam commanded thereunto: We the servants of the Highest and the same your God, and Reverently here present in his holy fear, do earnestly entreat, call upon, and move you all, O you Benevolent Angels or dignified powers of the Air, serving in orders, degree, and mansion (as aforesaid) OYube, Paoc, Vrbeneh, Diri, Jointly and severally, every and each one, for and by it self Respectively, in by and through this mighty and powerful name of your God Hacza, that you (at this our Earnest Addresses) would be so truly willing and friendly unto us that whensoever and wheresoever we shall Invocate, move or call you forth unto visible appearance and our Assistance, you then would readily and Immediately forthwith at our Invocations move, descend, appear, and show your selves corporally visible unto us in this Crystal Glass standing here before us or otherwise personally to appear out of the same visibly here before us, and so as that we may plainly see you and Audibly hear you speak unto us, and by such your Spiritual Revelations unto us, to make us partakers of that true knowledge and Sapience which by nature and office (given to[635] you of the Highest) may by such your visible appearance and verbal converse be showed forth and given to us; And furthermore also, that in, by, and through this great and powerful name of your God Palam, and the force and virtue thereof; we do likewise earnestly Invocate, and entreat you to do accomplish and fulfil whatsoever (accordingly[636] and is by nature and office given you of the Highest) we shall request and command you; Hear us therefore O ye Benevolent Servient Angels or dignified spiritual powers of the Air, Serving in orders, office, degree and mansion and by nature as aforesaid OYube, Paoc, Vrbeneh, Diri, you do yet further in this great name of your God Hacza, And by the virtue and Efficacy thereof, earnestly Invocate and entreat you, to yield up and give unto us your assuredly firm, free, full and obliged consent herein[637], that all or any of you which we shall at any time hereafter invocate move, or call forth to visible appearance, would certainly without any tarrying or delay Immediately move, descend, and

---

[633] S2: ~~"and of physick in all its parts and the curing of all diseases whatsoever that are incident to human bodies"~~.
[634] S2: "to".
[635] S2: Omits "to".
[636] S2: "~~and~~".
[637] S2: "therein".

visibly appear unto us in this Crystal Glass standing here before us or otherwise out of it, as it shall please God to give unto you, and thereby most beneficial, convenient and fit for us, in these both our present and other our future Actions and operations, and to speak plainly unto us, so, as that we may sensibly hear you and understand you, directing and instructing us in the true knowledge and Judgement of that your Spiritual Sapience and Science given you of the Highest; And in this undoubtedly true and great name of your God Palam, and by the virtue and power thereof, whereby we also earnestly Invocate & entreat you not only to reveal, declare,[638] show forth and make known unto us, the true and apprehensive knowledge of all such occult and mystical Arcanaes, in physick, and of[639] whatsoever else relates therein unto[640] as are unknown of mankind, but also do whatsoever we shall further command, request or desire to be done for us, relating to the said science and our benefits therein, as you by office of the Highest accordingly preordained and appointed; All which your obedience, readily & willingly fulfilling and accomplishing unto us, as here we have in the powerful and true name of your God earnestly entreated and besought you, shall be a song of Honour & the praise of your God in your Creation Amen.

———

Invocation by way of humble supplication & petition made to the four Benevolent Angels or Angelical powers of Light placed in orders and set over the third Lesser Angle or division of the great Quadrangle or Table of the East Cenbar[1], Enbarc[2], Barcen[3], Vrcenbe[4], by the great and powerful name of God Ecenbar.

O Ye great and glorious Angels or[641] Angelical powers of Light Cenbar, Enbarc, Barcen, Vrcenbe, governing or[642] set over the Third Lesser Angle, division or Quarter of the great Quadrangle of the East part of the Air, Respecting the like part or point of the compass, appropriated to the Earth serving your most high God Ecenbar, in orders and offices accordingly as you (by[643] Celestial Dignification) are in place and power more Aerially Superior, unto who is also given of the Highest by nature and office, the true

[638] S2: Inserts "and".
[639] S2: Omits "of".
[640] S2: Replaces "therein unto" with "thereunto".
[641] S2: "beneficial".
[642] S2: "and".
[643] S2: Repeats "by".

knowledge of (* all Mechanical crafts whatsoever), of the knitting together of natures, and also as well the destruction of nature and of things that may perish, as of conjoining, knitting them together;[644] And to Reveal, show forth, and communicate the same unto mankind (by your Angelical ministry) living on the Earth, whensoever you shall be invocated or moved thereunto, we the servants of the Highest (and the same your God) and Reverently here present in his holy fear, do earnestly entreat, humbly beseech and move you all; O ye Angels or Angelical powers of Light or celestially dignified Spirits of the Air, governing in orders, degree, mansion (as aforesaid) Cenbar, Enbarc, Barcen, Vrcenbe, Jointly and severally, every and each one, for and by it self Respectively, in, by and through this mighty and powerful name of your God Ecenbar, that you (at these our humble requests and Addresses) would be so favourable and friendly unto us as that whensoever or wheresoever we shall Invocate, move, or call you forth to visible appearance and our assistance, you would be thereby moved to descend and appear visibly unto us in this Crystal Stone or Glass Receptacle which stand here before us, or otherwise personally to appear out of the same visibly here before us, and so as that we may plainly see you, and Audibly here you speak unto us; And by such your friendly and verbal converse with us, to make us partakers of that undefiled knowledge and true sapience, which by nature and office (given you of the Highest) may by such your Angelical ministry be revealed given or administered unto us; Hear us therefore, O ye Sacred Angelical powers of Light or Celestial dignified Spirits of the Air by degree, and orders Superior and governing (as aforesaid) Cenbar, Enbarc, Barcen, Vrcenbe, we do yet further in this great name of your God Ecenbar, and by the force power and efficacy thereof, earnestly entreat and humbly beseech you, to grant these our supplications and petitions, and that all or any of you, that we shall at any time hereafter Invocate, move, or call forth to visible appearance, would readily and forthwith move, descend, and visibly appear unto us, whensoever we shall Invocate, call forth, or move you thereunto in this Crystal Glass standing here before us, or otherwise to appear out of it, as it shall please God and you his ministers of divine grace, and as befitted or shall be most convenient or beneficial for us, or unto us, in these our Actions and operations, Speaking Audibly unto us, and also thereby directing and Instructing us in the true knowledge of that your Angelical Sapience and Science given you of the Highest, and

---

[644] S2: This section is all struck out, thus "of the knitting together of natures, and also as well the destruction of nature and of things that may perish, as of conjoining, knitting them together".

wherein so[645] He hath accordingly by orders and office ordained and appointed you and this your Angelical benevolence in celestial grace and charity thus given and granted unto us; And also in the accomplishment & fulfilment of all these our humble desires and Requests and whatsoever else may[646] be requisite and fit for us to know, shall be a song of Honour and praise of your God in your creation Amen.

Invocation by way of humble supplication and petition made to the four Servient Angels or dignified Spirits of the Air placed in orders and serving in the Third Lesser or division of the greater Quadrangle or Table of the East, Abemo[1], Naco[2], Ocenem[3], Shael[4], who are moved and called forth by the great and powerful name of God Aiaoai, and constrained to do what they are commanded according to their office by the great name of God Oiiit.

O Ye Angelical powers or dignified spirits of the Air Abemo, Naco, Ocenem, Shael, serving in orders under superior powers your most high and omnipotent God Aiaoai, in the Third Lesser Angle, or division of the great Quadrangle or East part of the Air, Respecting the like part or point of the compass appropriated to the Earth accordingly as you therein are placed more Inferior and Subservient, and[647] unto whom is given of the Highest by nature & office the true knowledge of (*Transformation & transplantation,) physick in all its parts an the curing of diseases which are incident to Human bodies;[648] And to reveal, show forth and give the same unto mankind living on Earth whensoever you shall be moved and called forth by the great name of your God Oiiit, commanded thereunto; We the servants of the Highest (and the same your God) and Reverently here present in his holy fear, do earnestly entreat, call upon and move you all, O ye Benevolent Angels or dignified Spirits of the Air, serving in orders, degree, and mansion (as aforesaid) Abemo[1], Naco[2], Ocenem[3], Shael[4], Jointly and severally, every & each one for and by it self Respectively, in by and through this mighty and powerful name of your God Aiaoai, that you (at these our earnest Addresses) would be so truly willing and friendly unto us,[649] that whensoever and wheresoever we shall invoke

---

[645] S2: "also".
[646] S2: "shall".
[647] S2: "also".
[648] S2: Omits this section thus: "physick in all its parts an the curing of diseases which are incident to Human bodies".
[649] S2: Inserts "as".

move or call you forth, unto visible appearance and our Assistance, you then would readily and Immediately forthwith at our Invocations, move, Descend, appear, and show your selves corporally visible unto us in this Crystal Glass standing here before us, or otherwise personally to appear out of the same visibly here before us, and so, as that we may plainly see you, and audibly hear you speak unto us; And by such your Spiritual Revelations unto us, to make us partakers of that true knowledge and Sapience which by nature and office (given you of the Highest) may by such your visible appearance and verbal converse be showed forth and given to us; And furthermore also, that in by and through this great and powerful name of your God Oiiit, and the force and virtue thereof; we (the servants of the most high God) do likewise earnestly Invocate and Entreat you, to do, accomplish and fulfil whatsoever we shall request and command you; Hear us therefore O ye Benevolent Angels or dignified Spiritual powers of the Air, serving in orders, degree and mansion (as aforesaid) Abemo, Naco, Ocenem, Shael, you do yet further in this great name of your God Aiaoai, and by the virtue and efficacy thereof, Earnestly invocate and entreat you to yield up and give unto us, your assuredly firm free, full, and obliged consent herein, That all or any of you, which we shall at any time hereafter Invocate, move or call forth to visible appearance, would certainly without any Tarrying or delay, Immediately move, Descend, and visibly appear unto us in this Crystal Glass standing here before us, or otherwise out of it, as it shall please God to give unto you, and thereby most beneficial convenient and fit for us, in these both our present and other our future Actions and operations, and to speak plainly unto us, so as that we may sensibly hear you and understand you, directing and instructing us in the true knowledge and Judgement of that your Spiritual Sapience and Science (given you of the Highest) And in this undoubted true and great name of your God Oiiit, and by the virtue and power thereof, whereby we also earnestly Invocate and entreat you, not only to reveal, declare, show forth and make known unto us, the true and apprehensive knowledge of all such occult & mystical Arcanaes in physick, and of whatsoever else relates thereunto, as are unknown of mankind, but also do whatsoever we shall further command, Request or desire to be done Relating to the said Science and our Benefits therein (as you by office are of the Highest) accordingly preordained and appointed; All which your obedience, Readily and willingly fulfilling and accomplishing unto us, as here we have in the powerful and true names of your God Earnestly Entreated and besought you shall be a song of Honour and the praise of your God in your Creation Amen.

Invocation by way of humble supplication and petition made to the four Benevolent Angels or Angelical powers of Light placed in orders and set over the fourth Lesser Angle or division of the great Quadrangle or Table of the East Exgezod[1], Gezodex[2], Zodexge[3], Dexgezod[4], by the great and powerful name of God Eexgezod.

O Ye[650] great and glorious Angels or Angelical powers of Light Exgezod, Gezodex, Zodexge, Dexgezod, governing and set over the fourth Lesser Angle division or Quarter of the great Quadrangle of the East part of the Air, Respecting the like part or point[651] of the compass appropriated to the Earth serving your most high God Eexgezod in orders and office accordingly as you (by Celestial Dignification) are in place and power more Aerially Superior unto whom is given also of the Highest by nature and office the true knowledge (* of the Secrets of men knowing &c) (of physick in all its parts) and of the knitting together of natures, and also as well the destruction of nature and of things that may perish as of conjoining and knitting them together, [652] And to Reveal, show forth and communicate the same (by your Angelical ministry) unto mankind living on Earth, whensoever you shall be Invocated or moved thereunto; We the servants of the Highest (and the same your God) and Reverently here present in his holy fear, do earnestly entreat, humbly beseech and move you all, O ye Angels or Angelical powers of Light, or Celestially dignified Spirits of the Air governing in orders degree and mansion (as aforesaid) Exgezod, Gezodex, Zodexge, Dexgezod, Jointly & severally Every and Each one, for and by it self Respectively, In by and through this mighty and powerful name of your God Eexgezod, that you (at these our humble Requests and Addresses) would be favourable and friendly unto us, as that whensoever or wheresoever we shall Invocate, move, or call you forth to visible appearance & our Assistance, you would be thereby moved, to descend and appear visibly unto us in this Crystal Glass which stand here before us, or otherwise personally to appear out of the same visibly here before us; And so, as that we may plainly see you and Audibly hear you Speak unto us, and by such your friendly and verbal converse with us to make us partakers of that undefiled Knowledge and true Sapience, which by nature & office (given you of the Highest) may by such your Angelical ministry, be Revealed

---

[650] S2: "you".

[651] S2: "~~or point~~".

[652] S2: Has this section struck through, thus: "~~and of physick in all its parts and of the knitting together of natures, and also as well the destruction of nature and of things that may perish as of conjoining and knitting them together~~".

given or administered; Hear us therefore, O you[653] Sacred Angelical powers of Light or Celestially dignified Spirits of the Air, by degree and order Superior and governing (as aforesaid) Exgezod, Gezodex, Zodexge, Dexgezod, we do yet further in this great name of your God Eexgezod, And by the force power and efficacy thereof, to grant these our humble Supplications and petitions and that all or any of you, that we shall at any time hereafter Invocate move or call forth to visible appearance, would Readily and [654] forthwith move, Descend and visibly appear unto us in this Crystal Glass standing here before us or otherwise out of it as shall please God and you his ministers of divine grace, and as best befitted or shall be most convenient or Beneficial for us or unto us, in these our Actions and operations, Speaking Audibly unto us, and also thereby directing & Instructing us in the true knowledge of that your Angelical Sapience and Science (given you of the Highest) And wherein also he hath accordingly by order and office ordained and appointed you; And this your Angelical Benevolence in Celestial grace & charity thus given and granted unto us, and also in the Accomplishment and fulfilling of these our humble desires and requests and whatsoever else shall be requisite and fit for us to know, shall be a song of Honour, and the praise of your God in your Creation Amen.

Invocation by way of humble supplication and petition made to the four Servient Angels or dignified Spirits of the Air, placed in orders and serving in the fourth Lesser Angle or division of the great Quadrangle or Table of the East Acca[1], Enpeat[2], Otoi[3], Pemox[4], who are moved and called forth by the great & powerful name of God Aovararzod, and constrained thereunto to do what they are commanded according to their office by the great name of God Aloai.

O Ye Angelical powers of Light or dignified Spirits of the Air, Acca, Enpeat, Otoi, Pemox, serving in orders under superior powers your most high and omnipotent God, Aovararzod, in the fourth Lesser Angle, division of the great Quadrangle or East part of the Air, Respecting the like part or point of the Compass appropriated to the Earth accordingly as you therein are placed more Inferior and subservient, and unto whom is given of the Highest by nature and office, the true knowledge (* of all Elemental creatures amongst us,

---

[653] S2: "ye".
[654] S2: Omits "and".

how many Kinds,[655] their life[656] in the creation as they are severally placed in the 4 Elements, Air, Earth, fire & Water,) of physick in all its parts and the curing of all diseases, which are Incident to Human bodies,[657] and to reveal, show forth and give the same unto mankind living on Earth, whensoever you shall be moved and called forth by the great name of your God Aloai, commanded thereunto; we the servants of the Highest (and the same your God) and Reverently here present in his holy fear, do earnestly entreat, call upon and move you all; O you[658] Benevolent Angels or dignified powers of the Air, serving in orders degree and mansion (as aforesaid) Acca, Enpeat, Otoi, Pemox, Jointly and severally, every and each one, for and by itself respectively, In by and through this mighty and powerful name of your God Aovararzod, that you (at these our earnest Addresses) would be so truly willing and friendly unto us that whensoever and wheresoever we shall Invocate, move, or call you forth unto visible Appearance and our Assistance, you then would readily and forthwith at our Invocations move, Descend, appear and show your selves corporally visible unto us, in this Crystal Glass standing here before us[659], or otherwise personally to appear out of the same visibly here before us, and so as that we may plainly see you and Audibly hear you speak unto us; And by such your Spiritual Revelations to make us partakers of that true knowledge & Sapience which by nature & office (given you of the Highest) may be showed forth and given to us, and furthermore also that in by and through this great and powerful name of your God Aloai, and the force and virtue thereof, we do likewise Earnestly Invocate and entreat you, to do, accomplish, and fulfil whatsoever (accordingly and by its nature and office given you of the Highest) we shall request and command you; Hear us therefore, O ye Benevolent Angels or dignified Spiritual powers of the Air, serving in orders, degree and mansion (as aforesaid) Acca, Enpeat, Otoi, Pemox, you do yet further in this great name of your God Aovararzod, and by the virtue and efficacy thereof, Earnestly Invocate and Entreat you, to yield up, and give unto us your assuredly firm, free, full, and obliged consent herein, That all or any of you which we shall at any time hereafter, Invocate, move, or call forth to visible appearance, would certainly without any Tarrying or delay, Immediately, move, descend, and visibly appear unto us in this Crystal Glass standing here before us or otherwise out of it as

---

[655] S2: Inserts "&".

[656] S2: "use".

[657] S2: Has this section crossed out, thus: "~~of physick in all its parts and the curing of all diseases, which are Incident to Human bodies~~".

[658] S2: "ye".

[659] S2: "me".

it shall please God to give unto you, and thereby most beneficial convenient and fit for us in these both our present and other our future Actions & operations and to speak plainly unto us so as that we may sensibly hear you and understand you directing & Instructing[660] in the true knowledge and judgement of that your Spiritual Sapience (given you of the Highest) And in this undoubted true and great name of your God Aloai, and by the virtue and power thereof, whereby we also earnestly Invocate and Entreat you not only to instruct[661], declare, show forth and make known unto us the true and apprehensive knowledge of all such occult & mystical Arcanaes in physick, and of whatsoever else relates thereunto as are unknown of mankind, but also do whatsoever[662] we shall further command[663], request[664], desire to be done, relating to the said Science and our benefit therein (as you by office are of the Highest) accordingly preordained and appointed; All which your obedience readily and willingly fulfilling and accomplishing unto us as here we have in the powerful and true names of your God Earnestly Entreated,[665] besought you, shall be a song of Honour and the praise of your God in your Creation Amen.

---

[660] S2: Inserts "us".

[661] S2: "reveal".

[662] S1: Repeats the word "whatsoever" here.

[663] S2: Inserts "and".

[664] S2: Inserts "or".

[665] S2: Inserts "and".

[Invocation of the Kings, Seniors, Angels and Spirits of the West]

Humble Supplication and petition made to the great King RAAGIOS, principal governor and Celestial Angelical watchman set over the watch Tower or Terrestrial Angle of the West by the 3 mighty & powerful names of God Emph, Arsel, Gaiol.

O Thou Regal, great, mighty and powerful Angel of the most high, Immense, Immortal, and Incomprehensible God of Hosts RAAGIOS, who in the beginning of time by the divine decree and appointment of the Highest in the unity of the Blessed Trinity wast[666] set over the Terrestrial Angle of the West, as the only King, governor, overseer, principal watchman, protector and Keeper thereof, from the malice, misuse, Illusion, Temptation, Assault, Surprisal, Theft or other wicked Encroachments, usurping Blasphemy of the great Enemy of God's glory and the welfare of mankind, the Devil and Spirits of darkness; And as a snaffle to restrain their wickedness by the bit of God's boundless power and Justice, to the intent that (they being put on, into the earth) their Envious will may be bridled the determinations of the Highest fulfilled, and his creatures kept within the compass and measure of order; we humbly beseech, Invocate and Entreat you, O you Royal Angel RAAGIOS, In by and through these potent mighty and great names of your God Emph, Arsel, Gaiol, to preserve, defend, keep and protect us, from the wicked Illusions, Envious Temptations violent Assaults, or any other destructive Surprisals of all Evil Spirits or Infernal powers of darkness whatsoever and that we may not be thereby dismayed, vanquished or overcome, and that by the virtue, power & efficacy of those three said mighty names of God, Emph, Arsel, Gaiol, O you great potent and Royal Angel RAAGIOS, and by the true seal or character of your Creation, and by those Banners, Ensigns or Trophies of Honour and glory borne or standing before you as both divine Celestial Angelical, natural and Royal Tokens and Testimonies of Monarchy majesty and Imperial Authority (given and confirmed unto you in the beginning of the world), and by the Influence, Efficacy, force and virtue thereof; We most Earnestly Entreat and humbly beseech you to be gracious and friendly unto us herein, and furthermore likewise to help, aid, and assist us in all these as such our Temporal and Terrestrial operations, affairs, and concerns, as wherein you may or can by the Superior power of that

---

[666] S2: "wert".

your Kingly order and Authority (given you of the Highest) for the protection, defence, preservation, care, conduct, comfort, support, Assistance, Benefit and use of mankind living on Earth, and amongst the rest we also again humbly entreat and Earnestly beseech you, that all those six governing[667] Angels called Angelical Seniors, and all other governing or superior Angelical and Elemental powers of Light Celestially dignified, and also that all other dignified Servient and Subservient Spirits or Benevolent Aerially powers who are by nature and office friendly and good, and ordained (by divine appointment in the unity of the Blessed Trinity) for the use, Benefit and Service of mankind, of all degrees and offices from the Superior to the Inferior in the order and mansion serving the most high God, under your Imperial and Sovereign power, Authority, command, Subjection Service and obedience properly referred or appropriated to the West Angle of the Air, Respecting also the like point of the Compass, Quarter, Angle[668], division of the Earth, may by the force and power of our Invocations be moved to descend and appear visibly unto us in this Crystal Glass or otherwise out of the same, as either convenience or necessity of the occasion shall require, and that they may at the reading and repetition of our Invocations or calls on that account by us made unto them, moved, Descend and appear before us visible[669] to the Sight of our Eyes, and to speak Audibly unto us that we may plainly and perfectly both see and hear them and friendly to converse with us fulfilling our desires and requests in all things according to their several and respective offices, and to serve us therein, and also do for us as for the servants of the most high God, whensoever and wheresoever and whereunto we shall at any time and place move you both in power and presence whose works herein shall be a song of Honour to the glory and praise of the most high God both in your and their Creation Amen.

Invocation by way of humble supplication and petition made to the six great Angels or Angelical Seniors Lefarahpem[1], Saiinou[2], Laoaxarp[3], Selgaiol[4], Ligdisa[5], Soaixente[6], by the great and powerful name of their Imperial King RAAGIOS.

O Ye great Angels or Angelical Seniors Lefarahpem, Saiinou, Laoaxarp, Selgaiol, Ligdisa, Soaixente, serving your most high God

---

[667] S2: "great".
[668] S2: Inserts "or".
[669] S2: "visibly".

Emph, Arsel, Gaiol, before the mighty Angelical monarch King RAAGIOS, in the Angle, Region or division of the West, and who are dignified with Celestial power and Authority therein, and by office judging the government of the Angelical King, thereby fulfilling the divine will and pleasure of the Highest in all things appointed and committed to your charge, and placed in Superior (power[670] &) order under the said Angelical King and governing over all other, both superior Servient and subservient Angels or Angelical powers celestially dignified, and also all other Elemental Spirits whosever that in any wise hath power, mansion, Residence, orders, office, place or being, in the West part, Region or Angle of the Air with like respect also, from thence to be had to the west point of the Compass, Angle, part or division of the Earth, we the servants of the Highest, and Reverently here present in his holy fear, do humbly beseech, call upon, & Earnestly Entreat you all,[671] you Angelical Seniors Lefarahpem, Saiinou, Laoaxarp, Selgaiol, Ligdisa, Soaixente, In by and through this Imperial mighty and powerful name RAAGIOS, That all or some one severally[672] of you, Jointly and severally, in general and particular, Every and Each one, for and by it self respectively would be so favourable and friendly unto us as that whensoever or wheresoever we shall Invocate, move or call you forth unto visible appearance & our assistance, you then would be thereby moved to descend, and appear visibly unto us, in this Crystal Glass set here before us, and so, as that we may plainly see and Audibly hear you speak unto us, and by such your friendly Society and verbal converse with us, to Illuminate, Instruct, direct, help, Aid and assist us in all things whatsoever we shall humbly desire, beseech and request of you, wherein by nature and office (given you of the Highest) you may or can; Hear us therefore, O ye Blessed Angels or Angelical seniors Lefarahpem, Saiinou, Laoaxarp, Selgaiol, Ligdisa, Soaixente, and in the mighty name RAAGIOS, and by the virtue, power, Influence, Efficacy and force thereof, we earnestly entreat and humbly beseech you to grant these our supplications and petitions, that all or some[673] of you which we shall at any time hereafter Invocate, move[674], call forth to visible appearance would then be favourable and firmly placed in Celestial charity and Benevolence, forthwith & Immediately at such our Invocations and earnest requests accordingly of us made, be thereby moved, and also to move, descend, visibly appear and speak Audibly unto us, either in this Crystal Glass or otherwise out

---

[670] S2: "powers".
[671] S2: Inserts "O".
[672] S2: Replaces "severally" with "or any".
[673] S2: "any".
[674] S2: Inserts "or".

of the same as it shall please God and you his Angelical ministers or Celestial messengers of divine grace and Light and shall be most befitting, beneficial and convenient for us therein and to administer unto us the bountiful gifts of all Earthly benefits, and also endow us with the gift of true Sapience and science and such like other gifts of human Accomplishments & Enjoyments as may or shall be fit for us, and so beneficial unto us that we may thereby live happy with comfort during our continuance in this mortal being; All which we humbly beseech and earnestly entreat of all and every of you sacred Angels or Angelical Seniors, in the name of your God & King wherein these your friendly and benevolent works (thus graciously communicated and given to us) shall be a song of Honour and the praise of your God in your Creation Amen.

Invocation by way of humble Supplication and petition made to the four Benevolent Angels or Angelical powers of Light, placed in orders and set over the first Lesser Angle or division of the great Quadrangle or Table of the West Taad[1], Aadet[2], Adeta[3], Detaa[4], by the great and powerful name of God HETAAD.

O Ye great and glorious Angels or Angelical powers of Light Taad, Aadet, Adeta, Detaa, governing or set over the first Lesser Angle, division or Quarter of the great Quadrangle of the west part of the Air, respecting the like part or point of the compass appropriated to the Earth, serving your most high God Hetaad, in orders and office accordingly as you (by Celestial Dignification) are in place and power more Aerially Superior; unto whom is given also of the Highest by nature and office, the true knowledge of the knitting together of natures and also as well the destruction of nature and of things that may perish as of conjoining and knitting them together, and to reveal, show forth and communicate the same (by your Angelical ministry) unto mankind living on Earth, whensoever you shall be Invocated or moved thereunto; We the servants of the Highest (and the same your God) and reverently here present in his holy fear, do Earnestly Entreat, humbly beseech, and move you all; O you[675] Angels or Angelical powers of Light, or celestially dignified Spirits of the Air, governing in orders, degree, and mansion (as aforesaid) Taad, Aadet, Adeta, Detaa, Jointly and severally, Every and each one, for and by it self respectively, In by and through this mighty & powerful name of your God Hetaad, that you (at these humble requests and Addresses) would be favourable and friendly

---

[675] S2: "ye".

unto us, as that whensoever or wheresoever, we shall Invocate, move or call you forth to visible appearance & our Assistance, you would be thereby moved to descend and appear visibly unto us in this Crystal Glass which stand here before us, or otherwise personally to appear out of the same visibly here before us, and[676] as that we may plainly see you and Audibly hear you speak unto us, and by such your friendly and verbal converse with us, to make us partakers of that undefiled Knowledge and true Sapience, which by nature and office (given you of the Highest) may by such your Angelical ministry be revealed given or administered unto us. Hear us therefore O you[677] Sacred Angelical powers of Light or Celestially dignified Spirits of the Air, by degrees[678] & orders Superior, and governing (as aforesaid) Taad, Aadet, Adeta, Detaa, you do yet further in this great name of your God Hetaad, and by the force, power and Efficacy thereof, Earnestly Entreat, and humbly beseech you to grant these our Supplications & petitions, and that all or any of you that we shall at any time hereafter, Invocate, move or call forth to visible appearance, would readily & forthwith, move, Descend, & visibly appear unto us, whensoever we shall Invocate, call forth or move you thereafter[679] in this Crystal Glass standing here before us , or otherwise out of it, as it shall please God and you his ministers of divine grace, and as best befitted or shall be most convenient or beneficial for us, or unto us in these our Actions and operations, Speaking Audibly unto us and also thereby directing and instructing us in the true knowledge of that your Angelical Sapience and Science (given you of the Highest) wherein also he hath accordingly by order and office, ordained and appointed you; And this your Angelical Benevolence in Celestial grace and charity thus given and granted unto us, also in the accomplishment and fulfilling of these our humble desires and requests and of whatsoever else shall be requisite and fit for us to know shall be a song of Honour and the praise of your God in your Creation Amen.

Invocation by way of humble supplication and petition made to the four Servient Angels or dignified Spirits of the Air, placed in orders and serving in the first Lesser Angle or division of the great Quadrangle[680] or table of the West Toco[1], Nehded[2], Paax[3], Saix[4], who are moved and called forth by the great and powerful name of God Obegoca, and constrained to do what they are commanded

---

[676] S2: Inserts "so".
[677] S2: "ye".
[678] S2: "Degree".
[679] S2: "thereunto".
[680] S2: "of".

according to their office by the great name of God Aabeco.

O Ye Angelical powers of Light, or dignified Spirits of the Air, Toco, Nehded, Paax, Saix, serving in orders under superior powers your most high and Omnipotent God, Obegoca, in the first Lesser Angle, or division of the great Quadrangle or West part of the Air, respecting the like part or point of the Compass appropriated to the Earth, accordingly as you therein are placed more Inferior and subservient; and unto whom is given of the Highest by nature and office, the true knowledge of physick in all its parts and the curing of all diseases whatsoever that are incident to human bodies, and to reveal show forth & give the same unto mankind living on Earth, whensoever you shall be moved and called forth by the great name of your God Aabeco, commanded[681]; We the servants of the Highest (and the same your God) and reverently here present in his holy fear, do earnestly entreat, call upon, and move you all; O ye Benevolent Angels or dignified powers of the Air, serving in orders degree and mansion (as aforesaid) Toco, Nehded, Paax, Saix, Jointly & Severally, Every and each one, for and by itself respectively, In by and through this mighty & powerful name of your God Obegoca, that you (at these our Earnest Addresses) would be so truly willing and friendly unto us, that whensoever and wheresoever we shall Invocate, move, or call you forth unto visible appearance and our assistance; You then would readily and Immediately forthwith at our Invocations, move, Descend and appear, and show your selves corporally visible unto us in this Crystal Glass standing here before us, or otherwise plainly to appear visibly here before us, and so as that we may personally see you, and Audibly hear you speak unto us; And by such your Spiritual Revelations unto us to make us partakers of that true knowledge and Sapience which by nature and office (given you of the Highest) may by such your visible appearance and verbal converse, be showed forth and unto us; And furthermore also that In by and through this great and powerful name of your God Aabeco, and the force & virtue thereof; We do likewise Earnestly Entreat and Invocate you to do, accomplish and fulfil whatsoever (accordingly and by its[682] nature and office given you of the Highest) we shall request and command you; Hear us therefore, O ye Benevolent Servient Angels or dignified Spiritual powers of the Air, serving in orders, degree and mansion (as aforesaid) Toco, Nehded, Paax, Saix, you do yet further in this great name of your God Obegoca, and by the virtue and Efficacy thereof,

---

[681] S2: "commanding you thereunto".
[682] S2: Replaces 2by its" with "is by".

Earnestly Invocate and Entreat you, to yield up and give unto us, your assuredly firm, free, full, and obliged consent herein, that all or any of you which we shall at any time hereafter Invocate, move, or call forth to visible appearance, certainly without any Tarrying or delay, Immediately move, Descend, and visibly appear unto us in this Crystal Glass standing here before us, or otherwise out of it, as it shall please God to give unto you, and thereby most beneficial convenient and fit for us in these both our present and other our future Actions & operations, and to speak plainly unto us, so, as that we may sensibly hear you and understand you, directing and Instructing us, in the true knowledge and Judgement of that your Spiritual Sapience and Science given you of the Highest; And in this undoubted true and great name of your God Aabeco, and by the virtue and power thereof, whereby we also earnestly Invocate and Entreat, you not only to reveal, declare, show forth and make known unto us the true and apprehensive knowledge of all such occult and mystical Arcanaes, in physick, and of whatsoever else later thereunto, as are unknown of mankind, but also do whatsoever we shall further command, request or desire to be done for us, relating to the said Science and our benefits therein (as you by office are of the Highest) accordingly preordained and appointed; All which your obedience readily & willingly fulfilling and accomplishing unto us (as here we have in the powerful and true names of your God, Earnestly Entreated and besought you) shall be a song of Honour and the praise of your God in your Creation Amen.

Invocation by way of humble Supplication and petition made to the four Benevolent Angels or Angelical powers of Light, placed in orders and set over the Second Lesser Angle or division of the great Quadrangle or Table of the west Tedim[1], Dimet[2], Imtede[3], Emtedi[4], by the great & powerful name of God HETEDIM.

O Ye great and glorious Angels or Angelical powers of Light Tedim, Dimet, Imtede, Emtedi, governing or set over the second Lesser Angle, division or Quarter of the great Quadrangle of the west point of the Air respecting the like part or point of the Compass appropriated to the Earth serving your most high God Hetedim, in orders and office accordingly as you (by Celestial Dignification) are in place and power more Aerially Superior, unto whom is given also of the Highest by nature and office the true knowledge of (* Moving

171

from place to place[683] &c) the knitting together of natures, and also as well the destruction of nature and of things that may perish as of conjoining and knitting them together[684], and to invocate[685], show forth and communicate the same (by your Angelical ministry) unto mankind living on Earth, whensoever you shall be Invocated or moved thereunto; we the servants of the Highest (and the same your God) and reverently here present in his holy fear, do earnestly entreat, humbly beseech and move you all; O ye Angels or Angelical powers of Light or Celestially dignified Spirits of the Air, governing in orders degree, and mansion (as aforesaid) Tedim, Dimet, Imtede, Emtedi, Jointly and severally, Every and each one, for and by it self respectively, In by and through this mighty and powerful name of your God Hetedim, that you (at these humble requests and Addresses) would be favourable and friendly unto us, as that whensoever or wheresoever we shall Invocate, move or call you forth to visible appearance and our Assistance, you would be thereby moved to descend and appear visibly unto us in this Crystal Glass which stand here before us, or otherwise personally to appear out of the same visibly here before us, and so as that we may plainly see you and Audibly hear you speak unto us, and by such your friendly and verbal converse with us, to make us partakers of that undefiled knowledge and true Science, which by nature and office (given you of the Highest) may by such your Angelical ministry be revealed given or administered unto us, Hear us therefore O ye Sacred Angelical powers of Light or Celestially dignified Spirits of the Air, by degrees and orders Superior and governing (as aforesaid) Tedim, Dimet, Imtede, Emtedi, we do yet further in this great name of your God Hetedim, and by the force, power and Efficacy thereof, Earnestly Entreat and humbly beseech you, to grant these our Supplications and petitions, and that all or any of you that we shall at any time hereafter, Invocate, move, or call forth to visible appearance, would readily and forthwith, move, descend, and visibly appear unto us, whensoever we shall Invocate, call forth or move you thereafter[686] in this Crystal Glass standing here before us, or otherwise out of it, as it shall please God, and you his ministers of divine grace, and as best befitted or shall be most convenient or beneficial for or unto us, in these our Actions or operations, Speaking Audibly unto us and also thereby directing and instructing us, in the true knowledge of that your Angelical

---

[683] S2: Inserts "as unto this Country or that Country at pleasure".

[684] S2: This part is struck through in the manuscript, thus: "~~the knitting together of natures and also as well the destruction of nature and of things that may perish as of conjoining and knitting them together~~".

[685] S2: "reveal".

[686] S2: "thereunto".

172

Sapience and Science (given you of the Highest) and wherein also he hath accordingly by order and office ordained and appointed you; And this your Angelical Benevolence in Celestial grace and charity thus given and granted unto us, and also in the Accomplishment and fulfilling of these our humble desires and requests and of whatsoever else shall be requisite and fit for us to know shall be a song of Honour and the praise of your God in your Creation Amen.

Invocation by way of humble supplication and petition made to the four Servient Angels or dignified Spirits of the Air, placed in orders and serving in the Second Lesser Angle or division of the great Quadrangle or Table of the west Magem[1], Leoc[2], Vrsyl[3], Vrvoi[4], who are moved and called forth, by the great and powerful name of God Nelapar, and constrained thereunto to do what they are commanded according to their office, by the great name of God Omebeb.

O Ye Angelical powers of Light, or dignified Spirits of the Air, Magem, Leoc, Vrsyl, Vrvoi, serving in orders under superior powers your most high & omnipotent God, Nelapar, in the second Lesser Angle or division of the great Quadrangle or West part of the Air respecting the like part or point of the compass appropriated to the Earth accordingly as you therein are placed more Inferior and Subservient, and unto whom is given of the Highest by nature and office, the true knowledge of (* finding & use of metals, the Congelation of Stones &c[687]), physick in all its parts and the curing of all diseases whatsoever that are Incident to human bodies:[688] And to Reveal, show forth and give the same unto mankind living on Earth, whensoever you shall be moved and called forth by the great name of your God Omebeb commanded thereunto: We the servants of the Highest (and the same your God) and reverently here present in his holy fear, do earnestly Entreat, call upon and move you all; O ye Benevolent Angels or dignified powers of the Air, serving in orders degree and mansion (as aforesaid) Magem, Leoc, Vrsyl, Vrvoi, Jointly and severally, Every and Each one, for and by itself respectively, In by and through this mighty & powerful name of your God Nelapar, that you (at these our earnest Addresses) would be so truly willing and friendly unto us, that whensoever and wheresoever we shall Invocate, move or call you forth, unto visible

---

[687] S2: Inserts "and virtue of all stones".
[688] S2: This section is struck through, thus: "~~physick in all its parts and the curing of all diseases whatsoever that are incident to human bodies~~".

appearance and our assistance, you then would readily and Immediately forthwith at our Invocations, move, Descend, Appear, and show your selves corporally visible unto us in this Crystal Glass standing here before us, or otherwise personally to appear out of the same visibly here before us, and so, as that we may plainly see you, and audibly hear you speak unto us, and by such your Spiritual Revelations unto us, to make us partakers of that true knowledge and Sapience which by nature and office (given you of the Highest) may by such your visible appearance and verbal converse, be showed forth and given to us; And furthermore also that In by and through this great and powerful name of your God Omebeb, and the force and virtue thereof; we do likewise earnestly entreat and Invocate you, to do, accomplish, and fulfil, whatsoever (accordingly and[689] is by nature and office given you of the Highest) we shall request and command you; Hear us therefore, O you[690] Benevolent Angels or dignified Spiritual powers of the Air, serving in orders, office, degree and mansion (as aforesaid) Magem, Leoc, Vrsyl, Vrvoi, you do yet further in this great name of your God Nelapar, and by the virtue and Efficacy thereof, Earnestly Invocate and Entreat you, to yield up and give unto us, your assuredly firm, free, and obliged consent herein, that all or any of you, which we shall at any time hereafter, Invocate move or call forth to visible appearance would certainly without any Tarrying or delay, Immediately move, descend, and visibly appear unto us in this Crystal Glass standing here before us, or otherwise out of it as it shall please God to give unto you, & thereby most beneficial, convenient and fit for us, in these both our present and other our future Actions and operations, and to speak plainly unto us, so as that we may sensibly hear you and understand you, directing and Instructing us in the true knowledge and judgement of that your Spiritual Sapience and Science (given you of the Highest) And in this undoubted true and great name of your God Omebeb and by the virtue and power thereof, whereby we also earnestly Invocate and entreat you; not only to reveal, declare, show forth and make known unto us the true and apprehensive knowledge of all such Occult and mystical Arcanaes in physick, and of whatsoever else relates thereunto, as are unknown of mankind, but also do for us whatsoever we shall further command, request or desire to be done, relating to the said Science and our Benefits therein (as you by office are of the Highest) accordingly preordained & appointed All which your obedience readily and willingly fulfilling & accomplishing unto us (as here we have in the powerful and true

---

[689] S2: Replaces "and", with "~~and~~ as".
[690] S2: "ye".

names of your God Earnestly Entreated and besought you) shall be a song of Honour and the praise of your God in your Creation Amen.

Invocation by way of humble Supplication and petition made to the four Benevolent Angels or Angelical powers of Light placed in orders and set over the Third Lesser Angle or division of the great Quadrangle or Table of the West Magel[1], Agelem[2], Gelema[3], Lemage[4] by the great and powerful name of God HEMAGEL.

O Ye glorious and great Angels or Angelical powers of Light Magel, Agelem, Gelema, Lemage, governing or set over the Third Lesser Angle, division or Quarter of the great Quadrangle of the west point of the Air, respecting the like part or point of the compass appropriated to the Earth, Serving your most high God Hemagel, in orders and office accordingly, as you (by Celestial dignification) are in place and power more Aerially Superior; unto whom is given also of the Highest by nature & office, the true knowledge of (* all Mechanical Crafts whatsoever), the knitting together of natures, & also as well the destruction of nature and of things that may perish as of conjoining and knitting them together,[691] And to Reveal, Show forth and communicate the same (by your Angelical ministry) unto mankind living on Earth, whensoever you shall be Invocated or moved thereunto; We the servants of the Highest (and the same your God) and Reverently here present in his holy fear, do earnestly entreat, humbly beseech and move you all; O ye Angels or Angelical Spirits of Light, or Celestially dignified Spirits of the Air, governing in orders, degree, and mansion as aforesaid Magel, Agelem, Gelema, Lemage, Jointly and severally, Every and each one for and by it self respectively, In by and through this mighty and powerful name of your God Hemagel, that you (at these our humble requests and Addresses) would be favourable and friendly unto us, as that whensoever or wheresoever we shall Invocate, move, or call you forth to visible appearance and our Assistance, you would be thereby moved to descend and appear visibly unto us in this Crystal Glass which stand here before us, or otherwise personally to appear out of the same visibly here before us, and so as that we may plainly see you and Audibly hear you speak unto us, and by such your friendly and verbal converse with us to make us partakers of

---

[691] S2: This section is crossed out, thus: "~~the knitting together of natures, and also as well the destruction of nature and of things that may perish as of conjoining and knitting them together~~".

that undefiled knowledge and true Sapience, which by nature and office (given you of the Highest) may by such your Angelical ministry be revealed given or administered unto us, Hear us therefore O ye Sacred Angelical powers of Light, or Celestially dignified Spirits of the Air, by degree, and orders superior and governing as aforesaid Magel, Agelem, Gelema, Lemage, we do yet further in this great name of your God Hemagel, and by the force power and efficacy thereof, to grant these our humble Supplications, and that all or any of you, that we shall at any time hereafter Invocate, move or call forth to visible appearance, would readily and forthwith, move, descend, and visibly appear unto us, whensoever we shall Invocate, call forth or move you thereunto in this Crystal Glass standing here before us, or otherwise out of it, as it shall please God and you his ministers of divine grace and as best befitted or shall be most convenient or beneficial for us, or unto us in these, our Actions or operations, speaking Audibly unto us, and also thereby directing and Instructing us, in the true knowledge of that your Angelical Sapience and Science (given you of the Highest) and wherein also he hath accordingly by order and office ordained and appointed you, and this your Angelical Benevolence in Celestial grace and charity thus given and granted unto us, and also in the accomplishment and fulfilling of these our humble desires and requests, and whatsoever else shall be requisite and fit for us to know, shall be a song of Honour, and the praise of your God in your Creation Amen.

Invocation by way of humble Supplication and petition, made to the four Servient Angels or dignified Spirits of the Air placed in orders and serving in the Third Lesser Angle or division of the great Quadrangle or Table of the West Paco[1], Endezen[2], Jipo[3], Exarih[4], who are moved and called forth by the great and powerful name of God Maladi, And constrained thereunto to do what they are commanded, according to their office by the great name of God Olaad.

O Ye Angelical powers of Light or dignified Spirits of the Air, Paco, Endezen, Jipo, Exarih, serving in orders under superior powers, your most high and omnipotent God, Maladi, in the Third Lesser Angle or division of the great Quadrangle or West part of the Air, respecting the like part or point of the Compass appropriated to the Earth, accordingly as you therein are placed more Inferior and Subservient and unto whom is given of the Highest by nature and office the true knowledge of (* Transformation & transplantation), physick in all its parts and the curing of all diseases which are

Incident to human bodies,[692] and to reveal, show forth and give the same to mankind living on Earth whensoever you shall be moved and called forth by the great name of God Olaad, commanded thereunto; We the servants of the Highest (and the same your God) and reverently here present in his holy fear, do Earnestly Entreat, call upon and move you all; O ye Benevolent Angels or dignified powers of the Air, serving in orders, degree and mansion (as aforesaid) Paco, Endezen, Jipo, Exarih, Jointly and severally, Every and Each one, for and by itself respectively, In by and through this mighty & powerful name of your God Maladi, that you (at these our earnest Addresses) would be so truly willing and friendly unto us that whensoever we shall Invocate, move, or call you forth unto visible appearance and our Assistance, you then would readily and Immediately forthwith at our Invocations, move, descend, appear and show your selves corporally visible unto us in this Crystal Glass standing here before us, or otherwise personally to appear out of the same visibly here before us, and so as that we may plainly see you and Audibly hear you speak unto us; And by such your Spiritual Revelations unto us to make us partakers of that true knowledge and Sapience which by nature and office (given you of the Highest) may by such your visible appearance & verbal converse be showed forth and given to us: And furthermore also that In by and through this great and powerful name of your God Olaad, and the force and virtue thereof, we do likewise earnestly Invocate and Entreat you, to do, accomplish and fulfil whatsoever (accordingly and[693] is by nature and office given you of the Highest) we shall request & command you, Hear us therefore O ye Benevolent Angels or dignified Spiritual powers of the Air serving in orders, office, degrees, & mansion as aforesaid Paco, Endezen, Jipo, Exarih, you do yet further in this great name of your God Maladi, and by the virtue and Efficacy thereof, earnestly Invocate and Entreat you to yield up and give unto[694] us, your assuredly firm, free, and obliged consent herein, that all or any of you which we shall at any time hereafter Invocate move, or call forth to visible appearance would readily without any Tarrying or delay, Immediately, move descend, [695] appear visibly unto us in this Crystal Glass standing here before us, or otherwise out of it as it shall please God to give unto you, and thereby most beneficial convenient and fit for us, in these both our present and other our future Actions and operations, and to speak plainly unto us, so as

---

[692] S2: This section is struck through, thus: "physick in all its parts and the curing of all diseases which are Incident to human bodies".
[693] S2: "and as".
[694] S2: "unto".
[695] S2: Inserts "&".

that we may sensibly hear you and understand you, directing and Instructing us in the true knowledge and judgement of that your Spiritual Sapience and Science (given you of the Highest) And in this undoubted true, and great name of your God Olaad, and by the virtue and power thereof, whereby we also earnestly Invocate and entreat you, not only to reveal, declare, show forth and make known unto us, the true and apprehensive knowledge of all such Occult and mystical Arcanaes in physick and of whatsoever else relates thereunto, as are unknown of mankind, but also do whatsoever we shall further command, request or desire to be done, relating to the said Science and our Benefits therein (as you by office are of the Highest) accordingly preordained and appointed, All which your obedience, Readily and willingly fulfilling and accomplishing unto us as here we have in the powerful and true names of your God Earnestly Entreated and besought you, shall be a Song of Honour, & the praise of your God in your Creation Amen.

Invocation by way of humble Supplication and petition made to the four Benevolent Angels or Angelical powers of Light placed in orders and set over the fourth Lesser Angle or division of the great Quadrangle or Table of the West Enlarex, Larexen, Rexenel, Xenelar by the great & powerful name of God HENLAREX.

——

O Ye great and glorious Angels or Angelical powers of Light Enlarex, Larexen, Rexenel, Xenelar, governing and set over the fourth Lesser Angle division or Quarter of the great Quadrangle or West point of the Air, respecting the like part or point of the Compass appropriated to the Earth, Serving your most high God Henlarex, in orders and office accordingly as you (by Celestial Dignification)[696] are in place and power more Aerially Superior, unto whom is given also of the Highest by nature and office, the true knowledge of (* the Secrets of men knowing), the knitting together of natures, and also as well the destruction of nature and of things that may perish as of conjoining and knitting them together,[697] And to Reveal, Show forth and communicate the same (by your Angelical ministry) unto mankind living on Earth, whensoever you shall be invocated or moved thereunto; We the servants of the Highest (and the same

---

[696] S2: "are".

[697] S2: This section is struck through, thus: "the knitting together of natures, and also as well the destruction of nature and of things that may perish as of conjoining and knitting them together".

your God) and reverently here present in his holy fear, do earnestly entreat, humbly beseech and move you all; O ye Angels or Angelical powers of Light or Celestially dignified Spirits of the Air governing in orders, degree, and mansion as aforesaid Enlarex, Larexen, Rexenel, Xenelar, Jointly and severally, Every and each one for and by it self respectively, In by and through this mighty and powerful name of your God Henlarex, that you (at these humble requests and Addresses) would be favourable and friendly unto us, as that whensoever or wheresoever we shall Invocate move or call you forth to visible appearance and our assistance, you would be thereby moved to descend & appear visibly unto us in this Crystal Glass which stand here before us, or otherwise personally to appear out of the same visibly here before us, and so, as that we may plainly see you, and Audibly hear you speak unto us, and by such your friendly and verbal converse with us, to make us partakers of that undefiled knowledge and true Sapience, which by nature and office (given you of the Highest) may by such your Angelical ministry be revealed given or administered unto us; Hear us therefore O ye Sacred Angelical powers of Light or Celestially dignified Spirits of the Air by degree and orders Superior, and governing as aforesaid Enlarex, Larexen, Rexenel, Xenelar, we do yet further in this great name of your God Henlarex, and by the force power and efficacy thereof, to grant these our Supplications and petitions, and that all or any of you that we shall at any time hereafter, Invocate, move or call forth to visible appearance would readily and forthwith at our Invocations move, Descend, and visibly appear unto us, whensoever we shall Invocate or move you thereunto in this Crystal Glass standing here before us or otherwise out of it, as it shall please God and you his ministers of divine grace and as best befitted or shall be most convenient or beneficial for us or unto us in the true knowledge of that your Angelical Sapience and Science (given you of the Highest) And wherein also he hath accordingly by order and office ordained and appointed you, and this your Angelical Benevolence in Celestial grace & charity thus given and granted unto us, and also in the accomplishment and fulfilling of these our humble desires & requests and whatsoever else shall be requisite and fit for us to know, shall be a song of Honour and the praise of your God in your Creation Amen.

Invocation by way of humble Supplication and petition made to the four Servient Angels or dignified Spirits of the Air placed in orders, and serving in the Fourth Lesser Angle or division of the great Quadrangle or Table of the West Expecen[1], Vasa[2], Dapi[3], Reniel[4], who are moved and called forth by the great and powerful name of

God Jaaasde, and constrained thereunto to do what they are commanded according to their office by the great name of God Atapa.

O Ye Angelical powers of Light or dignified Spirits of the Air, Expecen, Vasa, Dapi, Reniel, serving in orders under superior powers, your most high & omnipotent God, Jaaasde, in the Fourth Lesser Angle or division of the great Quadrangle or West part of the Air, respecting the like part or point of the Compass appropriated to the Earth, accordingly as you therein are placed more Inferior and Subservient, and unto whom is given of the Highest by nature and office the true knowledge (* of all Elemental creatures among us how many Kinds & their life in the Creation &c,) of physick in all its parts and the curing of all diseases which are Incident to human bodies, [698] and to reveal, show forth and give the same unto mankind living on Earth whensoever you shall be moved and called forth by the great name of your God Atapa, commanded thereunto: We the servants of the Highest (and the same your God) and reverently here present in his holy fear, do earnestly entreat, call upon, and move you all, O ye Benevolent Angels or dignified powers of the Air, serving in orders, degree and mansion as aforesaid Expecen, Vasa, Dapi, Reniel, Jointly and severally, Every and Each one, for and by itself respectively, In by and through this mighty and powerful name of your God Jaasde, that you (at these our earnest Addresses) would be so truly willing and friendly unto us that whensoever & wheresoever we shall Invocate, move or call you forth unto visible appearance and our assistance, you then would readily and Immediately forthwith at our Invocations, move, Descend appear, and show your selves corporally visible unto us in this Crystal Glass standing here before us, or otherwise personally to appear out of the same visibly here before us, and so as that we may plainly see you, and Audibly hear you Speak unto us, and by such your Spiritual Revelations unto us to make us partakers of that true knowledge and Sapience, which by nature and office (given you of the Highest) may by such your visible appearance and verbal converse be showed forth and given to us, and furthermore also that In by and through this great and powerful name of your God Atapa, and the force and virtue thereof, we do likewise Earnestly Entreat and Invocate you, to do, accomplish, and fulfil whatsoever (accordingly and[699] is by nature and office, given you of

---

[698] S2: This section is struck through, thus: "~~of physick in all its parts and the curing of all diseases which are incident to human bodies~~".

[699] S2: "~~and~~ as".

the Highest) we shall request & command you, Hear us therefore O ye Benevolent Angels or dignified Spiritual powers of the Air serving in orders, degree, and mansion (as aforesaid) Expecen, Vasa, Dapi, Reniel, you do yet further in this great name of your God Jaaasde, and by the virtue and efficacy thereof, Earnestly Invocate and Entreat you to yield up and give unto us, your assuredly firm, free[700], and obliged consent herein, that all or any of you which we shall at any time hereafter Invocate, move, or call forth to visible appearance would certainly without any Tarrying or delay, Immediately move, Descend & visibly appear unto us in this Crystal Glass standing here before us, or otherwise out of it as it shall please God to give unto you and thereby most beneficial, convenient and fit for us, In these both our present and other our future Actions and operations, and to speak plainly unto us, so, as that we may sensibly hear you and understand you, directing and instructing us in the true knowledge & judgement, of that your Spiritual Sapience and Science (given you of the Highest) and in this undoubted true and great name of your God Atapa, and by the virtue and power thereof whereby we also earnestly Invocate and entreat you, not only to reveal, declare, show forth and make known unto us the true and apprehensive knowledge of all such occult and mystical Arcanaes, in physick and of whatsoever else relates thereunto, as are unknown of mankind but also do whatsoever we shall further command, request or desire to be done, relating to the said Science and our benefits therein (as you by office are of the Highest) accordingly preordained and appointed, All which your Obedience, readily & willingly fulfilling and accomplishing unto us, as here we have in the powerful and true names of your God Earnestly Entreated and besought you, shall be a Song of Honour and the praise of your God in your Creation Amen.

---

[700] S2: Inserts "will".

[Invocation of the Kings, Seniors, Angels and Spirits of the North]

Humble Supplication and petition made to the great King JCZODHEHCA, principal governor and Celestial Angelical Watchman, set over the Watch Tower or Terrestrial Table of the North by the 3 mighty & powerful names of God Emor, Dial, Hectega.

O Thou Regal, great mighty and powerful Angel of the most high, Immense, Immortal, and Incomprehensible God of Hosts JCZODHEHCA, who in the beginning of time by the divine decree and appointment[701] of the Highest in the unity of the blessed Trinity [wast set over the Terrestrial Angle of the North, as the only King,][702] Governor, Overseer, principal watchman, protector and Keeper thereof, from the malice, misuse, Illusion, Temptation, Assaults, Surprisal, Theft or other wicked Encroachments usurping Blasphemy of the great Enemy of God's glory and the welfare of mankind the Devil and Spirits of darkness, And as a snaffle to restrain their wickedness by the bit of God's boundless power and justice, to the intent,[703] that (they being put on into the earth) their envious will might be bridled the determinations of the Highest fulfilled and his creatures kept within the compass and measure of order; we humbly Invocate, Entreat and beseech you, O you Royal Angel JCZODHEHCA, In by and through these potent mighty and great names of your God Emor, Dial, Hectega, to preserve, defend, keep and protect us, from the wicked Illusions, envious Temptations violent assaults, or any other destructive Surprisals of all evil Spirits or Infernal powers of darkness whatsoever, and that we may not be thereby dismayed, vanquished or overcome, and that by the virtue power and efficacy of these three said mighty names of God, Emor, Dial, Hectega, O you great potent and Royal Angel JCZODHEHCA, and by the true Seal or character of[704] your Creation, and by those Banners Ensigns or Trophies of Honour and glory borne or standing before you, as both divine Celestial, Angelical natural and Royal Tokens and Testimonies of Monarchy majesty and Imperial Authority, given and confirmed unto you in

---

[701] S2: "Appointments".
[702] S1, S2: Section in square brackets is absent from S1 and S2, but this is surely an omission, see other Invocations to Kings. However combined with the crossed out sections on properties this does suggest that S2 was copied from S1.
[703] S2: "~~that~~".
[704] S2: "of" is repeated here.

182

the beginning of the world; And by the Influence, Efficacy force & virtue thereof, we most earnestly entreat, and humbly beseech you to be gracious and friendly unto us herein; and furthermore likewise to help, Aid, and assist us in all those, and such our Temporal and Terrestrial operations, affairs, & concerns, as wherein you may or can by the Superior power of that your Kingly power and Authority (given you of the Highest) for the protection, defence, preservation, care, conduct, comfort, support, Assistance, benefit and use of mankind living on Earth, And amongst the rest we also again humbly Entreat and earnestly beseech you, that all those six great Angels called Angelical Seniors, and all other governing or superior Angelical and Elemental powers of Light Celestially dignified. And also that all other dignified Servient and Subservient Spirits or Benevolent Aerial powers who are by nature and office friendly and good, and ordained (by divine appointment in the unity of the Blessed Trinity) for the use benefit and service of mankind of all degrees and offices from the Superior to the Inferior, in the orders & mansion serving the most high God, under your Imperial & sovereign power, Authority, command, Subjection, Service & obedience properly offered or appropriated to the north Angle of the Air, respecting the like point of the Compass, Quarter, Angle, or division of the Earth, may by the force and power of our Invocations be moved to descend and appear visibly unto us, in this Crystal Glass or otherwise out of the same, as either convenience or necessity of the occasion shall require, and that they may at the reading and repetition of our Invocations or calls on that account by us made unto them, move, descend & appear before us visibly to the sight of our Eyes and to speak Audibly unto us, as that we may plainly and perfectly both see and hear them, and friendly to converse with them fulfilling our desires and requests in all things according to their several and respective offices, and to serve us therein, and also do for us, as for the servants of the most high God whensoever and wheresoever and whereunto we shall at any time & place move them both in power and presence, whose works herein shall be a song of Honour to the glory and praise of the most high God both in your and their Creation Amen.

Invocation by way of humble Supplication and petition made to the six Angels or Angelical Seniors Laidrom Aczinor (or Aczodinor) Elzinopo Alhectega Elhiansa Acemliceve, by the great and powerful name of their Imperial King JCZODHEHCA.

O Ye great and glorious Angels or Angelical Seniors Laidrom,

Aczinor, Elzinopo, Alhectega, Elhiansa, Acemliceve, serving the most high God Emor, Dial, Hectega, before the mighty Angelical monarch King Jczodhehca, In the Angle Region or division of the north and who are dignified with Celestial power and Authority therein, and by office judging the government of the Angelical King, thereby fulfilling the divine will & pleasure of the Highest, in all things appointed and committed to your charge, and placed in Superior orders under the said Angelical King and governing over all other both Superior, Servient and Subservient Angels or Angelical powers Celestially dignified, and all other Elemental Spirits whatsoever that in any wise hath power, mansion, Residence, orders, office, place or being in the north part, Region or Angle of the Air, with like respect also from thence to be had, to the north point of the Compass, Angle, part or division of the Earth,:[705] we the servants of the most high God, and Reverently here present in his holy fear, do humbly beseech, & earnestly entreat you all, O ye Angelical Seniors Laidrom, Aczinor, Elzinopo, Alhectega, Elhiansa, Acemliceve, In by and through this Imperial mighty and powerful name Jczodhehca, that some one, or all or any of you, Jointly & severally Every Each one, for and by it self respectively; would be so favourable and friendly unto us as that whensoever or wheresoever we shall Invocate move or call forth unto visible appearance and our assistance, you then would be thereby moved to descend and appear visibly unto us in this Crystal Glass set here before us, and so as that we may plainly see and Audibly hear you speak unto us, And by such your friendly Society & verbal converse with us, to Illuminate, Instruct,[706] direct, help, aid and assist us in all things whatsoever we shall humbly desire, beseech and request of you, wherein by nature and office (given you of the Highest) you may or can; Hear us therefore O ye Blessed Angels or Angelical Seniors Laidrom, Aczinor, Elzinopo, Alhectega, Elhiansa, Acemliceve, and in the mighty name Jczodhehca, and by the virtue, power, Influence Efficacy and force thereof, we earnestly entreat & humbly beseech you to grant these our Supplications and petitions, that all or any of you which we shall at any time hereafter Invocate move or call forth to visible appearance would then be favourable and friendly in Celestial charity and Benevolence, forthwith and Immediately at such our Invocations and earnest requests accordingly of us be thereby moved, And also to move, Descend, visibly appear and speak Audibly unto us, either in this Crystal Glass or otherwise out of the same as it shall please God, and you his Angelical ministers or Celestial messengers of divine grace and

---

[705] S1: Though this punctuation may seem incorrect it is reproduced faithfully.
[706] S2: "instruct".

Light, and shall be most befitting beneficial and convenient for us therein, and to administer to us the bountiful gifts of all Earthly Benefits & also endow us[707] with the gift of[708] true Sapience and Science, and as may or shall be fit for us, and so beneficial unto us, that we may thereby live happy with comfort, during our continuance in this our mortal being, All which we humbly beseech and earnestly entreat of all and every of you Sacred Angels or Angelical Seniors, in the name of your God and King, wherein these [709] your friendly and Benevolent works (thus graciously communicated and given to us) shall be a song of Honour and the praise of your God in your Creation Amen.

Invocation by way of humble Supplication and petition made to the four Benevolent Angels or Angelical powers of Light, placed in orders and set over the first Lesser Angle or division of the great Quadrangle or Table of the North Boza[1], Ozab[2], Zabo[3], Aboz[4], by the great and powerful name of God ENBOZA.

O Ye great and glorious Angels or Angelical powers of Light Boza, Ozab, Zabo, Aboz, governing or set over the first Lesser Angle, division, or Quarter of the great Quadrangle of the north part of the Air, respecting the like part or point of the Compass appropriated to the Earth, serving your most high God Enboza, in orders and office accordingly as you (by Celestial Dignification) are in place and power more Aerially Superior, unto whom is given also of the Highest by nature and office, the true knowledge of the knitting together of natures, & also as well the destruction of nature and of things that may perish as of conjoining and knitting them together; And to Reveal, Show forth and communicate the same (by your Angelical ministry) unto mankind living on Earth, whensoever you shall be Invocated or moved thereunto; we the servants of the Highest (and the same your God) and Reverently here present in his holy fear, do Earnestly Entreat, humbly beseech, and move you all; O ye Angels or Angelical powers of Light or Celestially dignified Spirits of the Air governing in orders degree & mansion (as aforesaid) Boza, Ozab, Zabo, Aboz, Jointly and severally, every and each one, for and by it self Respectively, in by and through, this mighty and powerful name of your God Enboza, that you (at these humble requests and Addresses) would be favourable and friendly

---

[707] S2: "with the gift".
[708] S2: "ift".
[709] S2: "your".

unto us, as that whensoever or wheresoever, we shall Invocate move, or call you forth to visible appearance and our Assistance, you would be thereby moved, to descend, and appear visibly unto us in this Crystal Glass which stand here before us, or otherwise personally to appear out of the same visibly here before us, and so as that we may plainly See you and Audibly hear you speak unto us, and by such your friendly and verbal converse with us, to make us partakers of that undefiled knowledge and true Sapience, which by nature and office (given you of the Highest) may by such your Angelical ministry be revealed given or administered unto us; Hear us therefore O ye Sacred Angelical powers of Light or Celestial dignified Spirits of the Air, by degrees, and orders Superior and governing as aforesaid Boza, Ozab, Zabo, Aboz, we do yet further in this great name of your God Enboza, and by the force, power and Efficacy thereof, Earnestly Entreat, and humbly beseech you to grant these our humble supplications and petitions and that all or any of you, that we shall at any time hereafter, Invocate move or call forth to visible appearance, would Readily and forthwith, move, descend, and visibly appear unto us, whensoever we shall Invocate, call forth, or move you thereunto, in this Crystal Glass standing here before us or otherwise out of it as it shall please God and you his ministers of divine grace, and as best befitted or shall be most convenient for us, or unto us, in these our Actions and operations Speaking Audibly unto us, and also thereby directing and instructing us in the true knowledge of that your Angelical Sapience, and Science (given you of the Highest) wherein also he hath accordingly by order and office ordained and appointed you, And this your Angelical [710] Benevolence in Celestial grace and charity thus given and granted unto us, and also in the accomplishment and fulfilling of these our humble desires and requests and whatsoever else shall be requisite and fit for us to know shall be a song of Honour & the praise of your God in your Creation Amen.

Invocation by way of humble Supplication and petition made to the four Servient Angels or dignified Spirits of the Air, placed in orders, and serving in the first Lesser Angle or division of the great Quadrangle or Table of the North Aira[1], Ormen[2], Reseni[3], Jzodenar[4], who are moved and called forth by the great and powerful name of God Angepoi, and constrained to do what they are commanded according to their office by the great name of God Vnenax.

---

[710] S2: "sapience".

O Ye Angelical powers of Light, or dignified Spirits of the Air, Aira, Ormen, Reseni, Jzodenar, serving in orders under superior powers your most high and omnipotent God, Angepoi, in the first Lesser Angle or division of the great Quadrangle or north part of the Air, respecting the like part or point of the compass appropriated to the Earth, accordingly as you therein are placed more Inferior and Subservient and unto whom is given of the Highest by nature and office the true knowledge of physick in all its parts and the curing of all diseases whatsoever that are incident to human bodies and to Reveal show forth and give the same unto mankind living on Earth whensoever you shall be moved and called forth by the great name of your God Vnenax, commanded thereunto, we the servants of the Highest (and the same your God) and Reverently here present in his holy fear, do earnestly entreat, call upon, and move you all, O ye Benevolent Angels or dignified powers of the Air, serving in orders, degree and mansion as aforesaid Aira, Ormen, Reseni, Jzodenar, Jointly and severally Every and each one for and by itself respectively, In by and through this mighty and powerful name of your God Angepoi, that you (at these our earnest Addresses) would be so truly willing and friendly unto us that whensoever & wheresoever we shall Invocate move or call you forth to visible appearance and our assistance, you then would readily and Immediately forthwith at our Invocations, move, descend, appear, and show your selves corporally visible unto us in this Crystal Glass standing here before us or otherwise personally to appear out of the same visibly here before us, and so as that we may personally see you, and Audibly hear you speak unto us, And by such your Spiritual Revelations unto us to make us partakers of that true knowledge & Sapience which by nature and office (given you of the Highest) may by such your visible appearance and verbal converse, be showed forth and given to us, and furthermore also that in by & through this great and powerful name of your God Vnenax, and the force and virtue thereof, we do likewise Earnestly Invocate and Entreat you to do, accomplish and fulfil whatsoever (accordingly and is its nature and office given you of the Highest) we shall request and command you; Hear us therefore, O ye Benevolent Angels or dignified Spiritual powers of the Air, serving in orders, degree, & mansion as aforesaid Aira, Ormen, Reseni, Jzodenar, you do yet further in this great name of your God Angepoi, and by the virtue and efficacy thereof, earnestly Invocate and entreat you, to yield up and give unto us, your assuredly firm, free, and obliged consent herein, that all or any of you which we shall at any time hereafter Invocate, move, or call forth to visible appearance, would[711] certainly without any Tarrying or delay, Immediately move, Descend, and visibly appear unto us in this Crystal Stone standing here before us or otherwise out of it as it shall please God to give unto you and thereby most beneficial convenient and fit for us, in these both our present, & other our future Actions and operations, and to speak plainly unto us, so, as that we may sensibly hear you and understand you, directing and instructing us, in the true knowledge and judgement of that your Spiritual Sapience and Science given you of the Highest, And in this undoubted true and great name of your God Vnenax, and by the virtue and power thereof, whereby we also earnestly Invocate and Entreat you not only to Reveal, declare, show forth and make known unto us, the true and apprehensive knowledge of all such occult and mystical Arcanaes, in physick and of whatsoever else relates thereunto as are unknown of mankind, but also do whatsoever we shall further command, request or desire to be done for us, relating to the said Science and our benefits therein (as you by office are of the Highest accordingly preordained and appointed;) All which your obedience, readily and willingly fulfilling and accomplishing unto us, as here we have in the powerful and true names of your God Earnestly Entreated & besought you shall be a song of Honour, & the praise of your God in your Creation Amen.

Invocation by way of humble Supplication and petition made to the four Benevolent Angels or Angelical powers of Light, placed in orders and set over the Second Lesser Angle or division of the great Quadrangle or Table of the North Phara[1], Harap[2], Rapeh[3], Aphar[4], by the great and powerful name of God Enphara.

O Ye great and glorious Angels or Angelical powers of Light Phara, Harap, Rapeh, Aphar, governing or set over the second Lesser Angle, division or Quarter of the great Quadrangle of the north point of the Air, respecting the like part or point of the compass appropriated to the Earth, serving your most high God Enphara, in orders and office accordingly as you (by Celestial Dignification) are in place and power more Aerially Superior, unto whom is given also of the Highest by nature and office, the true knowledge of (* Moving from place to place &c[712],) the knitting together of natures and also as well the destruction of nature and of things that may perish, as

---

[711] S2: "would".
[712] S2: Omits "&c" and inserts "& moving from place to place as into this country or that country at pleasure".

188

of conjoining and knitting them together,[713] and to reveal, show forth and communicate the same (by your Angelical ministry) unto mankind living on Earth, whensoever you shall be Invocated or moved thereunto, We the servants of the Highest (and the same your God) and reverently here present in his holy fear, do earnestly entreat humbly beseech and move you all; O ye Angels or Angelical powers of Light or Celestially dignified Spirits of the Air, governing in orders, degree, & mansion as aforesaid Phara, Harap, Rapeh, Aphar, Jointly and severally every and each one for and by it self Respectively, In by and through this mighty and powerful name of your God Enphara, that you (at these humble requests and Addresses) would be favourable and friendly unto us, as that whensoever or wheresoever we shall Invocate move or call you forth to visible appearance and our assistance, you would be thereby moved to descend and appear visibly unto us in this Crystal Glass which stand here before us or otherwise personally to appear out of the same visibly here before us, and so as that we may plainly see you and Audibly hear you speak unto us, and by such your friendly and verbal converse with us, to make us partakers of that undefiled knowledge and true Science[714], which by nature and office (given you of the Highest) may by such your Angelical ministry be revealed given or administered unto us, Hear us therefore O ye Sacred Angelical powers of Light or Celestially dignified Spirits of the Air Phara, Harap, Rapeh, Aphar, we do yet further in this great name of your God Enphara, and by the force, power and Efficacy thereof, Earnestly Entreat and humbly [beseech][715] you, to grant these our Supplications and petitions, and that all or any of you, that we shall at any time hereafter, Invocate, move or call forth to visible appearance, would readily & forthwith, move, Descend, and visibly appear unto us, whensoever we shall Invocate call forth or move you thereunto in this Crystal Glass standing here before us, or otherwise out of it, as it shall please God and you his ministers of divine grace, and as best befitted or shall be most convenient or beneficial for us, or unto us, in these our Actions or operations, Speaking Audibly unto us, and also thereby directing and instructing us, in the true knowledge of that your Angelical Sapience and Science (given you of the Highest) And wherein also he hath accordingly by order and office ordained and appointed you, and this your Angelical Benevolence in Celestial grace and charity thus given & granted unto us, and also in the

---

[713] S2: This section is struck through, thus: "~~& the knitting together of natures and also as well the destruction of nature and of things that may perish, as of conjoining and knitting them together~~".

[714] S2: "Sapience".

[715] S1: The absence of the word "beseech" is clearly a copyist's error.

accomplishment and fulfilling of these our humble desires and requests and whatsoever else shall be requisite and fit for us to know, shall be a song of Honour, & the praise of your God in your Creation Amen.

Invocation by way of humble supplication and petition made to the four Servient Angels or dignified Spirits of the Air, placed in orders and serving in the second Lesser Angle or division of the great Quadrangle or Table of the North Omgege[1], Gebal[2], Relemu[3], Jahel[4], who are moved and called forth, by the great and powerful name of God Anacem, and constrained thereunto to do what they are commanded according to their office, by the great name of God Sonden.

O Ye Angelical powers of Light or dignified Spirits of the Air, Omgege, Gebal, Relemu, Jahel, serving in orders under Superior powers your most high and omnipotent God Anacem, in the Second Lesser Angle or division of the great Quadrangle or North part of the Air, Respecting the like part or point of the compass appropriated to the Earth, accordingly as you therein are placed more Inferior and Subservient, And unto whom is given of the Highest by nature and office, the true knowledge of[716] (* finding &[717] use of Metals, the Congelation of Stones[718] &c), physick in all its parts and the curing of all diseases whatsoever that are Incident to human bodies[719] and to Reveal, Show forth and give the same unto mankind living on Earth whensoever you shall be moved and called forth by the great name of your God Sonden, commanded thereunto: We the servants of the Highest (and the same your God) and Reverently here present in his holy fear, do earnestly entreat, call upon and move you all, O ye Benevolent Angels or dignified powers of the Air, serving in orders degree and mansion as aforesaid Omgege, Gebal, Relemu, Jahel, Jointly & severally, Every and Each one, for and by itself respectively, In by and through, this mighty and powerful name of your God Anacem, that you (at these our Earnest Addresses) would be so truly willing and friendly unto us, as that whensoever and wheresoever, we shall Invocate, move or call you forth unto visible appearance and our assistance, you then would readily and Immediately, forthwith at our Invocations, move, Descend, appear,

---

[716] S2: Omits "of"
[717] S2: "~~the~~".
[718] S2: Inserts "and the virtue of all Stones".
[719] S2: This section is crossed out, thus: "~~physick in all its parts and the curing of all diseases whatsoever that are Incident to human bodies~~".

and show your selves corporally visible unto us in this Crystal Glass standing here before us, [or otherwise personally to appear out of the same visibly here before us,] and so as that we may plainly see you, and Audibly hear you speak unto us, and by such your Spiritual Revelations unto us, to make us partakers of that true knowledge and Sapience, which by nature and office (given you of the Highest) may by such your visible appearance and verbal converse be showed forth and unto[720] us; And furthermore also, that In by and through this great & powerful name of your God Sonden, and the force and virtue thereof; we do likewise Earnestly Invocate & Entreat you, to do, accomplish and fulfil whatsoever (accordingly and is by nature and office given you of the Highest) we shall request and command you; Hear us therefore, O ye Benevolent Angels or dignified Spiritual powers of the Air serving in orders, office, degree, and mansion as aforesaid Omgege, Gebal, Relemu, Jahel, you do yet further in this great name of your God Anacem, And by the virtue and efficacy thereof, earnestly entreat and Invocate you, to yield up and give unto us, your assuredly firm free and obliged consent herein, that all or any of you which we shall at any time hereafter, Invocate, move, or call forth to visible appearance, would certainly without any Tarrying or delay, Immediately move, descend, and visibly appear unto us in this Crystal Glass standing here before us, or otherwise out of it as it shall please God to give unto you and thereby most beneficial, convenient and fit for us, in these both our present and other our future Actions & operations, and to speak plainly unto us, so as that we may sensibly hear you and understand you, directing and Instructing us, in the true knowledge and judgement of that your Spiritual Sapience and Science given you of the Highest, And in this undoubted true and great name of your God Sonden and by the virtue and power thereof, whereby we also earnestly Invocate and Entreat you, not only to reveal, declare, show forth and make known unto us the true and apprehensive knowledge of all such Occult and mystical Arcanaes in physick, and of whatsoever else relates thereunto, as are unknown of mankind, but also do for us whatsoever we shall further command, request or desire to be done, relating to the said Science and our benefits therein (as you by office are of the Highest accordingly preordained and appointed;) All which your obedience readily and willingly fulfilling and accomplishing unto us, as here we have in the powerful and true names of your God, Earnestly Entreated and besought you, shall be a song of Honour and the praise of your God in your Creation Amen.

---

[720] S2: "given to".

Invocation by way of humble Supplication & petition made to the four Benevolent Angels or Angelical powers of Light placed in orders and set over the Third Lesser Angle or division of the great Quadrangle or Table of the North Æoan[1], Oanæ[2], Anæo[3], Næoa[4] by the great and powerful name of God NÆOAN.

O Ye great and glorious Angels or Angelical powers of Light Æoan, Oanæ, Anæo, Næoa, governing or set over the Third Lesser Angle, division or Quarter of the great Quadrangle of the north point of the Air, respecting the like part or point of the compass appropriated also[721] to the Earth, Serving your most high God Næoan, in orders and office accordingly as you (by Celestial Dignification) are in place and power more Aerially Superior, unto whom is given also of the Highest by nature and office, the true knowledge (* of all the mechanical Crafts whatsoever), of the knitting together of natures and also as well the destruction of nature and of things that may perish as of conjoining and knitting them together,[722] And to reveal show forth and communicate the same (by your Angelical ministry) unto mankind living on Earth whensoever you shall be invocated or moved thereunto; We the servants of the Highest (and the same your God) and reverently here present in his holy fear, do earnestly entreat, humbly beseech and move you all; O you[723] Angels or Angelical powers of Light or Celestially dignified Spirits of the Air, governing in orders, degree, and mansion as aforesaid Æoan, Oanæ, Anæo, Næoa, Jointly & severally, every and each one, for and by it self respectively, In by and through this mighty and powerful name of your God Næoan, that you (at these humble requests and Addresses) would be favourable and friendly unto us, as that whensoever or wheresoever we shall Invocate, move or call you forth to visible appearance and our assistance, you would be thereby moved to descend and appear visibly unto us in this Crystal Glass which stand here before us or otherwise personally to appear out of the same visibly here before us, and so as that we may plainly see you and Audibly hear you, speak unto us, And by such your friendly and verbal converse with us to make us partakers of that undefiled Knowledge and true Sapience which by nature and office (given you of the Highest) may by such your Angelical ministry

---

[721] S2: Omits "also".

[722] S2: This section is crossed out, thus: "~~of the knitting together of natures and also as well the destruction of nature and of things that may perish as of conjoining and knitting them together~~".

[723] S2: "ye".

192

be revealed given or administered unto us, Hear us therefore O ye Sacred Angelical powers of Light or Celestially dignified Spirits of the Air, by degree and orders Superior, and governing as aforesaid Æoan, Oanæ, Anæo, Næoa, we do yet further in this great name of your God Næoan and by the force power and efficacy thereof Earnestly Entreat and humbly beseech you to grant these our humble Supplications and petitions, and that all or any of you that we shall at any time hereafter Invocate move or call forth to visible appearance, would readily and forthwith, move, Descend, and visibly appear unto us in this Crystal Glass standing here before us, or otherwise out of it, as it shall please God and you his ministers of divine grace, and as best befitted or shall be most convenient or beneficial for us or unto us, in these our Actions or operations, speaking Audibly unto us and also thereby directing and Instructing us in the [724] true knowledge of that your Angelical Sapience and Science (given you of the Highest) and wherein also he hath accordingly by order and office ordained & appointed you, and this your Angelical Benevolence in celestial grace and charity thus given and granted unto us, and also in the Accomplishment and fulfilling of these our humble desires and requests, and whatsoever else shall be requisite and fit for us to know, shall be a song of Honour and the praise of your God in your Creation Amen.

Invocation by way of humble Supplication and petition made to the four Servient Angels or dignified Spirits of the Air placed in orders and serving in the Third Lesser Angle or division of the great Quadrangle or Table of the North Opena[1], Doope[2], Rexao[3], Axir[4], who are moved and called forth by the great and powerful name of God Cebalpet, and constrained thereunto to do what they are commanded according to their office by the great name of God Arbizod.

O Ye Angelical powers of Light, or dignified Spirits of the Air, Opena, Doope, Rexao, Axir, serving in orders under Superior powers your most high and omnipotent God, Cebalpet, in the Third Lesser Angle or division of the great Quadrangle or North part of the Air, Respecting the like part or point of the compass appropriated to the Earth, according as you therein are placed more Inferior and Subservient, and unto whom is given of the Highest by nature and office, the true knowledge of (* Transformation & transplantation), physick in all its parts and the curing of all diseases whatsoever

---

[724] S2: "the".

that are incident to human bodies,[725] and to reveal, show forth and give the same unto mankind living on Earth whensoever you shall be moved and called forth by the great name of God Arbizod, commanded thereunto; We the Servants of the Highest (and the same your God) and reverently here present in his holy fear, do earnestly entreat, call upon and move you all; O ye Benevolent Angels or dignified powers of the Air, serving in orders degree and mansion as aforesaid Opena, Doope, Rexao, Axir, Jointly and Severally, Every and Each one, for and by itself respectively, In by and through this mighty and powerful name of your God Cebalpet, that you (at these our earnest Addresses) would be so truly willing and friendly unto us, that whensoever and wheresoever we shall Invocate move or call forth unto visible appearance and our assistance, you then would readily and Immediately forthwith at our Invocations, move, Descend, appear, and show your selves corporally visible unto us in this Crystal Glass standing here before us, or otherwise personally to appear out of the same, visibly here before us and so as that we may plainly see you and Audibly hear you speak unto us; And by such your Spiritual Revelations unto us, to make us partakers of that true knowledge and Sapience, which by nature & office (given you of the Highest) may by such your visible appearance & verbal converse (with us) be showed forth and given to us, And furthermore also, that In by and through this great and powerful name of your God Arbizod and by the force and virtue thereof, we do likewise Earnestly Invocate and Entreat you, to do, accomplish and fulfil whatsoever (accordingly and is by nature and office given you of the Highest) we shall request and command you; Hear us therefore, O ye Benevolent Angels or dignified Spiritual powers of the Air, Serving in orders, degree and mansion as aforesaid Opena, Doope, Rexao, Axir, you do yet further in this great name of your God Cebalpet, and by the virtue and Efficacy thereof earnestly Invocate, and entreat you to yield up and give unto us, your assuredly firm, free, and obliged consent herein, that all or any of you which we shall at any time hereafter Invocate move or call forth to visible appearance would certainly without any Tarrying or delay, Immediately move, Descend, and visibly appear unto us in this Crystal Glass standing here before us, or otherwise out of it as it shall please God to give unto you, and thereby most beneficial convenient and fit for us in these both our present & other our future Actions and operations, and to speak plainly unto us, so as that we may sensibly hear you & understand you, directing and instructing us in the true knowledge and judgement of that your

---

[725] S2: This section is crossed out, thus: "physick in all its parts and the curing of all diseases whatsoever that are incident to human bodies".

Spiritual Sapience and Science (given you of the Highest;) And in this undoubted true and great name of your God Arbizod, and by the virtue & power thereof whereby we also earnestly Invocate and entreat you, not only to reveal, declare, show forth and make known unto us, the true and apprehensive knowledge of all such occult and mystical Arcanaes in physick, and of whatsoever else relates thereunto as are unknown of mankind, but also do for us whatsoever we shall further command, request or desire to be done for us, relating to the said Science and our benefits therein; (as you by office are of the Highest accordingly preordained and appointed) All which your obedience readily and willingly fulfilling and accomplishing unto us, as here we have in the powerful and true names of your God Earnestly Entreated and besought you, shall be a Song of Honour, and the praise of your God in your Creation Amen.

Invocation by way of humble Supplication & petition made to the four Benevolent Angels or Angelical powers of Light, placed in orders & set over the Fourth Lesser Angle or division of the great Quadrangle or Table of the North Jaom[1], Aomi[2], Omia[3], Maio[4], by the great and powerful name of God NIAOM.

O Ye great and glorious Angels or Angelical powers of Light Jaom, Aomi, Omia, Maio, governing & set over the Fourth Lesser Angle division or Quarter of the great Quadrangle or north point of the Air appropriated to the Earth, serving your most high God Naiom, in orders and office accordingly, as you (by Celestial dignification) are in place and power more Aerially Superior, unto whom is given also of the Highest by nature and office, the true knowledge of (* the Secrets of men Knowing), the knitting together of natures, and also as well the destruction of nature and of things that may perish as of conjoining and knitting them together,[726] And to reveal, show forth and communicate the same (by your Angelical ministry) unto mankind living on Earth, whensoever you shall be invocated or moved thereunto: we the servants of the Highest (and the same your God) and reverently here present in his holy fear, do earnestly entreat humbly beseech and move you all, O ye Angels or Angelical powers of Light or Celestially dignified Spirits of the Air, governing in orders degree and mansion (as aforesaid) Jaom, Aomi, Omia,

---

[726] S2: This section is crossed through, thus: "the knitting together of natures, and also as well the destruction of nature and of things that may perish as of conjoining and knitting them together".

Maio, Jointly and severally every and each one, for and by it self respectively, In by and through this mighty and powerful name of your God Naiom, that you (at these our earnest and humble requests and Addresses) would be favourable and friendly unto us, as that whensoever or wheresoever we shall Invocate, move, or call you forth to visible appearance and our Assistance, you then would be thereby moved, to descend and appear visibly unto us in this Crystal Glass which stand here before us, or otherwise personally to appear out of the same visibly here before us, and so, as that we may plainly see you and Audibly hear you speak unto us, and by such your friendly & verbal converse with us, to make us partakers of that undefiled knowledge and true Sapience, which by nature and office (given you of the Highest) may by such your Angelical ministry be revealed given or administered unto us, Hear us therefore, O ye Sacred Angelical powers of Light or Celestially dignified Spirits of the Air, by degree, & orders Superior & governing as aforesaid Jaom, Aomi, Omia, Maio, we do yet further in this great name of your God Naiom, and by the force, power and efficacy thereof, to grant these our Supplications and petitions, and that all, or any of you that we shall at any time hereafter invocate, move or call forth to visible appearance, would readily and forthwith move, Descend, and visibly appear unto us in this Crystal Glass standing here before us, or otherwise out of it as it shall please God & you his ministers of divine grace, & as best befitted, or shall be most convenient for us, or unto us in the true knowledge of that your Angelical Sapience and Science (given you of the Highest) and wherein also he hath accordingly by order and office ordained and appointed you, and this your Angelical benevolence in Celestial grace and charity thus given and granted unto us, and also in the accomplishment and fulfilling of these our humble desires and requests and whatsoever else shall be requisite and fit for us to know, shall be a song of Honour & the praise of your God in your Creation Amen.

Invocation by way of humble Supplication & petition made to the four Servient Angels or dignified Spirits of the Air placed in orders and serving in the Fourth Lesser Angle or division of the great Quadrangle or Table of the North Mefael[1], Jaba[2], Jezexpe[3], Estim[4], who are moved & called forth by the great and powerful name of God Espemenir, and constrained thereunto to do what they are commanded, according to their office by the great name of God Hpizod.

O Ye Angelical powers of Light or dignified Spirits of the Air, Mefael, Jaba, Jezexpe, Estim, serving in orders under Superior powers, your most high & omnipotent God, Espemenir, in the Fourth Lesser Angle or division of the great Quadrangle or north part of the Air, respecting the like part or point of the compass appropriated to the Earth, accordingly as you therein are placed more Inferior and Subservient, and unto whom is given of the Highest by nature & office the true knowledge (* of Elemental Creatures [727] &c,) of physick in all its parts, & the curing of all diseases which are Incident to human bodies,[728] and to reveal, show forth and give the same unto mankind living on Earth, whensoever you shall be moved and called forth by the great name of God Hpizod, commanded thereunto: We the servants of the Highest (and the same your God) and reverently here present in his holy fear, do earnestly entreat call upon, and move you all, O ye Benevolent Angels or dignified powers of the Air, serving in orders, degree, & mansion (as aforesaid) Mefael, Jaba, Jezexpe, Estim, Jointly & severally, every & each one, for and by itself respectively In by and through this mighty and powerful name of your God Espemenir, that you (at these our earnest Addresses) would be so truly willing and friendly unto us, that whensoever and wheresoever we shall invocate move, or call you forth unto visible appearance and our Assistance, you then would readily and Immediately forthwith at our Invocations, move, Descend, appear, and show your selves corporally visible unto us in this Crystal Glass standing here before us, and so as that we may plainly see you and Audibly hear you speak unto us, And by such your Spiritual Revelations unto us to make us partakers of that true knowledge and Sapience, which by nature and office (given you of the Highest) may by such your visible appearance and verbal converse be showed forth and given unto us, And furthermore also, that In by and through this great and powerful name of your God Hpizod, and the force and virtue thereof: We do likewise Earnestly invocate you, to do, accomplish and fulfil whatsoever (accordingly and is by nature and office given you of the Highest) we shall request and command you; Hear us therefore O ye Benevolent Angels or dignified Spiritual powers of the Air serving in orders, office degree, and mansion (as aforesaid) Mefael, Jaba, Jezexpe, Estim, you do yet further in this great name of your God Espemenir, and by the virtue and efficacy thereof, Earnestly Invocate & entreat you to yield up and give unto us, your

---

[727] S2: Inserts "amongst us, how many kinds & their use in the Creation as they are severally placed in the four Elements, Air, Water, Earth & Fire".

[728] S2: This section is crossed through, thus: "~~of physick in all its parts, & the curing of all diseases which are incident to human bodies~~".

assuredly firm, free and obliged consent herein, that all or any of you, which we shall at any time hereafter Invocate move or call forth to visible appearance, would certainly without any Tarrying or delay, Immediately move, descend, & visibly appear unto us, in this Crystal Glass standing here before us, or otherwise out of it, as it shall please God to give unto you, and thereby most beneficial convenient and fit for us, in these both our present and other our future Actions and operations, and to speak plainly unto us, so as that we may sensibly hear you & understand you, directing and instructing us in the true knowledge and judgement of that your Spiritual Sapience and Science (given you of the Highest) And in this undoubted true and great name of your God Hpizod, and by the virtue and power thereof, whereby we also earnestly Invocate and entreat you, not only to reveal, declare, and make known unto us the true and apprehensive knowledge of all such occult and mystical Arcanaes, in physick, and of whatsoever else relates thereunto, as are unknown of mankind but also do for us whatsoever we shall further command, request or desire to be done for us, relating to the said Science and our benefits therein (as you by office are of the Highest) accordingly preordained and appointed, All which your obedience readily and willingly fulfilling and accomplishing unto us, as here we have in the powerful and true names of your God, Earnestly Entreated & besought you, shall be a Song of Honour and the praise of your God in your Creation Amen.

[Invocation of the Kings, Seniors, Angels and Spirits of the South]

Humble Supplication and petition made to the great King EDELPERNA, principal governor & Celestial Angelical Watchman, set over the Watch Tower or Terrestrial Table of the South by the three mighty & powerful names of God Oip, Teaa, Pedoce.

O Thou Regal[729] great mighty and powerful Angel of the most high, Immense, Immortal, and Incomprehensible God of Hosts EDELPERNA, who in the beginning of time by the divine decree & appointment of the Highest, in the unity of the blessed Trinity, governor, overseer, principal watchman, protector & keeper thereof, from the malice, misuse, Illusion, Temptation, assaults, Surprisals, Theft, or other wicked Encroachments, usurping Blasphemy of the great Enemy of God's glory and the welfare of mankind, the Devil and Spirits of darkness, and as a snaffle to restrain their wickedness by the bit of God's boundless power & Justice, to the intent, that (they being put on, into the earth) their Envious will may be bridled the determinations of the Highest fulfilled, and his creatures kept within the compass and measure of order; We humbly Invocate, Entreat and beseech you, O you Royal Angel EDELPERNA, In by and through, these potent mighty and great names of your God Oip Teaa Pedoce, to preserve, defend, Keep and protect us, from the wicked Illusions, envious Temptations violent assaults or any other destructive Surprisals of all evil Spirits or Infernal powers of darkness whatsoever and that we may not be thereby dismayed, vanquished or overcome, and that by the virtue power, and efficacy of these three said mighty names of[730] God, Oip, Teaa, Pedoce,[731] O you great potent & Royal Angel EDELPERNA, and by the true Seals or Character of your Creation, and by those Banners, Ensigns or Trophies of Honour and glory, borne or standing before you as both divine, Celestial Angelical, natural and Royal Tokens and Testimonies of Monarchy, majesty and Imperial Authority given and confirmed unto you in the beginning of the world and by the influence, Efficacy, force and virtue thereof, we most Earnestly Entreat and humbly beseech you to be gracious and friendly unto us herein, and furthermore likewise to help, aid and assist us, in all those and such our Temporal and Terrestrial

---

[729] S2: "Royal".
[730] S2: Inserts "your".
[731] S2: "~~to preserve Defend Keep and protect us from the wicked Illusions, Envious Temptations~~".

operations and affairs & concerns, as wherein you may or can, by the Superior power of that your kingly power[732] & Authority (given you of the Highest) for the protection, defence, preservation, care, conduct, comfort, support, assistance, benefit and use of mankind living on Earth: And amongst the rest we also again humbly entreat and earnestly beseech you, that all those six Angels called Angelical Seniors and all other governing or Superior Angelical and Elemental powers of Light, Celestially dignified, and also that all other dignified Servient and Subservient Spirits, or Benevolent Aerial powers, who are by nature and office friendly & good, and ordained (by divine appointment in the unity of the blessed Trinity) for the use, benefit & service of mankind, of all degrees & offices from the Superior to the Inferior, In the orders and mansion serving the most high God, under your Imperial & Sovereign power, Authority, command, Subjection, Service and obedience properly offered[733] or appropriated to the South Angle of the Air, respecting the like point of the Compass, Quarter Angle or division of the Earth, may by the force and power of our Invocations be moved to descend and appear visibly unto us, in this Crystal Glass or otherwise out of the same, as either convenience or necessity of the occasion shall require, and that they may at the repetition and reading of our Invocations or calls on that account by us made unto them, move, Descend, and appear before us visibly to the sight of our Eyes, and to speak Audibly unto us, As that we may plainly and perfectly both see and hear them, and friendly to converse with us, fulfilling our desires and requests in all things according to their several and respective offices and to serve us therein, and also do for us as for the servants of the most high God, whensoever, & wheresoever & whereunto we shall at any time and place move them, both in power and presence whose works herein shall be a song of Honour to the glory and praise of the most high God both in your and their Creation Amen.

Invocation by way of humble Supplication and petition made to the Six great Angels or Angelical Seniors Aaetpio[1], Adoeoet[2], Aapedoce[3], Alendood[4], Arinnaquu[5], Anodoin[6], by the great and powerful name of their Imperial King EDELPERNA.

O Ye great and glorious Angels or Angelical Seniors Aaetpio, Adoeoet, Aapedoce, Alendood, Arinnaquu, Anodoin, serving the

---

[732] S2: "office".
[733] S2: "referred".

most high God Oip, Teaa, Pedoce, before the mighty Angelical monarch King EDELPERNA, in the Angle, Region, or division of the South, and who are dignified with Celestial power and Authority therein, And by office judging the government of the Angelical King, thereby fulfilling the divine will and pleasure of the Highest in all things appointed and committed to your charge and placed in Superior orders under the said Angelical King, and governing[734] over all other both Superior Servient and Subservient Angels or Angelical powers Celestially dignified, and also all other Elemental Spirits whatsoever, that in any wise hath power, mansion, Residence, orders, office, place or being in the South [735] part, Region, or Angle of the Air, with like respect also from thence to be had to the South point of the compass, Angle, part, or division of the Earth. We the servants of the most high God, and Reverently here present in his holy fear, do humbly beseech and move you all, O ye Angelical Seniors Aaetpio, Adoeoet, Aapedoce, Alendood, Arinnaquu, Anodoin, In by & through this Imperial mighty & powerful name EDELPERNA, that some one, or all or any of you Jointly and Severally, in general and particular, every and each one for and by it self respectively, would be so favourable and friendly unto us, as that whensoever or wheresoever we shall Invocate, move or call you forth unto visible appearance and our assistance, you then would be thereby moved to descend & appear visibly unto us, in this Crystal Glass set here before us, and so as that we may plainly see you, and audibly hear you speak unto us, and by such your friendly Society & verbal converse with us, to Illuminate, Instruct, direct, help, Aid & assist us in all things whatsoever we shall humbly desire, beseech & request of you wherein by nature and office (given you of the Highest) you may or can; Hear us therefore O ye Blessed Angels or Angelical Seniors Aaetpio, Adoeoet, Aapedoce, Alendood, Arinnaquu, Anodoin, And in the mighty name EDELPERNA, and by the virtue, power, Influence Efficacy and force thereof, we Earnestly Entreat and humbly beseech you, to grant these our Supplications & petitions, that all or any of you, which we shall at any time hereafter Invocate move or call forth to visible appearance would then be favourable and friendly in Celestial charity & Benevolence forthwith and Immediately at such our Invocations & earnest requests accordingly of us made be thereby moved, And also to move, descend, visibly appear and speak Audibly unto us, either in this Crystal Glass or otherwise out of the same; as it shall please God, and you his Angelical ministers or Celestial messengers of divine grace and Light, and shall be most

---

[734] S2: "are".
[735] S2: "South".

befitting, beneficial and convenient for us therein, and to administer unto us, the bountiful gifts of all Earthly benefits, and also endow us with the gift of true Science and Sapience, and such other gifts of human Accomplishments and enjoyments, as may or shall be fit for us, and so beneficial unto us that we may thereby live happy with comfort, during our continuance in this our mortal being, All which we humbly beseech, and earnestly entreat of all and every of you Sacred Angels or Angelical powers, in the name of your God & King, wherein these your friendly and benevolent works (thus graciously communicated and given to us) shall be a song of Honour, & the praise of your God in your Creation Amen.

Invocation by way of humble Supplication and petition made to the four Benevolent Angels or Angelical powers of Light placed in orders & set over the first Lesser Angle or division of the great Quadrangle or Table of the South Dopa[1], Opad[2], Pado[3], Adop[4], by the great & powerful name of God Bedopa.

O Ye great and glorious Angels or Angelical powers of Light Dopa, Opad, Pado, Adop, governing or set over the first Lesser Angle, division or Quarter of the great Quadrangle of the South part of the Air, respecting the like part or point of the compass appropriated to the Earth, serving your most high God Bedopa, in orders and office accordingly, as you (by Celestial Dignification) are in place and power more Aerially Superior, unto whom is given also of the Highest by nature and office the true knowledge of the knitting together of natures, and also as well the destruction of nature and of things that may perish, as of conjoining and knitting them together; And to reveal, Show forth and communicate the same (by your Angelical ministry) unto mankind living on Earth: whensoever you shall be Invocated or moved thereunto, We the servants of the Highest (and the same your God) and reverently here present in his holy fear, do earnestly entreat, humbly beseech[736], and move you all, O ye Angels or Angelical powers of Light, or Celestially dignified Spirits of the Air governing in orders, degree and mansion (as aforesaid) Dopa, Opad, Pado, Adop, Jointly & severally every and each one, for and by it self respectively, In by and through this mighty and powerful name of your God Bedopa, that you (at these humble requests & Addresses) would be favourable and friendly unto us, as that whensoever & wheresoever we shall Invocate move,

---

[736] S2: Inserts "you".

or call you forth[737] to visible appearance, and our assistance, you would be thereby moved to descend and appear visibly unto us, into this Crystal Glass which stand here before us, or otherwise personally to appear out of the same visibly here before us, and so as that we may plainly See you and Audibly hear you speak unto us, and by such your friendly and verbal converse with us, to make us partakers of that undefiled knowledge and true Sapience, which by nature & office (given you of the Highest) may by such your Angelical ministry be revealed given or administered unto us; Hear us therefore O ye Sacred Angelical powers of Light or Celestially dignified Spirits of the Air, by degrees and orders governing as aforesaid Dopa, Opad, Pado, Adop, we do yet further in this great name of your God Bedopa, And by the force, power and efficacy thereof, to grant these our supplications and petitions, and that all or any of you that we shall at any time hereafter, Invocate, move, or call forth to visible appearance, would readily and forthwith, move, descend, and visibly appear unto us, whensoever we shall Invocate or move you thereunto in this Crystal Glass standing here before us, or otherwise out of it, as it shall please God and you his ministers of divine grace, and as best befitted, or shall be most convenient and beneficial for us, or unto us, in the true knowledge of that Angelical Sapience, and Science (given you of the Highest) and wherein also he hath accordingly by order and office ordained and appointed you, And this your Angelical Benevolence in Celestial grace and charity, thus given and granted unto us, and also in the accomplishment and fulfilling of these our humble desires and requests, and whatsoever else shall be requisite and fit for us to know, shall be a song of Honour and the praise of your God in your Creation Amen.

Invocation by way of humble Supplication and petition made to the four Servient Angels or dignified Spirits of the Air placed in orders and serving in the first Lesser Angle or division of the great Quadrangle or Table of the South Opemen[1], Apeste[2], Scio[3], Vasge[4], who are moved and called forth by the great and powerful name of God Noalmar, and constrained thereunto to do what they are commanded according to their office, by the great name of God Oloag.

O Ye Angelical powers of Light, or dignified Spirits of the Air, Opemen, Apeste, Scio, Vasge, serving in orders under Superior

[737] S2: Transposes this phrase to "move or Call or Invocate you".

203

powers, your most high and Omnipotent God, Noalmar, in the first Lesser Angle or division of the great Quadrangle or South part of the Air, respecting the like part or point of the compass appropriated to the Earth, accordingly as you therein are placed more Inferior and Subservient, & unto whom is given of the Highest by nature and office the true knowledge of physick in all its parts and the curing of all diseases which are incident to human bodies, and to reveal Show forth and give the same unto mankind living on Earth, whensoever you shall be moved and called forth by the great name of God Oloag, commanded thereunto; we the servants of the Highest (and the same your God) and reverently here present in his holy fear, do earnestly entreat, call upon and move you all, O ye Benevolent Angels or dignified powers of the Air, serving in orders, degree and mansion (as aforesaid) Opemen, Apeste, Scio, Vasge, Jointly and severally, Every and each one, for and by itself respectively, In by and through this mighty and powerful name of your God Noalmar, that you (at these our earnest Addresses) would be so truly willing and friendly unto us, that whensoever and wheresoever we shall Invocate, move, or call you forth unto visible appearance and our assistance, you then would readily and Immediately, forthwith at our Invocations, move, Descend, appear, and show your selves corporally visible unto us in this Crystal Glass standing here before us, or otherwise personally to appear out of the same visibly here before us, and so as that we may plainly see you, and Audibly hear you speak unto us, and by such your Spiritual Revelations unto us, to make us partakers of that true knowledge and Sapience, which by nature & office (given you of the Highest) may by such your visible appearance & verbal converse be showed forth and given unto us, And furthermore also, that in by and through this great and powerful name of your God Oloag, and [738] the force and virtue thereof: We do likewise, earnestly Invocate and entreat you, to do, accomplish, and fulfil whatsoever (accordingly and is by nature and office given you of the Highest) we shall request and command you: Hear us therefore, O ye Benevolent Angels or dignified Spiritual powers of the Air, serving in orders, degree and mansion (as aforesaid) Opemen, Apeste, Scio, Vasge, you do yet furthermore in this great name of your God Noalmar, and by the virtue and efficacy thereof, earnestly Invocate & entreat you to yield up and give unto us, your assuredly firm, free, and obliged consent herein, that all or any of you, which we shall at any time hereafter, Invocate, move, or call forth to visible appearance and our assistance, would certainly without any Tarrying or delay, Immediately move, descend, and visibly appear unto us, in this

---

[738] S2: Inserts "by".

Crystal Glass standing here before us, or otherwise out of it as it shall please God to give unto you, and thereby most beneficial, convenient, and fit for us, in these both our present, and other our future Actions and operations, and to speak plainly unto us, so as that we may sensibly hear you and understand you, directing and Instructing us, in the true knowledge and judgement of that your Spiritual Sapience and Science (given you of the Highest) And in this undoubted true and great name of your God Oloag, and by the virtue and power thereof, whereby we also earnestly Invocate and entreat you, not only to reveal, direct, show forth and make known unto us, the true apprehensive knowledge of all such occult and mystical Arcanaes in physick, and of whatsoever else relates thereunto, as are unknown of mankind, but also do whatsoever we shall further command, request, or desire to be done for us, relating to the said Science and our benefits therein (as you by office are of the Highest accordingly preordained and appointed) All which your obedience readily and willingly fulfilling and accomplishing unto us, as here we have in the powerful and true names of your God, earnestly entreated and besought you shall be a song of Honour & the praise of your God in your Creation Amen.

Invocation by way of humble Supplication and petition made to the four Benevolent Angels or Angelical powers of Light placed in orders and set over the Second Lesser Angle or division of the great Quadrangle or Table of the South Anaa[1], Naaa[2], Aaan[3], Aana[4], by the great and powerful name of God BANAA.

O Ye great and glorious Angels or Angelical powers of Light Anaa, Naaa, Aaan, Aana, governing or set over, the Second Lesser Angle, division or Quarter of the great Quadrangle of the South point of the Air, respecting the like part or point of the compass appropriated to the Earth, serving your most high God Banaa, in orders and office accordingly as you (by Celestial Dignification) are in place and power more Aerially Superior, unto whom is given also of the Highest by nature and office the true knowledge of (* moving from place to place,[739]) the knitting together of natures, and also as well the destruction of nature and of things that may perish as of conjoining and knitting them together,[740] and to reveal show forth

---

[739] S2: Inserts "as into this Country or that at pleasure".
[740] S2: This section is struck through, thus: "~~and of the knitting together of natures, and also as well the destruction of nature and of things that may perish as of conjoining and knitting them together~~".

and communicate the same (by your Angelical ministry) unto mankind living on Earth, whensoever you shall be Invocated or moved thereunto: We the servants of the Highest (and the same your God) and reverently here present in his holy fear, do earnestly entreat humbly beseech, and move you all, O ye Benevolent Angels or Angelical powers of Light or Celestially dignified Spirits of the Air, governing in orders, degree and mansion (as aforesaid) Anaa, Naaa, Aaan, Aana, Jointly and severally, every and each one, for and by it self respectively, In by and through this mighty and powerful name of your God Banaa, that you (at these humble requests and addresses) would be favourable and friendly unto us, as that whensoever or wheresoever we shall Invocate move or call you forth to visible appearance and our Assistance, you would be thereby moved to descend and appear visibly unto us in this Crystal Glass which stand here before us, or otherwise personally to appear out of the same visibly here before us, and so, as that we may plainly see you, and audibly hear you speak unto us, And by such your friendly and verbal converse with us, to make us partakers of that undefiled knowledge and true Sapience, which by nature and office (given you of the Highest) may by such your Angelical ministry be revealed given or administered unto us: Hear us therefore O ye Sacred Angelical powers of Light or Celestially dignified Spirits of the Air, by degree, and orders Superior, & governing as aforesaid Anaa, Naaa, Aaan, Aana, we do yet further in this great name of your God Banaa, and by the force power and efficacy thereof, Earnestly Entreat[741] and humbly beseech you, to grant these our Supplications and petitions, and that all or any of you, that we shall at any time hereafter Invocate, move or call forth to visible appearance, would ready and forthwith, move descend, and visibly appear unto us, whensoever we shall Invocate, move or call you forth in this Crystal Glass standing here before us, or otherwise out of it as it shall please God & you his ministers of divine grace and as best befitted or shall be most convenient or beneficial for us, or unto us, in these our Actions or operations, Speaking Audibly unto us, and also thereby directing and instructing us in the true knowledge of that your Angelical Sapience and Science given you of the Highest, and wherein also he hath accordingly by order and office ordained and appointed you, and this your Angelical Benevolence in Celestial grace and charity, thus given and granted unto us, and also in the accomplishment and fulfilling of these our humble desires and requests and whatsoever else shall be requisite and fit for us to know, shall be a song of Honour and the praise of your God in your Creation Amen.

---

[741] S2: "~~and~~".

Invocation by way of humble supplication & petition made to the four Servient Angels or dignified Spirits of the Air, placed in orders and serving in the Second Lesser Angle or division of the great Quadrangle or Table of the South Gemenem[1], Ecope[2], Amox[3], Berape[4], who are moved and called forth by the great and powerful name of God Vadali, and constrained thereunto to do what they are commanded according to their office by the great name of God Obavi.

O Ye Angelical powers of Light or dignified Spirits of the Air, Gemenem, Ecope, Amox, Berape, serving in orders under Superior powers, your most high and omnipotent God Vadali, in the Second Lesser Angle or division of the great Quadrangle or South part of the Air, respecting the like part or point of the compass appropriated to the Earth, accordingly as you therein are placed more inferior and subservient, and unto whom is given of the Highest by nature and office the true knowledge of (* finding & use of Metals &c[742]), physick in all its parts and the curing of all diseases whatsoever that are incident to human bodies[743], and to reveal, show forth and give the same unto mankind living on Earth whensoever you shall be moved & called forth by the great name of your God Obavi, commanded thereunto: we the servants of the Highest (& the same your God) and reverently here present in his holy fear, do earnestly entreat, call upon and move you all, O ye Benevolent Angels or dignified powers of the Air serving in orders degree and mansion (as aforesaid) Gemenem, Ecope, Amox, Berape, Jointly and severally, every and each one, for and by itself respectively, In by & through this mighty & powerful name of your God Vadali, that you (at these our Earnest addresses) would be so truly willing and friendly unto us, that whensoever and wheresoever we shall Invocate move or call you forth unto visible appearance and our assistance, you then would readily and Immediately, forthwith at our Invocations, move, Descend, appear, & show your selves corporally visible unto us, in this Crystal Glass standing here before us, or otherwise personally to appear out of the same visibly here before us, and so as that we may plainly see you, and Audibly hear you speak unto us, and by such your Spiritual Revelations

---

[742] S2: Omits "&c" and inserts "the Congelation of Stones & the Virtue of all Stones".
[743] S2: This section is struck through, thus: "~~and of physick in all its parts and the curing of all diseases whatsoever that are incident to human bodies~~".

unto us, to make us [partakers]⁷⁴⁴ of that true knowledge and Sapience, which by nature and office (given you of the Highest) may by such your visible appearance and verbal converse, be showed forth and given to us; And furthermore also that in by and through this great and powerful name of your God Obavi, and the force and virtue thereof; we do likewise earnestly Invocate and entreat you, to do, accomplish and fulfil whatsoever (accordingly and is by nature and office given you of the Highest) we shall request and command you, Hear us therefore, O ye Benevolent Angels, or dignified Spiritual powers of the Air, serving in orders, office, degree & mansion as aforesaid Gemenem, Ecope, Amox, Berape, you do yet further in this great name of your God Vadali, and by the virtue and efficacy thereof, earnestly Invocate and entreat you, to yield up and give unto us, your assuredly firm, free, and obliged consent herein, that all or any of you, which we shall at any time hereafter, Invocate, move, or call forth to visible appearance, would certainly without any Tarrying or delay, Immediately move, descend, and visibly appear unto us in this Crystal Glass standing here before us, or otherwise out of it, as it shall please God to give unto you, and thereby most beneficial convenient and fit for us, in these both our present and other our future Actions and operations, and to speak plainly unto us, so as that we may sensibly hear you and understand you, directing & Instructing us in the true knowledge and judgement of that your Spiritual Sapience and Science given you of the Highest; And in this undoubted true and great name of your God Obavi, and by the virtue and power thereof, whereby we also earnestly Invocate and entreat you, not only to reveal, declare, show forth and make known unto us, the true & apprehensive knowledge of all such Occult & mystical Arcanaes in physick, and of whatsoever else relates thereunto, as are unknown of mankind, but also do for us whatsoever we shall further command, request, or desire to be done, relating to the said Science & our benefits therein (as you by office are of the Highest accordingly preordained and appointed) All which your obedience readily & willingly fulfilling & accomplishing unto us, as here we have in the powerful & true names of your God Earnestly entreated & besought you, shall be a song of Honour, & the praise of your God in your Creation Amen.

Invocation by way of humble Supplication & petition made to the four Benevolent Angels or Angelical powers of Light placed in orders and set over the Third Lesser Angle or division of the great Quadrangle or Table of the South Pesac, Sacepe, Acepes, Cepesa, by

---

⁷⁴⁴ S1: "partakers" is missing here but this is clearly a copying error.

the great and powerful name of God BEPESAC.

O Ye great and glorious Angels or Angelical powers of Light Pesac, Sacepe, Acepes, Cepesa, governing or set over the Third Lesser Angle division or Quarter of the great Quadrangle of the South part of the Air, respecting the like part or point of the Compass appropriated to the Earth serving your most high God Bepesac, in orders and office accordingly as you (by Celestial Dignification) are in place and power more Aerially Superior, unto whom is given also of the Highest by nature and office, the true knowledge (* of all Mechanical Crafts whatsoever), of the knitting together of natures, and also as well the destruction of nature and of things[745] that may perish as of conjoining and knitting them together,[746] And to reveal, show forth, and communicate the same (by your Angelical ministry) unto mankind living on Earth, whensoever you shall be invocated or moved thereunto; we the servants of the Highest (and the same your God) and reverently here present in his holy fear, do earnestly entreat, humbly beseech and move you all, O ye Angels or Angelical powers of Light or Celestially dignified Spirits of the Air, governing in orders, degree, and mansion as aforesaid Pesac, Sacepe, Acepes, Cepesa, Jointly and severally, every and each one, for and by it self respectively, In by and through this mighty and powerful name of your God Bepesac, that you (at these humble requests and Addresses) would be favourable and friendly unto us, as that whensoever or wheresoever we shall Invocate, move or call forth to visible appearance and our assistance, You would be thereby moved to descend and appear visibly unto us, in this Crystal Glass which stand here before us, or otherwise personally to appear out of the same that we may plainly see you, And audibly hear you speak unto us, and by such your friendly and verbal converse with us to make us partakers of that undefiled knowledge and true Sapience, which by nature and office (given you of the Highest) may by such your Angelical ministry be revealed given or administered unto us, Hear us therefore O ye Sacred Angelical powers of Light or Celestially dignified Spirits of the Air, by degree and orders governing (as aforesaid) Pesac, Sacepe, Acepes, Cepesa, we do yet further in this great name of your God Bepesac, and by the force, power and efficacy thereof, to grant these our Supplications and petitions, and that all or any of you, that we shall at any time hereafter, Invocate,

---

[745] S1: The word "things" is repeated.
[746] S2: This section is crossed through, thus: "~~of the knitting together of natures, and also as well the destruction of nature and of things that may perish as of conjoining and knitting them together~~".

move, or call forth to visible appearance, would readily and forthwith move, Descend and visibly appear unto us, whensoever we shall Invocate, or move you thereunto in this Crystal Glass standing here before us, or otherwise out of it, as it shall please God, and you his ministers of divine grace, and as best befitted or shall be most convenient, or beneficial for us, or unto us, in the true knowledge of that your Angelical Sapience and Science (given you of the Highest) and wherein also he hath accordingly by order and office ordained and appointed you, and this your Angelical Benevolence in Celestial grace and charity thus given and granted unto us, and also in the accomplishment and fulfilling of these our humble requests and desires, and whatsoever else shall be requisite and fit for us to know, shall be a song of Honour, and the praise of your God in your Creation Amen.

Invocation by way of humble Supplication & petition, made to the four Servient Angels, or dignified Spirits of the Air, placed in orders and serving in the Third Lesser Angle, or division of the great Quadrangle or Table of the South Datete[1], Diom[2], Oopezpd[3], Vrgan[4], who are commanded and called forth by the great and powerful name of God Volexdo, and constrained thereunto to do what they are commanded according to their office by the great name of God Sioda.

O Ye Angelical powers of Light or dignified Spirits of the Air, Datete, Diom, Oopezpd, Vrgan, Serving in orders under Superior powers your most high and omnipotent God, Volexdo, in the Third Lesser Angle or division of the great Quadrangle, or South part of the Air, respecting the like part or point of the compass appropriated to the Earth, accordingly as you therein are placed more inferior and subservient, and unto whom is given of the Highest by nature and office, the true knowledge of (* Transformation & transplantation), physick in all its parts and the curing of all diseases whatsoever that are incident to human bodies,[747] And to reveal, show forth, and give the same unto mankind living on Earth whensoever you shall be moved and called forth by the great name of your God Sioda, commanded thereunto; We the Servants of the Highest (and the same your God) and reverently here present in his holy fear, do earnestly entreat, call upon, and move you all: O ye Benevolent Angels or dignified powers of the Air, serving in orders, degree and

---

[747] S2: This section is crossed through, thus: "physick in all its parts and the curing of all diseases whatsoever that are incident to human bodies".

mansion (as aforesaid) Datete, Diom, Oopezpd, Vrgan, Jointly and Severally, every and each one, for and by it self respectively, In by & through this mighty & powerful name of your God Volexdo, that you (at these our earnest addresses) would be so truly willing and friendly unto us, that whensoever & wheresoever we shall Invocate move or call you forth unto visible appearance and our assistance, you then would readily and Immediately forthwith at our Invocations, move, descend, appear, and show your selves corporally visible unto us, in this Crystal Glass standing here before us, or otherwise personally to appear out of the same visibly here before us, and so as that we may plainly see you and Audibly hear you speak unto us; And by such your Spiritual Revelations, to make us partakers of that true knowledge & Sapience which by nature and office (given you of the Highest) may by such your visible appearance and verbal converse, be showed forth and given to us, And furthermore also that In by and through this great and powerful name of your God Sioda, and the force and virtue thereof; we do likewise Earnestly Invocate and entreat you, to do, accomplish, and fulfil whatsoever (accordingly and is by nature and office given you of the Highest) we shall request and command you, Hear us therefore, O ye Benevolent Angels or dignified Spiritual powers of the Air, Serving in orders, office, degree and mansion (as aforesaid) Datete, Diom, Oopezpd, Vrgan, you do yet further in this great name of your God Volexdo, And by the virtue and efficacy thereof, earnestly Invocate and entreat you, to yield up, and give unto us, your assuredly firm, free and obliged consent herein, that all or any of you, which we shall at any time hereafter Invocate move or call forth to visible appearance, would certainly without any Tarrying or delay, Immediately move, descend, and visibly appear unto us, in this Crystal Glass standing here before us, or otherwise out of it, as it shall please God to give unto you, and thereby most beneficial convenient and fit for us, in these both our present and other our future Actions and operations, and to speak plainly unto us, so as that we may plainly see you & understand you, directing and instructing us in the true knowledge and Judgement of that your Spiritual Sapience and Science given you of the Highest, And in this undoubted true and great name of your God Sioda, and by the virtue and power thereof, whereby we also earnestly Invocate and entreat you, not only to reveal, declare, show forth and make known unto us the true and apprehensive knowledge of all such occult and mystical Arcanaes in physick and of whatsoever else relates thereunto, as[748] are unknown of mankind but also do for us whatsoever we shall further command, request,

---

[748] S2: "are".

or desire to be done, relating to the said Science and our benefits therein, (as you by office are of the Highest accordingly preordained and appointed;) All which your obedience readily & willingly fulfilling and accomplishing unto us, as here we have in the powerful and true names of your God Earnestly Entreated and besought you, shall be a Song of Honour, & the praise of your God in your Creation Amen.

Invocation by way of humble Supplication and petition made to the four Benevolent Angels or Angelical powers of Light, placed in orders and set over the Fourth Lesser Angle or division of the great Quadrangle or Table of the South Ziza[1], Jzaz[2], Zazi[3], Aziz[4], by the great & powerful name of God BEZIZA.

O Ye great and glorious Angels or Angelical powers of Light Ziza, Jzaz, Zazi, Aziz, governing or set over the fourth Lesser Angle, division or Quarter of the great Quadrangle of the South part of the Air, respecting the like part or point of the Compass appropriated to the Earth, Serving your most high God Beziza, in orders and office accordingly as you (by Celestial Dignification) are in place and power more Aerially Superior, unto whom is given also of the Highest by nature and office, the true knowledge of (*the Secrets of men knowing), the knitting together of natures and things that may perish as of conjoining and knitting them together,[749] And to Reveal show forth and communicate the same (by your Angelical ministry) unto mankind living on Earth whensoever you shall be Invocated or moved thereunto. We the servants of the Highest (& the same your God) and reverently here present in his holy fear, do earnestly entreat, humbly beseech and move you all, O ye Angels or Angelical powers of Light or Celestially dignified Spirits of the Air, governing in orders degree and mansion as aforesaid Ziza, Jzaz, Zazi, Aziz, Jointly and severally every and each one, for and by it self respectively, In by and through this mighty and powerful name of your God Beziza, that you (at these our Earnest Addresses) would be favourable and friendly unto us, as that whensoever or wheresoever we shall Invocate move or call you forth to visible appearance and our Assistance, you would be thereby moved to Descend and appear, visibly unto us in this Crystal Glass which stands here before us, or otherwise personally to appear out of the same visibly here before us, And so as that we may plainly see you,

---

[749] S2: This section is crossed through, thus: "~~the knitting together of natures and things that may perish as of conjoining and knitting them together~~".

and Audibly hear you speak unto us, and by such your friendly and verbal converse with us to make us partakers of that undefiled knowledge and true Sapience, which by nature and office (given you of the Highest) may by such your Angelical ministry be revealed given or administered unto us. Hear us therefore O ye Sacred Angelical powers of Light or Celestially dignified Spirits of the Air, by degree and orders, governing as aforesaid Ziza, Jzaz, Zazi, Aziz, we do yet further in this great name of your God Beziza, and by the force and efficacy thereof to grant these our Supplications and petitions, and that all or any of you, that we shall at any time hereafter, Invocate, move or call forth to visible appearance, would readily and forthwith, move descend and visibly appear unto us, whensoever we shall Invocate or move you thereunto in this Crystal Glass standing here before us or otherwise out of it, as it shall please God and you his ministers of divine grace, and as best befitted, or shall be most convenient or beneficial for us, or unto us, in the true knowledge of that your Angelical Sapience and Science (given you of the Highest) And wherein also he hath accordingly by order and office ordained and appointed you, And this your Angelical benevolence in Celestial grace and charity thus given and granted unto us and also in the accomplishment and fulfilling of these our humble desires and requests, and whatsoever else shall be requisite and fit for us to know, shall be a song of Honour and the praise of your God in your Creation Amen.

Invocation by way of humble Supplication and petition made to the four Servient Angels or dignified Spirits of the Air placed in orders, and serving in the Fourth Lesser Angle or division of the great Quadrangle or Table of the South Adre[1], Sispe[2], Pali[3], Acar[4], who are moved and called forth by the great and powerful name of God Arzodionar, and constrained thereunto to do what they are commanded according to their office by the great name of God Narzefem.

O Ye Angelical powers of Light or dignified Spirits of the Air, Adre, Sispe, Pali, Acar, serving in orders under superior powers, your most high and omnipotent God, Arzodionar, in the Fourth Lesser Angle, or division of the great[750] Quadrangle or South part of the Air, respecting the like part or point of the Compass appropriated to the Earth, accordingly[751] as you therein are placed more Inferior

---

[750] S2: "at".
[751] S2: "according".

and Subservient, And unto whom is given of the Highest by nature and office the true knowledge (* of all Elemental Creatures &c[752],) of physick in all its parts, and the curing of all diseases which are incident to human bodies,[753] and to Reveal, show forth and give the same unto mankind living on Earth, whensoever you shall be moved and called forth by the great name of God Narzefem, commanded thereunto, We the servants of the Highest (and the same your God) and Reverently here present in his holy fear, do earnestly entreat, call upon and move you all; O ye Benevolent Angels, or dignified powers of the Air, serving in orders, degree, and mansion as aforesaid Adre, Sispe, Pali, Acar, Jointly and severally, every and each one, for and by itself respectively, In by and through this mighty and powerful name of your God Arzodionar, that you (at these our earnest Addresses) would be so truly willing and friendly unto us, that whensoever and wheresoever, we shall invocate move or call you forth, unto visible appearance and our Assistance you then would readily and Immediately forthwith at our Invocations move, descend, appear, and show your selves corporally visible unto us in this Crystal Glass standing here before us, and so, as that we may plainly see you and Audibly hear you speak unto us, or otherwise personally to appear out of the same; And by such your Spiritual Revelations unto us, to make us partakers of that true knowledge and Sapience, which by nature and office (given you of the Highest) may by such your visible appearance and verbal converse be showed forth and given to us; And furthermore also that In by and through this great and powerful name of your God Narzefem, and the force and virtue thereof, We do likewise earnestly Invocate and entreat you, to do, accomplish, and fulfil, whatsoever (accordingly and is by nature and office given you of the Highest) we shall request and command you; Hear us therefore O ye benevolent Angels or dignified Spiritual powers of the Air, serving in orders, degree and mansion as aforesaid Adre, Sispe, Pali, Acar, you do yet further in this great name of your God Arzodionar, and by the virtue and efficacy thereof, earnestly Invocate and entreat you to yield up, and give unto us, your assuredly firm, free and obliged consent herein, that all, or any of you, which we shall at any time hereafter, Invocate, move or call forth to visible appearance, would certainly without any Tarrying or delay, Immediately, move, descend, and visibly appear unto us, in this Crystal Glass standing here before us, or otherwise out of it, as it shall please God to give unto you,

---

[752] S2: Omits "&c" and inserts "amongst us, how many kinds, & their use in the Creation, as they are severally placed in the 4 Elements Air Water Earth & fire".

[753] S2: This section is crossed through, thus: "~~of physick in all its parts, and the curing of all diseases which are incident to human bodies~~".

and thereby most beneficial convenient and fit for us, In these both our present and other our future Actions and operations, and to speak plainly unto us, so as that we may sensibly hear you and understand you, directing and instructing us in the true knowledge and judgement of that your Spiritual Sapience and Science (given you of the Highest) And in this undoubted true and great name of your God Narzefem, and the virtue and power thereof, whereby we also earnestly Invocate and entreat you, not only to reveal, declare, show forth and make known unto us, the true and apprehensive knowledge of all such occult and mystical Arcanaes in physick and of whatsoever else relates thereunto, as are unknown of mankind, but also do whatsoever we shall command, request, or desire to be done for us, relating to the said Science and our benefits therein (as you by office are of the Highest accordingly preordained and appointed;) All which your Obedience readily and willingly fulfilling and accomplishing unto us, as here we have in the powerful and true names of your God, earnestly entreated and besought you, shall be a Song of Honour and the praise of your God in your Creation Amen.

Janua Orientalis Reserata

or the Key opening and giving entrance into the Region, Angle or division of the East.

THE Prayer, to be said before Invocation[754]
O beginning, And fountain of all wisdom gird up thy Loins in misery, & Shadow our [ioe] Lord be merciful unto us & forgive us our Trespasses, for That Rise up Saying there is No god, have Risen up [a....nfius] Saying Let us Confound them, our Strength is [....] Neither are our bones full of marrow, Help therefore O Eternal god of mercy, Help therefore O Eternal god of Salvation, Help therefore O Eternal god & Comfort, Who is like Unto the one [emalter?] of Immense, before whom the choir of Heaven sing, Omappa-la-man-hallelujah, visit us O God, with a Comprehending fire brighter than the Stars in your fourth heaven, be merciful unto us O God, & Continue with us, For thou art almighty, to Whom all things of thy breath in Heaven & Earth, Sing glory, Praise & Honour, Saying Come Lord for thy Mercy's Sake.

O Almighty & Everlasting the true & Living god Have mercy pity & Compassion on me & my dear Companions, Who being now on our bended knees, in all Reason of humility, obedience & faith [fill....], To serve Thy Divine Majesty, with all your gifts & graces which thou hast hitherto, Endowed us with, & with all other which of Thy most bountiful & Fatherly mercies thou wilt therefore [aid] us and bestow upon us; Lighten therefore O Lord god almighty our Eyes, & open thou our Ears, guide us Instruct & Confirm in us & unto us, our directions Judgements Understandings memories & Utterances, that we may be true & Perfect Seers Hearers declarers, & witnesses of Such things which Either Immediately of your Divine Majesty, or mediately by your Ministry of thy holy faithful Angels Shall be manifested declared or revealed unto us, Now & at all times & occasions for the admiring of thy prayer honour & glory Amen.[755]

Invocation or Key, moving and calling forth to visible appearance the 6 Angelical Seniors of the East Habioro, Aaoxaif, Hetemorda, Ahaozpi, Hipotga, Autotar, by the great & mighty name BATAIVA.

---

[754] R1: This prayer only occurs in this manuscript R1. The edge of the MSS is frayed, resulting in some unintelligible words, indicated by [...].
[755] R1: The prayer ends here.

O Ye glorious Angels or Angelical Seniors Celestially dignified Habioro, Aaoxaif, Hetemorda, Ahaozpi, Hipotga, Autotar, serving before the great & mighty Angel or Angelical monarch BATAIVA, in the mansion, Region, Angle, or division of the East, unto whom is given of the Highest by office Scientiam, Rerum, Humanarum et Judicium. And to declare, show forth, & reveal the same unto mankind living on Earth, whensoever you shall be called or moved thereunto, by visible appearance & verbal converse. We[756] servants of the most high God, do Invocate, adjure, move, and call you forth to visible appearance, friendly society & verbal converse with us, all or some one or any of you, O all ye Celestially dignified Angels or benevolent Angelical Seniors of the East Habioro, Aaoxaif, Hetemorda, Ahaozpi, Hipotga, Autotar, In by & through, this mighty &[757] powerful, great, & Royal name BATAIVA, And the most Imperial efficacy & virtue thereof. Move therefore we say, O all ye Benevolent Angels or Angelical Seniors of the East Habioro, Aaoxaif, Hetemorda, Ahaozpi, Hipotga, Autotar, And in this Royal & mighty name BATAIVA, either some one, or all, or any of you, Descend, appear, and visibly show your selves unto the sight of our Eyes, in this Crystal Glass or otherwise out of the same, visibly here before us, as the pleasure of the Highest & you his messengers of divine grace shall seem best & most fit, or requisite for us, both now & at all times hereafter, speaking plainly and showing forth unto us, by verbal converse, whatsoever is given you by office to declare, discover, and make known for the benefit of his servants the sons of men, move therefore we say, & by the signal virtue & power of all aforesaid, Descend, appear, & some one, or all, or any of you, visibly show your selves here before us, and be friendly unto us. Open the mysteries of your creation, & make us partakers of undefiled knowledge, whereunto we move you, both in power & presence, whose works shall be a Song of Honour, & the praise of your God in your Creation Amen.

Invocation or Key, moving & calling forth to visible appearance, the four Angels or Angelical powers of the Air, Celestially dignified Vrzela, Zelar, Larzod, & Arzel by the great name of God Erzela, governing and set over the first Lesser Angle or Quarter of the great Quadrangle or Table of the East.

---

[756] S2: Inserts "the".
[757] S2: Omits "&".

O Ye Benevolent Angels or angelical powers of the Air Celestially dignified Vrzela, Zelar, Larzod, & Arzel as governing & set over the first Lesser Angle or division (of the great Quadrangle,) of the Region or Angle of the East, unto whom is given of the Highest by office (& nature) the true knowledge of the Knitting together of natures, and also as well the destruction of nature and of things that may perish, as of conjoining and knitting them together, and to declare show forth, & reveal the same unto mankind living on Earth, whensoever you shall be called or moved thereunto by visible appearance & verbal converse. We the servants of the Highest, do Invocate, adjure, move & call forth to visible appearance, friendly society and verbal converse with us, all or some one, or any of you, O all ye Benevolent Angels or Angelical powers of the Air, Celestially dignified set over the first Quarter part of the East Angle Vrzela, Zelar, Larzod, & Arzel, In by & through, this great & powerful name of your God Erzela, & the signal virtue thereof: move therefore we say O ye Benevolent Angels or Angelical powers of the Air Celestially dignified & placed in orders (as aforesaid) Vrzela, Zelar, Larzod, & Arzel, And in this powerful name of your God Erzela, either some one, or all, or any of you, descend, appear & visibly show your selves, unto the sight of our eyes in this Crystal Glass or otherwise out of the same visibly here before us, as the pleasure of the Highest and you his messengers of divine grace & permission shall seem best, & most fit, or requisite for us, both now and at all times hereafter, speaking audibly unto us, and showing forth by verbal converse whatsoever is given you by office, to declare, discover, & make known for the benefit of his servants the sons of men, Move therefore we say, and by the signal virtue & power of all aforesaid, Descend, appear, & some one, or all of you, visibly show your selves here before us, and be friendly unto us, open the mysteries of your Creation and make us partakers of undefiled knowledge, whereunto we move you both in power & presence whose works shall be a song of Honour, & the praise of your God in your Creation Amen.

Invocation or Key moving & calling forth to visible appearance the four[758] Angelical powers of Light or dignified spirits of Air Cezodines, Totet, Sias, & Efemende,[759] by the great name of God Jdoigo, and also to do what they are commanded (according to their offices) by

---

[758] S2: "~~Angels or~~".

[759] S1: This is clearly a copyist's mistake as the name is incorrectly given here as Efende and then Efemende and it is used elsewhere throughout the text. In S2 the letters "me" are added in, further suggesting that Sloane 3821 was copied from Sloane 307.

the name of God Ardeza, serving & set under the first Lesser Angle, or Quarter part of the greater Quadrangle or Table of the East.

O Ye Angels of Light or dignified Spirits of the Air Cezodines, Totet, Sias, & Efemende, serving in orders under superior Angelical powers your most high God by his great name Jdoigo, And doing all his commandments by his great name Ardeza as being set under, and servient spirits in the first Lesser Angle, or division of the Region, or greater Angle of the East, unto which is given of the Highest by office, the true knowledge of physick in all its parts, & the curing of all diseases whatsoever that are incident to Human Bodies, And to reveal, show forth, & give the same to mankind living on Earth, whensoever you shall be called or moved thereunto by visible appearance & verbal converse. We the servants of the most high God do Invocate, adjure, move, and call forth to visible appearance, friendly society, & verbal converse with us, All, or some one, or any of you, O all ye Angelical powers of Light or dignified Spirits of the Air, set under, & serving in the first Quarter part of the East Angle, Cezodines, Totet, Sias, Efemende, In by and through this powerful & great name of your God Jdoigo, And also do for us, whatsoever we shall request & command you by this great name of your God Arderza, and by the signal virtues thereof[760] move therefore, We say O all ye Benevolent powers or dignified Spirits of the Air, placed in order (as aforesaid) Cezodines, Totet, Sias, Efemende, Either some one, or all, or any of you, Descend, appear, & visibly show your selves unto the sight of our Eyes, in this Crystal Glass or otherwise out of the same, visibly here before us as the pleasure of the Highest shall seem best, and most fit, or requisite for us, both now, & at all times hereafter speaking plainly And showing forth unto us by verbal converse, whatsoever is given you by office to declare, discover & make known, for the benefit of his servants the sons of men, move therefore we say, and by signal virtue & power of this great name of your God Jdoigo, Descend, appear, & some one, or all, or any of you, visibly show your selves here before us, In manner & form as it shall please God & you his messengers of Celestial grace accordingly (as aforesaid) And is this great name of your God Ardeza, be friendly unto us, and do for us whatsoever we shall command, effectually fulfilling all our desires according to your offices, opening the mysteries of your Creation & make us partakers of undefiled knowledge whereunto we move you both in power & presence, whose works shall be a song of Honour & the praise of your God in your Creation Amen.

---

[760] S2: "of them".

Invocation, or Key, moving & calling forth to visible appearance, the four Angels or Angelical powers of the Air, Celestially Dignified Vtepa, Tepau, Paute, Autepe, by the great name of God Eutepa, governing & set over the Second Lesser Angle or quarter of the great Quadrangle or Table of the East.

O Ye Benevolent Angels or Angelical powers of the Air Vtepa, Tepau, Paute, Autepe, as governing & set over the second Lesser Angle or division of the Region, or greater Angle of the East, unto whom is given of the Highest by office the true knowledge of (* Moving from place to place[761],) the knitting together of natures, and also as well the destruction of nature, & of things that may perish, as of conjoining & knitting them together[762], And to declare, show forth, reveal, the same unto mankind living on Earth, whensoever you shall be called or moved thereunto by visible appearance & verbal converse. We the servants of the most high God, do Invocate, adjure, move & call forth to visible appearance, friendly society & verbal converse with us, All, or some one, or any of you, O all ye Benevolent Angels or Angelical powers of the Air, Vtepa, Tepau, Paute, Autepe, (Celestially dignified, & set over the Second quarter part of the East Angle,) In by & through this great & powerful name of your God Eutepa, and the signal virtue thereof, move therefore we say, O ye Benevolent Angels or Angelical powers of the Air Celestially dignified & placed in orders as aforesaid, Vtepa, Tepau, Paute, Autepe, and in this powerful name of your God Eutepa, either some one, or all, or any of you, Descend, appear, & visibly show your selves unto the sight of our Eyes, in this Crystal Glass or otherwise out of the same visibly here before us, as the pleasure of the Highest & you his messengers of divine grace shall seem best, and most fit or requisite for us, both now and at all times hereafter, speaking plainly & showing forth unto us by verbal converse whatsoever is given you by office to declare, discover, and make known, for the benefit of his servants the sons of men, Move therefore we say, & by the signal virtue & power of all aforesaid, Descend, appear, & some one, or all, or any of you, visibly show your selves here before us, and be friendly unto us, open the mysteries of your Creation & make us partakers of

---

[761] S2: Inserts "as into this Country or that Country at will & pleasure".
[762] S2: This section is crossed through, thus: "~~the knitting together of natures, and also as well the destruction of nature, & of things that may perish, as of conjoining & knitting them together~~".

undefiled Knowledge, whereunto we move you both in power & presence whose works shall be a song of Honour, and the praise of your God in your Creation Amen.

Invocation or Key moving & calling forth to visible appearance, the four Angelical powers of Light, or dignified spirits of Air OYube, Paoc, Vrbeneh, Diri, by the great name of God Hacza, and also to do what they are commanded (according to their offices) by the name of God Palam serving and set under the second Lesser Angle or Quarter part of the greater Quadrangle or Table of the East.

O Ye Angels of Light or dignified Spirits of the Air OYube, Paoc, Vrbeneh, Diri, serving in orders under Superior Angelical powers, your most high God, by his great name Hacza, & doing all his commandments by his great name Palam, as being set under, & servient spirits in the Second Lesser Angle, or division of the Region or greater Angle of the East, unto which[763] is given of the Highest by office, the true knowledge of (* finding & also the Methods of Congelation of Stones &c[764]) physick in all its parts & the curing of all diseases whatsoever that are Incident to Human Bodies,[765] And to reveal, show forth & give the same to[766] mankind living on Earth, whensoever you shall be called or moved thereunto by visible appearance & verbal converse. We the servants of the most high God, do Invocate, adjure, move, & call forth to visible appearance, friendly society, & verbal converse with us, all, or some one, or any of you, O all ye Angelical powers of Light or dignified Spirits of the Air set under & serving in the second Quarter part of the East Angle, OYube, Paoc, Vrbeneh, Diri, In by & through this powerful & great name of your God Hacza, And also[767] do for us, whatsoever we shall request & command you, by this great name of your God Palam, and by the signal virtues of them, move therefore we say O all ye Benevolent powers or dignified Spirits of the Air, placed in orders as aforesaid OYube, Paoc, Vrbeneh, Diri, Either some one, or all, or any of you, Descend, appear, & visibly show your selves unto the sight of our Eyes, in this[768] Crystal Glass or otherwise out of the

---

[763] S2: "whom".
[764] S2: Replaces "finding & also the Methods of Congelation of Stones &c", with "finding out & also the use of metals, the Congelation of Stones & the virtue of all stones &c".
[765] S2: This section is crossed through, thus: "physick in all its parts & the curing of all diseases whatsoever that are Incident to Human Bodies".
[766] S2: "unto".
[767] S2: Inserts "to".
[768] S2: "the".

same visibly here before us, both now, & at all times hereafter, speaking plainly, & showing forth unto us, by verbal converse, whatsoever is given you by office, to declare, discover, & make known, for the benefit of his servants the sons of men, move therefore we say, & by the signal virtue & power of this great name of your God Hacza, Descend, appear, & some one, or all, or any of you, visibly show your selves here before us, In manner & form, as it shall please God, & you his messengers of divine grace, accordingly as aforesaid, And in this great name of your God Palam, be friendly unto us, & do for us, in whatsoever we shall command you, effectually fulfilling all our desires, according to your offices, Opening the mysteries of your Creation & make us partakers of undefiled knowledge, whereunto we move you, both in power & presence, whose works shall be a Song of Honour, & the praise of your God in your Creation Amen.

Invocation or Key, moving & calling forth to visible appearance, the four Angels, or Angelical powers of the Air, Celestially Dignified Cenbar, Enbarc, Barcen, Vrecenbe, by the great name of your[769] God Ecenbar, governing & set over, the Third Lesser Angle or Quarter of the great Quadrangle or Table of the East.

O Ye Benevolent Angels or Angelical powers of the Air, Celestially dignified Cenbar, Enbarc, Barcen, Vrecenbe, serving your God Ecenbar as governing & set over the 3rd Lesser Angle, or division of the Region or greater Angle of the East, unto whom is given of the Highest by office, the true knowledge (* of all the mechanical crafts whatsoever) of the knitting together of natures, & also as well the destruction of nature, & of things that may perish, as of conjoining & knitting them together,[770] And to declare, show forth, & reveal the same unto mankind living on Earth, whensoever you shall be called or moved thereunto by visible appearance & verbal converse, We the servants of the most high God, do Invocate[771], adjure, move & call forth to visible appearance, friendly society, & verbal converse with us, All, or some one, or any of you, O all ye Benevolent Angels or Angelical powers of the Air, Cenbar, Enbarc, Barcen, Vrecenbe, Celestially dignified, & set over the 3rd Quarter part of the East Angle, In by & through, this great & powerful name of your God

---

[769] S2: Omits "your".
[770] S2: This section is crossed through, thus: "of the knitting together of natures, & also as well the destruction of nature, & of things that may perish as of conjoining & knitting them together".
[771] S2: "friendly society, & verbal converse with us all".

Ecenbar, And the signal virtue thereof, Move therefore we say, O ye Benevolent Angels or Angelical powers of the Air Celestially dignified & placed in orders as aforesaid, Cenbar, Enbarc, Barcen, Vrecenbe, And in this powerful name of your God Ecenbar, either some one, or all, or any of you, Descend, appear, and visibly show your selves unto the sight of our Eyes in this Crystal Glass or otherwise out of the same visibly here before us, as the pleasure of the Highest & you his messengers of divine grace shall seem best, & most fit or requisite for us, both now and at all times hereafter, speaking plainly & showing forth unto us by verbal converse, whatsoever is given you by office to declare, discover, & make known, for the benefit of his servants the sons of men, move therefore we say, and by the signal virtue & power of all aforesaid, Descend, appear, & some one, or all, or any of you, visibly show your selves here before us & be friendly unto us, open the mysteries of your Creation, & make us partakers of undefiled knowledge, whereunto we move you both in power & presence, whose works shall be a song of Honour, and the praise of your God in your Creation Amen.

Invocation or Key, moving and calling forth to visible appearance, the four Angelical powers of Light, or dignified spirits of the Air Abemo, Naco, Ocenem, Shael, by the great name of God Aiaoai, and also to do what they are commanded (according to their offices) by the name of God Oiiit, serving & set under the Third Lesser Angle, or Quarter part[772] of the great Quadrangle or Table of the East.

O Ye Angels of Light, or dignified Spirits of the Air Abemo, Naco, Ocenem, Shael, serving in orders under superior Angelical powers your most high God Aiaoai, And doing all his commandments by his great name Oiiit, as being set under, & servient spirits in the Third Lesser Angle or division of the Region or greater Angle of the East, unto which is given of the Highest by office, the true knowledge of (* Transformation & transplantation,) physick in all its parts & the curing of all diseases whatsoever that are Incident to Human Bodies,[773] And to reveal, show forth, & give the same to mankind living on Earth, whensoever you shall be called or moved thereunto, by visible appearance & verbal converse, We the servants of the most high God, do Invocate, adjure, move, & call forth to visible appearance, friendly society, & verbal converse with us, All, or some

---

[772] S2: Omits "part".
[773] S2: This section is crossed through, thus: "~~physick in all its parts & the curing of all diseases whatsoever that are incident to Human Bodies~~".

one, or any of you, O all ye Angelical powers of Light or dignified Spirits of the Air, set under & serving in the Third (Lesser) or Quarter part of the East Angle, Abemo, Naco, Ocenem, Shael, In, by and through, this powerful and great name of your God Aiaoai, And also do for us whatsoever we shall request & command you by this great name of your God Oiiit and by the signal virtues of them, Move therefore we say, O all ye Benevolent powers or dignified Spirits of the Air, placed in orders as aforesaid Abemo, Naco, Ocenem, Shael, Either some one, or all, or any of you, Descend, appear, & visibly show your selves unto the sight of our Eyes in this Crystal Glass or otherwise out of the same, visibly here before us, as the pleasure of the Highest, shall seem best, & most fit or requisite for us, both now and at all times hereafter, speaking plainly and showing forth unto us, by verbal converse, whatsoever is given you by office, to declare, discover, and make known for the benefit of his servants the sons of men, Move therefore we say, & by the signal virtue & power of this great name of your God Aiaoai, Descend, appear, & some one, or all, or any of you, visibly show your selves here before us, in manner and form, as it shall please God and you his ministers of Celestial grace accordingly as aforesaid, And in this great name of your God Oiiit, be friendly unto us, and do for us, In whatsoever we shall command you, effectually fulfilling all our desires according to your offices, opening the mysteries of your Creation & make us partakers of undefiled knowledge whereunto we move you both in power & presence, whose works shall be a Song of Honour, and the praise of your God in your Creation Amen.

Invocation or Key moving & calling forth to visible appearance, the four Angels, or Angelical powers of the Air Exgezod, Gezodex, Zodexge, Dexgezod, by the great name of your God Eexgezod, governing & set over the fourth Lesser Angle or Quarter of the great Quadrangle, or Table of the East.

O Ye Benevolent Angels or Angelical powers of the Air Celestially dignified Exgezod, Gezodex, Zodexge, Dexgezod, serving your God Eexgezod, as governing and set over the fourth Lesser Angle, or division of the Region or greater Angle of the East, unto whom is given of the Highest by office, the true knowledge of (* the secrets of men knowing,) the knitting together of natures and also as well the destruction of nature, & of things that may perish, as of conjoining and knitting them together, [774] And to declare, show forth, and reveal the same unto mankind living on Earth, whensoever you shall be called or moved thereunto by visible appearance, & verbal converse. We the servants of the most high God, do Invocate, adjure, move & call forth to visible appearance, friendly society & verbal converse with us, all, or some one, or any of you, O all ye Benevolent Angels or Angelical powers of the Air, Celestially dignified, set over the fourth quarter part of the East Angle, Exgezod, Gezodex, Zodexge, Dexgezod, In, by, and through this great & powerful name of your God Eexgezod, and the signal virtue thereof, move therefore we say, O ye Benevolent Angels or Angelical powers of the Air, Celestially dignified & placed in orders as aforesaid, Exgezod, Gezodex, Zodexge, Dexgezod, And in this powerful name of your God Eexgezod, either some one, or all, or any of you, Descend, appear, and visibly show your selves unto the sight of our Eyes, in this Crystal Glass or otherwise out of the same visibly here before us, as the pleasure of the Highest and you his messengers of divine grace, shall seem best & most fit or requisite for us, both now & at all times hereafter, speaking plainly and showing forth unto us by verbal converse, whatsoever is given you by office to declare, discover, and make known, for the benefit of his servants the sons of men, move therefore we say, and by the signal virtue and power of all aforesaid, Descend, appear, and some one, or all, or any of you visibly show your selves here before us and be friendly unto us, open the mysteries of your Creation, & make us partakers of undefiled knowledge, whereunto we move you both in power & presence, whose works shall be a song of Honour, & the praise of your God in your Creation Amen.

Invocation or Key, moving & calling forth to visible appearance, the four Angelical powers of Light or dignified spirits of the Air Acca, Enpeat, Otoi, Pemox, by the great name of your God Aovararzod and also to do what they are commanded (according to their offices) by the name of God Aloai, serving & set under the fourth Lesser Angle, or Quarter part of the greater Quadrangle or Table of the East.

O Ye Angels of Light, or dignified Spirits of the Air Acca, Enpeat, Otoi, Pemox, serving in orders under superior Angelical powers,

---

[774] S2: This section is crossed through, thus: "~~the knitting together of natures and also as well the destruction of nature, & of things that may perish, as of conjoining and knitting them together~~".

your most high God by his great name Aovararzod, and doing all his commandments by his great name Aloai, as being set under & servient spirits in the fourth Lesser Angle, or division of the Region or greater Quadrangle of the East, unto which is given of the Highest by office, the ~~true knowledge~~[775] (*of all Elemental Creatures amongst us, how many Kinds, their use in the creation as they are severally placed in the 4 Elements, fire, & air, earth, water) ~~of physick in all its parts, and the curing of all diseases whatsoever that are Incident to Human Bodies~~, And to reveal show forth and give the same to mankind living on Earth, whensoever you shall be called, or moved thereunto by visible appearance and verbal converse. We the Servants of the most high God, do Invocate, adjure, move, & call forth to visible appearance, friendly society and verbal converse with us, all, or some one, or any of you, O all ye Angelical powers of Light or dignified Spirits of the Air, set under and serving in the fourth Quarter part of the East Angle, Acca, Enpeat, Otoi, Pemox, In by & through, this powerful and great name of your God Aovararzod, and also to do for us whatsoever we shall request and command you, by this great name of your God Aloai, and by the signal virtues of them, Move therefore we say, O all ye Benevolent powers or dignified Spirits of the Air, placed in orders, as aforesaid Acca, Enpeat, Otoi, Pemox, Either some one, or all, or any of you, Descend, appear, and visibly show your selves unto the sight of our Eyes in this Crystal Glass or otherwise out of the same visibly here before us, as the pleasure of the Highest, shall seem best, and most fit or requisite for us, both now & at all times hereafter, speaking plainly & showing forth unto us, by verbal converse, whatsoever is given you by office to declare, discover, & make known for the benefit of his servants the sons of men, Move therefore we say, & by the signal virtue and power of this great name of your God Aovararzod, Descend, appear, and some one, or all, or any of you, visibly show your selves here before us, in manner & form, as it shall please God, and you his messengers of Celestial grace, accordingly as aforesaid, And in this great name of your God Aloai, be friendly unto us, and do for us, in whatsoever we shall command[776] you, effectually fulfilling all our desires according to your offices, opening the mysteries of your Creation, and make us partakers of undefiled Knowledge whereunto we move you both in power and presence, whose works shall be a Song of Honour and the praise of your God in your Creation Amen.

---

[775] S2: Inserts "true knowledge".
[776] S2: "~~and~~".

Janua Occidentalis Reserata

or the Key opening and giving entrance into the Region, Angle or division of the West.

Invocation or Key, moving & calling forth to visible appearance, the 6 Angelical Seniors of the West, Lesurahpem, Saiinou, Laoaxarp, Selgaiol, Ligdisa, Soaixente, by the great and mighty name RAAGIOS.

O Ye glorious Angels or Angelical Seniors, Celestially dignified Lesurahpem, Saiinou, Laoaxarp, Selgaiol, Ligdisa, Soaixente, serving before the great & mighty Angel or Angelical monarch RAAGIOS, In the mansion, Region, Angle, or division of the West, unto whom is given (by office), of the Highest[777] Scientiam, Rerum, Humanarum, et Judicium, and to declare, show forth & reveal the same unto mankind living on Earth, whensoever you shall be called or moved thereunto, by visible appearance & verbal converse. We[778] servants of the most high God, do Invocate, adjure, move & call you forth to visible appearance, friendly society, & verbal converse with us, all, or some one, or any of you, O all ye Celestially dignified Angels or Benevolent Angelical Seniors of the West Lesurahpem, Saiinou, Laoaxarp, Selgaiol, Ligdisa, Soaixente, In by & through, this mighty powerful, great, & Royal name RAAGIOS, and the most Imperial efficacy & virtue thereof, move therefore we say O all ye Benevolent Angels or Angelical Seniors of the West Lesurahpem, Saiinou, Laoaxarp, Selgaiol, Ligdisa, Soaixente, And in this Royal & mighty name RAAGIOS, either some one, or all, or any of you, Descend, appear, and visibly show your selves unto the sight of our Eyes in this Crystal Glass or otherwise out of the same, visibly here before us, as the pleasure of the Highest & you his messengers of divine grace shall seem best and most fit or requisite for us, both now, and at all times hereafter, speaking plainly & showing forth unto us, by verbal converse, whatsoever is given you by office, to declare, discover, & make known, for the benefit of his servants the sons of men, move therefore we say, & by the signal virtue and power of all aforesaid, Descend, appear, & some one, or all, or any of you, visibly show your selves here before us, and be friendly unto

---

[777] S2: "highest".
[778] S2: Inserts "the".

us, open the mysteries of your creation and make us partakers of undefiled knowledge, whereunto we move you both in power & presence, whose works shall be a Song of Honour & the praise of your God in your Creation Amen.

Invocation or Key, moving & calling forth to visible appearance, the four Angels or Angelical powers of the Air Celestially dignified Taad, Aadet, Adeta, Detaa, by the great name of God Hetaad governing & set over the first Lesser Angle or Quarter of the great Quadrangle or Table of the West.

O Ye Benevolent Angels or Angelical powers of the Air, Celestially dignified Taad, Aadet, Adeta, Detaa, as governing and set over the first Lesser Angle or division of the Region, or Greater Angle of the West, unto whom is given of the Highest by office, the true knowledge of the knitting together of natures, and also as well the destruction of nature, and of things that may perish, as of conjoining & knitting them together, And to declare, show forth, & reveal the same unto mankind living on Earth, whensoever you shall be called or moved thereunto by visible appearance and verbal converse. We the servants of the Highest, do Invocate, adjure, move & call forth to visible appearance, friendly society & verbal converse with us, All, or some one, or any of you, O all ye Benevolent Angels or Angelical powers of the Air, Celestially dignified, set over the first Quarter part of the West Angle Taad, Aadet, Adeta, Detaa, In by & through this great and powerful name of your God Hetaad, and the signal virtue thereof, move therefore we say O ye Benevolent Angels or Angelical powers of the Air, Celestially dignified & placed in orders as aforesaid Taad, Aadet, Adeta, Detaa, And in this powerful name of your God Hetaad, either some one, or all, or any of you, Descend, appear, & visibly show your selves, unto the sight of our eyes in this Crystal Glass or otherwise out of the same visibly here before us, as the pleasure of the Highest & you his messengers of divine grace & permission shall seem best, and most fit or requisite for us, both now & at all times hereafter speaking plainly unto us and showing forth by verbal converse whatsoever is given you by office to declare, discover, and make known for the benefit of his servants the sons of men, Move therefore we say, and by the signal virtue & power of all aforesaid, Descend, appear, & some one, or all, or any of you, visibly show your selves here before us, and be friendly unto us, open the mysteries of your Creation and make us partakers of undefiled knowledge, whereunto we move you, both in power & presence whose works shall be a song of Honour, & the praise of your God in your Creation Amen.

Invocation or Key, moving & calling forth to visible appearance the four Angelical powers of Light or dignified Spirits of the Air Toco, Nehded (or Enehded), Paax, Saix, by the great name of God Obegoca, and also to do what they are commanded (according to their offices) by the name of God Aabeco, serving & set under the first Lesser Angle or Quarter part of the greater Quadrangle, or Table of the West.

O Ye Angels of Light or dignified Spirits of the Air Toco, Enehded, Paax, Saix, serving in orders under superior Angelical powers your most high God, by his[779] great name Obegoca, and doing all his commandments by his great name Aabeco as being set under, and servient[780] spirits in the first Lesser Angle or division of the Region or greater Angle of the West, unto which[781] is given of the Highest by office the true knowledge of physick in all its parts, and the curing of all diseases whatsoever, that are Incident to Human Bodies, And to reveal, show forth, & give the same to mankind living on Earth, whensoever you shall be called or moved thereunto by visible appearance & verbal converse. We the servants of the most high God, do Invocate, adjure, move, and call forth to visible appearance, friendly society, & verbal converse with us, All or some one, or any of you, O all ye Angelical powers of Light, or dignified Spirits of the Air, set under, & serving in the first Quarter part of the West Angle Toco, Enehded, Paax, Saix, In by and through this powerful & great name of your God Obegoca, And also to do for us, whatsoever we shall request & command you, by this great name of your God Aabeco, & by the signal virtues of them, move therefore we say O all ye benevolent powers, or dignified Spirits of the Air, placed in order (as aforesaid) Toco, Enehded, Paax, Saix, Either some one, or all, or any of you, Descend, appear, and visibly show your selves unto the sight of our Eyes in this Crystal Glass or otherwise out of the same visibly here before us, as the pleasure of the Highest, shall seem best and most fit or requisite for us, both now & at all times hereafter, speaking[782] plainly & showing forth unto us by verbal converse whatsoever is given you by office to declare, discover, & make known, for the benefit of his servants the

---

[779] S2: "the".
[780] S2: "serving".
[781] S2: "whom".
[782] S2: "~~plainly~~".

sons of men, Move therefore we say, and by the signal virtue & power of this great name of your God[783] Obegoca, Descend, appear, & some one, or all, or any of you, visibly show your selves here before us, in manner and form, as it shall please God & you his messengers of Celestial grace, accordingly as aforesaid, And in this great[784] name of your God Aabeco, be friendly unto us, & do for us in whatsoever we shall command you, effectually fulfilling all our desires, according to your offices, Opening the mysteries of your Creation, and make us partakers of undefiled knowledge, whereunto we move you both in power and presence, whose works shall be a song of Honour and the praise of your God in your Creation Amen.

Invocation or Key, moving & calling forth to visible appearance, the four Angels or Angelical powers of the Air, Celestially dignified Tedim, Dimet, Imtede, Emtedi, by the great name of God Hetedim, governing & set over the Second Lesser Angle or Quarter of the great Quadrangle or Table of the West.

O Ye Benevolent Angels, or Angelical powers of the Air, Celestially dignified Tedim, Dimet, Imtede, Emtedi, serving your God Hetedim, as governing & set over the second Lesser Angle or division of the Region or greater Angle of the West unto whom is given of the Highest by office the true knowledge of (* Moving from place to place &c [785],) the knitting together of natures, and also as well the destruction of nature and of things that may perish, as of conjoining & knitting them together[786], And to declare, show forth, and reveal the same unto mankind living on Earth, whensoever you shall be called or moved thereunto, by visible appearance & verbal converse. We the servants of the most high God, do Invocate, adjure, move & call forth, to visible appearance, friendly society, & verbal converse with us, all, or some one, or any of you, O all ye Benevolent Angels or Angelical powers of the Air, Celestially dignified and set over the second Quarter part of the West Angle Tedim, Dimet, Imtede, Emtedi, In by & through, this great & powerful name of your God Hetedim, & the signal virtue thereof, move therefore we say, O ye Benevolent Angels or Angelical powers

---

[783] S2: "Obegoca be friendly unto".

[784] S1: The word "great" is given twice here.

[785] S2: Omit "&c" and inserts "as into this place or that place at pleasure".

[786] S2: This section is crossed through, thus: "the knitting together of natures, and also as well the destruction of nature and of things that may perish, as of conjoining & knitting them together".

of the Air, Celestially dignified & placed in orders as aforesaid, Tedim, Dimet, Imtede, Emtedi, And in this powerful name of your God Hetedim, either some one, or all, or any of you, Descend, appear, and visibly show your selves unto the sight of our Eyes in this Crystal Glass or otherwise out of the same, visibly here before us, as the pleasure of the Highest & you his messengers of divine grace, & permission shall seem best & most fit, or requisite for us, both now and at all times hereafter, Speaking plainly & showing forth unto us by verbal converse, whatsoever is given you by office to declare, discover & make known, for the benefit of his servants, the sons of men, Move therefore we say, and by the signal virtue & power of all aforesaid Descend, appear, and some one, or all, or any of you, visibly show your selves here before us, and be friendly unto us, Open the mysteries of your Creation, and make us partakers of[787] undefiled knowledge whereunto we move you, both in power and presence, whose works shall be a song of Honour, & the praise of your God in your Creation Amen.

Invocation or Key, moving & calling forth to visible appearance, the four Angelical powers of Light or dignified spirits of the Air Magem, Leoc, Visyl, Vrvoi, by the great name of God Nelapar, and also to do, what they are commanded (according to their offices) by the name of God Omebeb, serving & set over, the second Lesser Angle or Quarter part of the greater Quadrangle or Table of the West.

O Ye Angels of Light or dignified Spirits of the Air Magem, Leoc, Visyl, Vrvoi, serving in orders under Superior Angelical powers, your most high God, by his great name Nelapar, And doing all his commandments by his great name Omebeb, as being set under & servient Spirits in the Second Lesser Angle or division of the Region or greater Angle of the West, unto which is given of the Highest by office, the true knowledge of (* finding[788] & use of Metals &c,) physick in all its parts, & the curing of all diseases, whatsoever that are Incident to human bodies[789], & to reveal, show forth, & give the same to mankind living on Earth, whensoever you shall be called or moved thereunto by visible appearance & verbal converse, we the servants of the most high God, do Invocate, adjure, move, & call forth to visible appearance friendly society & verbal converse with

---

[787] S2: Inserts "and of".
[788] S2: Inserts "out", and also has "~~the use~~".
[789] S2: This section is crossed through, thus: "~~physick in all its parts, & the curing of all diseases, whatsoever that are incident to human bodies~~".

us, all, or some one, or any of you, O all ye Angelical powers of Light
or dignified Spirits of the Air, set under & serving in the second
Quarter part of the West Angle, Magem, Leoc, Visyl, Vrvoi, In, by, &
through, this powerful & great name of your God Nelapar, And also
to do for us, whatsoever we shall request & command you, by this
great name of your God Omebeb, and by the signal virtue of them,
Move therefore we say, O all ye Benevolent powers or Dignified
Spirits of the Air, placed in orders as aforesaid Magem, Leoc, Visyl,
Vrvoi, Either some one, or all, or any of you, Descend, appear, &
visibly show your selves unto the sight of our Eyes in this Crystal
Glass or otherwise out of the same visibly here before us, as the
pleasure of the Highest, shall[790] seem best, & most fit, or requisite
for us, both now and at all times hereafter, speaking plainly &
showing forth unto us by verbal converse, whatsoever is given you,
by office to declare, discover & make known for the benefit of his
servants the sons of men, Move therefore, we say, and by the signal
virtue & power of this great name of your God Nelapar, Descend,
appear, & some one, or all, or any of you, visibly show your selves
here before us, in manner and form as it shall please God, and you
his messengers of Celestial grace accordingly as aforesaid, And in
this great name of your God Omebeb, be friendly unto us, & do for
us, in whatsoever we shall command you, Effectually fulfilling all
our desires according to your offices, opening the mysteries of your
Creation and make us partakers of undefiled knowledge, whereunto
we move you both in power and presence whose works shall be a
Song of Honour, & the praise of your God in your Creation Amen.

Invocation or Key, Moving & calling forth to visible appearance, the
four Angels or Angelical powers of the Air, Celestially dignified
Magel, Agelem, Gelema, Lemage, by the great name of God
Hemagel, governing and set over the Third Lesser Angle or Quarter
of the great Quadrangle or Table of the West.

O Ye Benevolent Angels or Angelical powers of the Air Celestially
dignified Magel, Agelem, Gelema, Lemage, serving your God
Hemagel, as governing & set over the Third Lesser Angle or division
of the Region, or greater Angle of the West, unto whom is given of
the Highest by office, the true knowledge of (* All Mechanical crafts
whatsoever,) the knitting together of natures, and also as well the
destruction of nature, & of things that may perish, as of conjoining

---

[790] S2: "~~seem~~".

& knitting them together[791], And to declare, show forth, & reveal the same unto mankind living on Earth whensoever you shall be called or moved thereunto, by visible appearance & verbal converse, we the servants of the most high God, do Invocate, adjure, move & call forth, to visible appearance, friendly society, & verbal converse with us, all, or some one, or any of you, O all ye Benevolent Angels or Angelical powers of the Air, Celestially dignified, set over the Third Quarter part of the West Angle Magel, Agelem, Gelema, Lemage, In by & through this great & powerful name of your God Hemagel, & the signal virtue thereof, Move therefore we say O ye Benevolent Angels or Angelical powers of the Air, Celestially Dignified, & placed in orders as aforesaid, Magel, Agelem, Gelema, Lemage, And in this powerful name of your God Hemagel, either some one, or all, or any of you, Descend, appear, & visibly show your selves unto the sight of our Eyes, in this Crystal Glass or otherwise out of the same visibly here before us, as the pleasure of the Highest & you his messengers of divine grace & permission, shall seem best, And most fit or requisite for us, both now & at all times hereafter, speaking plainly & showing forth unto us by verbal converse whatsoever is given you by office to declare, discover, and make known for the Benefit of his servants the sons of men, Move therefore we say, & by the signal virtue & power of all aforesaid, Descend[792], appear, & some one, or all, or any of you, visibly show your selves here before us & be friendly unto us, open the mysteries of your Creation, and make us partakers of undefiled Knowledge, whereunto we move you both in power & presence, whose works shall be a song of Honour, and the praise of your God in your Creation Amen.

Invocation, or Key, moving & calling forth to visible appearance the four Angelical powers of Light, or dignified Spirits of the Air Paco, Endezen, Jipo, Exarih, by the great name of God Maladi, And also to do what they are commanded (according to their offices) by the name of God Olaad, serving & set under the Third Lesser Angle, or Quarter part of the greater Quadrangle or Table of the West.

O Ye Angels of Light, or dignified Spirits of the Air Paco, Endezen, Jipo, Exarih, serving in orders under superior Angelical powers, your most high God, by his great name Maladi, And doing all his

---

[791] S2: This section is crossed through, thus: "~~the knitting together of natures, and also as well the destruction of nature, & of things that may perish, as of conjoining & knitting them together~~".
[792] S2: "~~and~~".

commandments by his great name Olaad, as being set under, and servient spirits in the Third Lesser Angle or division of the Region, or greater Angle of the West, unto whom is given of the Highest by office, the true knowledge of (* Transformation & transplantation &c,) physick in all its parts, and the curing of all diseases whatsoever, that are Incident to Human Bodies[793], and to reveal, show forth, and give the same to mankind living on Earth, whensoever you shall be called or moved thereunto by visible appearance & verbal converse, we the servants of the most high God, do Invocate, adjure, move & call forth to visible appearance, friendly society, & verbal converse with us, All, or some one, or any of you, O all ye Angelical powers of Light or dignified Spirits of the Air, set under, & serving in the Third (Lesser Angle) or Quarter part of the West Angle, Paco, Endezen, Jipo, Exarih, In by and through, this powerful & great name of your God Maladi, and also to do for us whatsoever we shall request & command you, by this great name of your God Olaad, and by the signal virtues of them, Move therefore we say O all ye Benevolent powers or dignified Spirits of the Air, placed in orders as aforesaid Paco, Endezen, Jipo, Exarih, Either some one, or all, or any of you, Descend, appear, and visibly show your selves unto the sight of our Eyes, in this Crystal Glass or otherwise out of the same, visibly here before us, as the pleasure of the Highest shall seem best, and most fit or requisite for us, both now & at all times hereafter, speaking plainly and showing forth unto us by verbal converse, whatsoever is given you by office, to declare, discover, and make known for the benefit of his servants the sons of men. Move therefore we say, and by the signal virtue & power, of this great name of your God Maladi, Descend, appear, & some one, or all, or any of you visibly show your selves here before us, in manner & form, as it shall please God, and you his messengers of Celestial grace accordingly as aforesaid, And is this great name of your God Olaad, be friendly unto us, & do for us, in whatsoever we shall command you, effectually fulfilling all our desires according to your offices, opening the mysteries of your Creation, & make us partakers of undefiled knowledge, whereunto we move you both in power & presence, whose works shall be a Song of Honour, & the praise of your God in your Creation Amen.

Invocation or Key, moving and calling forth to visible appearance, the four Angels or Angelical powers of the Air, Celestially Dignified Nelarex, Larexen, Rexenel, Xenelar, by the great name of God

---

[793] S2: This section is struck through, thus: "~~physick in all its parts, and the curing of all diseases whatsoever, that are incident to Human Bodies~~".

HENLAREX, governing and set over the fourth Lesser Angle or Quarter of the great Quadrangle or Table of the West.

O Ye Benevolent Angels or Angelical powers of the Air Celestially dignified Nelarex, Larexen, Rexenel, Xenelar, serving your God Henlarex, as governing & set over the fourth Lesser Angle, or division of the Region or greater Angle of the West, unto whom is given of the Highest by office, The true knowledge of[794] (* The secrets of men Knowing) the knitting together of natures And also as well the destruction of nature, and of things that may perish, as of conjoining and knitting them together[795], And to declare, show forth, and reveal the same unto mankind living on Earth, whensoever you shall be called or moved thereunto, by visible appearance and verbal converse. We the servants of the most high God, do Invocate, adjure, move, & call forth to visible appearance, friendly society and verbal converse with us, all, or some one, or any of you, O all ye Benevolent Angels or Angelical powers of the Air, Celestially dignified, set over the Fourth Quarter part of the West Angle, Nelarex, Larexen, Rexenel, Xenelar, In by and through, this great and powerful name of your God HENLAREX, and the signal virtue thereof, Move therefore we say, O ye Benevolent Angels or Angelical powers of the Air Celestially dignified, Nelarex, Larexen, Rexenel, Xenelar, (and placed in orders as aforesaid) And in this powerful name of your God HENLAREX, either some one, or all, or any of you, Descend, appear, and visibly show your selves unto the sight of our Eyes in this Crystal Glass or otherwise out of the same visibly here before us, as the pleasure of the Highest, and you his messengers of divine grace and permission, shall seem best and most fit or requisite for us, both now and at all times hereafter, speaking plainly, & showing forth unto us by verbal converse, whatsoever is given you by office to declare, discover, and make known for the Benefit of his servants the sons of men, Move therefore we say, and by the signal virtue and power of all aforesaid, Descend, appear and some one, or all, or any of you, visibly show your selves here before us, and be friendly unto us Open the mysteries of your Creation, and make us partakers of undefiled Knowledge, whereunto we move you both in power and presence, whose works shall be a song of Honour, and the praise of your God in your Creation Amen.

---

[794] S2: "and".

[795] S2: This section is crossed out, thus: "~~the knitting together of natures and also as well the destruction of nature, and of things that may perish, as of conjoining and knitting them together~~".

Invocation or Key, moving and calling forth to visible appearance, the four Angelical powers of Light or dignified spirits of the Air Expecem, Vasa, Dapi, Reniel, by the great name of God Jaaasde, And also to do, what they are commanded (according to their offices) by the name of God Atapa, serving and set under the fourth Lesser Angle, or Quarter part of the greater Quadrangle or Table of the West.

O Ye Angels of Light, or dignified Spirits of the Air Expecem, Vasa, Dapi, Reniel, serving in orders under superior Angelical powers, your most high God by his great name Jaaasde, and doing all his commandments by his great name Atapa, as being set under, and servient spirits in the fourth Lesser Angle or division of the Region or greater Angle of the West, unto whom is given of the Highest by office, the true knowledge (* Of all Elemental creatures &c[796],) of physick in all its parts, and the curing of all diseases, whatsoever that are incident to Human bodies[797], And to Reveal, show forth, and give the same to mankind living on Earth, whensoever you shall be called or moved thereunto by visible appearance and verbal converse, we the servants of the most high God, do Invocate, adjure, move, and call forth to visible appearance, friendly society, and verbal converse with us, all, or some one, or any of you, O all ye Angelical powers of Light or dignified Spirits of the Air, set under and serving in the fourth Quarter part of the West Angle, Expecem, Vasa, Dapi, Reniel, In by and through, this powerful and great name of your God Jaaasde, And also to do for us, whatsoever we shall request and command you by this great name of your God Atapa, and by the signal virtues of them, Move therefore we say O all ye Benevolent powers or dignified Spirits of the Air, placed in orders as aforesaid Expecem, Vasa, Dapi, Reniel, either some one, or all, or any of you, Descend, appear, & visibly show your selves unto the sight of our Eyes in this Crystal Glass or otherwise out of the same, visibly here before us, as the pleasure of the Highest shall seem best, and most fit or requisite for us, both now and at all times hereafter, speaking plainly unto us and showing forth by verbal converse whatsoever is given you by office, to declare, discover, and make known for the benefit of his servants the sons of men, Move therefore we say, and by the signal virtue and power of

---

[796] S2: Omits "&c".
[797] S2: This section is crossed out, thus: "of physick in all its parts, and the curing of all diseases, whatsoever that are incident to human bodies".

236

this great name of your God Jaaasde, Descend, appear, and some one, or all, or any of you, visibly show your selves here before us in manner and form as it shall please God, and you his messengers of Celestial grace accordingly as aforesaid, and is this great name of your God Atapa, be friendly unto us, and do for us in whatsoever we shall command you, effectually fulfilling all our desires according to your offices opening the mysteries of your Creation, and make us partakers of undefiled knowledge, whereunto we move you both in power and presence, whose works shall be a song of Honour, and the praise of your God in your Creation Amen.

Janua Septentrialis Reserata

or the Key opening and giving entrance into the Region, Angle, or division of the North.

Invocation or Key, moving & calling forth to visible appearance, the 6 Angelical Seniors of the North Laidrom[1], Aczinor[2], (or Aczodinor) Elzinopo[3], Althectega[4], Elhiansa[5], Acemliceve[6], by the great and mighty name JCZODHEHCA.

O Ye glorious Angels or Angelical Seniors Celestially dignified Laidrom, Aczinor (or Aczodinor), Elzinopo, Althectega, Elhiansa, Acemliceve, serving before the great & mighty Angel or Angelical monarch JCZODHEHCA, in the Region, mansion, Angle or division of the North, unto whom is given of the Highest by office Scientiam, Rerum, Humanarum et Judicium, And to declare, show forth, and reveal the same unto mankind living on Earth, whensoever you shall be called or moved thereunto, by visible appearance and verbal converse. We the servants of the most high God, do Invocate, adjure, move & call you forth to visible appearance, friendly[798] society, and verbal converse with us, All, or some one, or any of you, O all ye Celestially dignified Angels or Angelical Seniors of the North Laidrom, Aczinor, Elzinopo, Althectega, Elhiansa, Acemliceve, In, by and through, this mighty, powerful, great, and Royal name JCZODHEHCA, and the most Imperial efficacy and virtue thereof, Move therefore we say, O all ye Benevolent Angels, or Angelical Seniors of the north Laidrom, Aczinor, Elzinopo, Althectega, Elhiansa, Acemliceve, And in this Royal and mighty name Jczodhehca, either some one, or all, or any of you, Descend, appear, and visibly show your selves unto the sight of our Eyes, in this Crystal Glass or otherwise out of the same visibly here before us, as the pleasure of the Highest, and you his messengers of divine grace, shall seem best, & most fit or requisite for us, both now and at all times hereafter, speaking plainly & showing forth unto us, by verbal converse, whatsoever is given you by office to declare, discover, & make known, for the Benefit of his servants the sons of men, move therefore, we say, and by the signal virtue, & power of all aforesaid, Descend appear, & some one, or all, or any of you, visibly show your selves here before us, and be friendly unto us,

---

[798] S2: "ђ".

Open the mysteries of your creation, & make us partakers of undefiled knowledge whereunto we move you both in power & presence, whose works shall be a Song of Honour and the praise of your God in your Creation Amen.

Invocation, or Key, moving & calling forth to visible appearance, the four Angels or Angelical powers of the Air Celestially dignified Boza, Ozab, Zabo, Aboz, by the great name of God Enboza, governing and set over the first Lesser Angle or Quarter of the great Quadrangle or Table of the North.

O Ye Benevolent Angels or angelical powers of the Air, Celestially dignified Boza, Ozab, Zabo, Aboz, governing and set over the first Lesser Angle or division of the Region or Greater Angle of the North, unto whom is given of the Highest by office, the true knowledge of the knitting together of natures, and also as well the destruction of nature & of things that may perish, as of conjoining & knitting them together, And to declare, show forth & reveal the same unto mankind living on Earth, whensoever you shall be called or moved thereunto by visible appearance & verbal converse, we the servants of the most high God, do Invocate, adjure, move & call forth to visible appearance, friendly society & verbal converse with us, All, or some one, or any of you, O all ye Benevolent Angels or Angelical powers of the Air, Celestially dignified, & set over the first Quarter part of the North Angle Boza, Ozab, Zabo, Aboz, In by & through, this great & powerful name of your God Enboza, & the signal virtue thereof, move therefore we say O ye Benevolent Angels or Angelical powers of the Air Celestially dignified & placed in orders as aforesaid Boza, Ozab, Zabo, Aboz, And in this powerful name of your God Enboza, either some one, or all, or any of you, Descend, appear, & visibly show your selves unto the sight of our eyes, in this Crystal Glass or otherwise out of the same visibly here before us, as the pleasure of the Highest, and you his messengers of divine grace and permission, shall seem best & most fit, or requisite for us, both now & at all times hereafter, speaking plainly unto us, and showing forth by verbal converse, whatsoever is given you by office to declare, discover, & make known for the benefit of his servants the sons of men, move therefore we say, And by the signal virtue & power, of all aforesaid, Descend, appear, and some one, or all, or any of you, visibly show your selves here before us, and be friendly unto us, Open the mysteries of your Creation, and make us partakers of undefiled knowledge whereunto we move you both in power and presence whose works shall be a song of Honour, and the praise of your God in your Creation Amen.

Invocation or Key moving & calling forth to visible appearance, the four Angelical powers of Light or Dignified spirits of the Air Aira, Ormen, Reseni, Jzodenar, by the great name of God Angepoi, and also to do what they are commanded (according to their offices) by the name of God Vnenax serving & set under the first Lesser Angle, or Quarter part of the greater Quadrangle or Table of the North.

O Ye Angels of Light or dignified Spirits of the Air Aira, Ormen, Reseni, Jzodenar, serving in orders under superior Angelical powers your most high God by his great name Angepoi, and doing all his commandments by his great name, Vnenax, as being set under, & servient spirits in the first Lesser Angle or division of the Region, or greater Angle of the North, unto whom is given of the Highest by office the true knowledge of physick in all its parts, & the curing of all diseases whatsoever, that are incident to human Bodies, & to reveal, show forth and give the same to mankind living on Earth whensoever you shall be called or moved thereunto by visible appearance and verbal converse. We the servants of the most high God, do Invocate, adjure, move & call forth to visible appearance, friendly society, & verbal converse with us, All, or some one, or any of you, O all ye Angelical powers of Light or dignified Spirits of the Air, set under, & serving in the first Quarter part of the North Angle, Aira, Ormen, Reseni, Jzodenar, In, by & through, this powerful and great name of your God Angepoi; and also do for us whatsoever we shall request & command you, by this great name of your God Vnenax, and by the signal virtues thereof[799] move therefore we say O all ye Benevolent powers or dignified Spirits of the Air, placed in order as aforesaid, Aira, Ormen, Reseni, Jzodenar, either some one, or all, or any of you, Descend, appear, & visibly show your selves unto the sight of our Eyes in this Crystal Glass or otherwise out of the same visibly here before us, as the pleasure of the Highest shall seem best, & most fit or requisite for us, both now and at all times hereafter, speaking plainly, & showing forth unto us, by verbal converse whatsoever is given you by office to declare, discover, & make known for the benefit of his servants the sons of men, Move therefore we say, & by signal virtue & power of this great name of your God Angepoi, Descend, appear, & some one, or all, or any of you, visibly show your selves here before us, in manner and form as it shall please God & you his messengers of Celestial grace,

---

[799] S2: "of them".

accordingly as aforesaid, And is this great name of your God Vnenax, be friendly unto us, and do for us in whatsoever we shall command you, effectually fulfilling all our desires according to your offices, opening the mysteries of your Creation and make us partakers of undefiled Knowledge whereunto we move you both in power & presence, whose works shall be a song of Honour and the praise of your God in your Creation Amen.

Invocation or Key, moving and calling forth to visible appearance the four Angels or Angelical powers of the Air, Celestially Dignified Phara, Harap, Rapeh, Aphar, by the great name of God Enphara, governing and set over the Second Lesser Angle or Quarter of the great Quadrangle or Table of the North.

O Ye Benevolent Angels or Angelical powers of the Air Celestially dignified Phara, Harap, Rapeh, Aphar, serving your God Enphara,[800] as governing & set over the Second Lesser Angle or division of the Region, or greater Angle of the north, unto whom is given of the Highest by office The true knowledge of (* Moving from place to place &c[801],) the knitting together of natures, and also as well the destruction of nature and of things that may perish as of conjoining and knitting them together[802], And to declare, show forth, and reveal the same unto mankind living on Earth, whensoever you shall be called or moved thereunto by visible appearance & verbal converse. We the servants of the most high God, do Invocate, adjure, move & call forth, to visible appearance, friendly society, & verbal converse with us, all, or some one, or any of you, O all ye Benevolent Angels or Angelical powers of the Air, Celestially dignified set over the Second quarter part of the North Angle, Phara, Harap, Rapeh, Aphar, In by & through, this great and powerful name of your God Enphara, & the signal virtue thereof, Move therefore we say, O ye Benevolent Angels or Angelical powers of the Air, Celestially dignified and placed in orders as aforesaid, Phara, Harap, Rapeh, Aphar, And in this powerful name of your God Enphara, either some one, or all, or any of you, Descend, appear, & visibly show your selves unto the sight of our Eyes in this Crystal Glass or otherwise out of the same visibly here before us, as the pleasure of the Highest and you his messengers of

---

[800] S2: Inserts "and".
[801] S2: Omits "&c" and inserts "as unto this Country or that Country at pleasure".
[802] S2: This section is crossed through, thus: "the knitting together of natures, and also as well the destruction of nature and of things that may perish as of conjoining and knitting them together".

divine grace & permission, shall seem best, and most fit or requisite for us, both now and at all times hereafter, speaking plainly, & showing forth unto us by verbal converse, whatsoever is given you, by office to declare, discover, and make known for the benefit of his servants the sons of men, Move therefore we say and by the signal virtue & power of all aforesaid, Descend, appear, & some one, or all, or any of you, visibly show your selves here before us & be friendly unto us, Open the mysteries of your Creation and make us partakers of undefiled Knowledge, whereunto we move you both in power and presence, whose works shall be a song of Honour, and the praise of your God in your Creation Amen.

Invocation or Key, moving & calling forth to visible appearance the four Angelical powers of Light or dignified spirits of the Air Omgege, Gebal, Relemi, Jahel, by the great name of God Anaeem, and also to do what they are commanded (according to their offices) by the name of God Sonden serving & set under the second Lesser Angle or Quarter part of the greater Quadrangle, or Table of the North.

O Ye Angels of Light or Dignified Spirits of the Air Omgege, Gebal, Relemi, Jahel, serving in orders under Superior Angelical powers, your most high God, by his great name Anaeem, & doing all his commandments by his great name Sonden, as being set under, and servient Spirits in the second Lesser Angle, or division of the Region, or greater Angle of the North, unto whom is given of the Highest by office The true knowledge of (* finding out & use of Metals &c,) physick in all its parts, & the curing of all diseases whatsoever that are Incident to human bodies,[803] And to reveal, show forth, & give the same to mankind living on Earth, whensoever you shall be called, or moved thereunto by visible appearance & verbal converse. We the servants of the most high God, do Invocate, adjure, move & call forth to visible appearance, friendly society, & verbal converse with us, all or some one, or any of you, O, all ye Angelical powers of Light, or dignified Spirits of the Air, set under & serving in the Second Quarter part of the North Angle, Omgege, Gebal, Relemi, Jahel, In by & through, this powerful & great name of your God Anaeem, and also do for us, whatsoever we shall request and command you, by this great name of your God Sonden, and by the signal virtues of them, Move therefore we say O

---

[803] S2: This section is crossed through, thus: "physick in all its parts, & the curing of all diseases whatsoever that are incident to human bodies".

all ye Benevolent powers or dignified [Spirits][804] of the Air, placed in orders as aforesaid Omgege, Gebal, Relemi, Jahel, either some one, or all, or any of you, Descend, appear, and visibly show your selves unto the sight of our Eyes in this Crystal Glass or otherwise out of the same, visibly here before us, as the pleasure of the Highest shall seem best, and most fit or requisite for us, both now and at all times hereafter, Speaking plainly and showing forth unto us, by verbal converse, whatsoever is given you by office, to declare, discover, & make known, for the benefit of his servants the sons of men. Move therefore we say, & by the signal virtue and power of this great name of your God Anaeem, Descend, appear, & some one, or all, or any of you, visibly show your selves here before us, in manner & form, as it shall please God, and you his messengers of Celestial grace, accordingly as aforesaid, And is this great name of your God Sonden, be friendly unto us, & do for us, in whatsoever we shall command you, effectually fulfilling all our desires, according to your offices Opening the mysteries of your Creation and make us partakers of undefiled knowledge, whereunto we move you both in power & presence, whose works shall be a Song of Honour, and the praise of your God in your Creation Amen.

Invocation or Key, moving & calling forth to visible appearance, the four Angels or Angelical powers of the Air Celestially Dignified Æoan, Oanæ, Anæo, Næoa, by the great name of your[805] God NÆOAN, governing and set over the Third Lesser Angle or Quarter of the great Quadrangle or Table of the North.

O Ye Benevolent Angels or Angelical powers of the Air Celestially dignified Æoan, Oanæ, Anæo, Næoa, serving your God NÆOAN, as governing & set over the Third Lesser Angle, or division of the Region, or greater Angle of the North, unto whom is given of the Highest by office, The true knowledge of[806] (* The secrets of all Mechanical Crafts &c,) of the knitting together of Natures and also as well the destruction of nature & of things that may perish, as of conjoining & knitting them together[807], And to declare, show forth, & reveal the same unto mankind living on Earth, whensoever you shall be called or moved thereunto, by visible appearance, & verbal

---

[804] S1: The word "Spirits" is absent, which is obviously a copying error.
[805] S2: Omits "your".
[806] S2: "and".
[807] S2: This section is crossed out, thus: "of the knitting together of natures and also as well the destruction of nature and of things that may perish as of conjoining and knitting them together".

converse. We the servants of the most high God, do Invocate, adjure, move & call forth to visible appearance, friendly society, & verbal converse with us, all, or some one, or any of you, O all ye Benevolent Angels, or Angelical powers of the Air, Celestially dignified, set over the Third Quarter part of the North Angle, Æoan, Oanæ, Anæo, Næoa, In, by, and through, this great & powerful name of your God NÆOAN, & the signal virtue thereof, Move therefore we say, O ye Benevolent Angels or Angelical powers of the Air, Celestially Dignified and placed in orders as aforesaid, Æoan, Oanæ, Anæo, Næoa, And in this powerful name of your God Næoan, either some one, or all, or any of you, Descend, appear, And visibly show your selves unto the sight of our Eyes in this Crystal Glass or otherwise out of the same, visibly here before us, as the pleasure of the Highest and you his messengers of divine grace & permission, shall seem best, and most fit or requisite for us, both now & at all times hereafter, Speaking plainly and showing forth unto us, by verbal converse, whatsoever is given you by office to declare, discover, and make known for the benefit of his servants the sons of men. Move therefore we say, and by the signal virtue and power of all aforesaid, Descend, appear, & some one, or all, or any of you, visibly show your selves here before us, and be friendly unto us, Open the mysteries of your Creation, and make us partakers of undefiled knowledge, whereunto we move you, both in power and presence, whose works shall be a song of Honour, and the praise of your God in your Creation Amen.

Invocation or Key, moving & calling forth to visible appearance, the four Angelical powers of Light or dignified spirits of the Air Opena, Doope, Rexao, Axir, by the great name of God Cebalpet, and also to do what they are commanded (according to their offices) by the name of God Arbizod, serving and set under the Third Lesser Angle, or Quarter part of the great Quadrangle or Table of the North.

O Ye Angels of Light or dignified Spirits of the Air Opena, Doope, Rexao, Axir, serving in orders under superior Angelical powers, your most high God, by his great name Cebalpet, and doing all his commandments by his great name Arbizod as being set under, and servient spirits in the Third Lesser Angle or division of the Region or greater Angle of the North, unto whom is given of the Highest by office the true knowledge of (* Transformation and Transplantation,) physick in all its parts, & the curing of all diseases whatsoever, that are Incident to Human Bodies[808], & to reveal, show forth and give the same to mankind living on Earth, whensoever you shall be called or moved thereunto, by visible appearance and verbal converse. We the servants of the most high God, do Invocate, adjure, move, and call forth to visible appearance, friendly society & verbal converse with us, all, or some one, or any of you, O all ye Angelical powers of Light, or dignified Spirits of the Air, set under & serving in the Third Quarter part of the North Angle, Opena, Doope, Rexao, Axir, In, by, and through, this powerful & great name of your God Cebalpet, and also to do for us whatsoever we shall request and command you, by this great name of your God Arbizod, and by the signal virtues of them, Move therefore we say, O all ye Benevolent powers, or dignified Spirits of the Air, placed in orders as aforesaid Opena, Doope, Rexao, Axir, Either some one, or all, or any of you, Descend, appear and visibly show your selves unto the sight of our Eyes in this Crystal Glass or otherwise out of the same visibly here before us, as the pleasure of the Highest shall seem best, and most fit or requisite for us, both now and at all times hereafter, speaking plainly & showing forth unto us, by verbal converse, whatsoever is given you by office to declare, discover, and make known, for the benefit of his servants the sons of men. Move therefore we say and by the signal virtue & power of this great name of your God Cebalpet, Descend, appear, and some one, or all, or any of you, visibly show your selves here before us, in manner and form as it shall please God, and you his messengers of Celestial grace accordingly as aforesaid, And is this great name of your God Arbizod, be friendly unto us, and do for us in whatsoever we shall command you, Effectually fulfilling, all our desires according to your offices, Opening the mysteries of your Creation, & make us partakers of undefiled knowledge, whereunto we move you, both in power and presence, whose works shall be a Song of Honour, & the praise of your God, in your Creation Amen.

Invocation or Key moving & calling forth to visible appearance, the four Angels, or Angelical powers of the Air Celestially Dignified Jaom, Aomi, Omia, Miao, by the great name of your God NIAOM, governing and set over the fourth Lesser Angle or Quarter of the great Quadrangle or Table of the North.

O Ye Benevolent Angels or Angelical powers of the Air, Celestially

---

[808] S2: This section is crossed through, thus: "~~physick in all its parts & the curing of all diseases whatsoever that are incident to human bodies~~".

dignified Jaom, Aomi, Omia, Miao, serving your God Niaom, as governing & set over the fourth Lesser Angle or division of the Region or greater Angle of the North, unto whom is given of the Highest by office the true knowledge of (* The secrets of men knowing,) the knitting together of natures, & also as well the destruction of nature and of things that may perish, as of conjoining & knitting them together[809], And to declare, show forth, & reveal the same unto mankind living on Earth, whensoever you shall be called or moved thereunto, by visible appearance and verbal converse. We the servants of the most high God, do Invocate, adjure, Move, & call forth to visible appearance, friendly society, & verbal converse with us, all, or some one, or any of you, O all ye Benevolent Angels or Angelical powers of the Air, Celestially dignified, set over the fourth Quarter part of the North Angle, Jaom, Aomi, Omia, Miao, In by and through this[810] great & powerful name of your God Niaom[811], and the signal virtue thereof, Move therefore we say, O ye Benevolent Angels or Angelical powers of the Air, Celestially dignified and placed in orders as aforesaid, Jaom, Aomi, Omia, Miao, And in this powerful name of your God Niaom, Either some one, or all, or any of you, Descend, appear, and visibly show your selves unto the sight of our Eyes in this Crystal Glass or otherwise out of the same visibly here before us, as the pleasure of the Highest, and you his messengers of divine grace & permission, shall seem best, and most fit or requisite for us both now & at all times hereafter, speaking plainly and showing forth unto us by verbal converse whatsoever is given you by office, to declare, discover, and make known, for the Benefit of his servants the sons of men, Move therefore we say, & by the signal virtue and power of all aforesaid, Descend, appear, and some one, or all, or any of you, visibly show your selves here before us, and be friendly unto us; Open the mysteries of your Creation, and make us partakers of undefiled knowledge, whereunto we move you, both in power and presence, whose works shall be a song of Honour, and the praise of your God in your Creation Amen.

Invocation or Key, moving & calling forth to visible appearance, the four Angelical powers of Light or dignified spirits of the Air Mesad, Jaba, Jezexpe, Estim, by the great name of God Espemenir, And also to do what they are commanded (according to their offices) by

---

[809] S2: This section is crossed through, thus: "~~the knitting together of natures and also as well the destruction of nature and of things that may perish as of conjoining and knitting them together~~".

[810] S2: "~~this~~".

[811] S1: Gives "Niam" as the name here but it is clearly a copyist's error.

the name of God Hpizod, serving and set under the 4th Lesser Angle or Quarter part of the greater Quadrangle or Table of the North.

O Ye Angels of Light, or dignified Spirits of the Air Mesad, Jaba, Jezexpe, Estim, serving in orders, under Superior Angelical powers your most high God by his great name Espemenir, and doing all his Commandments by his great name Hpizod, as being set under, and Servient Spirits in the fourth Lesser Angle or division of the Region or greater Angle of the North, unto which is given of the Highest by office, the true knowledge (* of all Elemental creatures[812] &c,) of physick in all its parts, and the curing of all diseases whatsoever that are incident to Human bodies[813], And to reveal show forth, and give the same to mankind living on Earth, whensoever you shall be called or moved thereunto, by visible appearance and verbal converse, We the servants of the most high God, do Invocate, adjure, move, & call forth to visible appearance, friendly society, and verbal converse with us, all, or some one, or any of you, O all ye Angelical powers of Light or dignified Spirits of the Air set under, & serving in the Fourth Quarter part of the North Angle Mesad, Jaba, Jezexpe, Estim, In by and through, this powerful & great name of your God Espemenir, and also to do for us whatsoever we shall request and command you, by this great name of your God Hpizod, and by the signal virtues of them, Move therefore we say O all ye Benevolent powers or dignified Spirits of the Air, placed in orders as aforesaid Mesad, Jaba, Jezexpe, Estim, Either some one or all, or any of you, Descend appear and visibly show your selves unto the sight of our Eyes in this Crystal Glass or otherwise out of the same visibly here before us, as the pleasure of the Highest shall seem best, and most fit or requisite for us, both now and at all times hereafter, speaking plainly and showing forth unto us by verbal converse, whatsoever is given you by office to declare, discover and make known for the benefit of his servants the sons of men. Move therefore we say, & by the signal virtue and power of this great name of your God Espemenir, Descend, appear, & some one, or all, or any of you, visibly show your selves here before us, in manner and form as it shall please God & you his Messengers of Celestial grace, accordingly as aforesaid, And is this great name of your God Hpizod be friendly unto us, and do for us in whatsoever we shall command you, Effectually fulfilling all our desires according to your

---

[812] S2: Inserts "amongst us, how many kinds & their use in the Creation as they are severally placed in the 4 Elements".
[813] S2: This section is crossed through, thus: "~~of physick in all its parts and the curing of all diseases whatsoever that are incident to human bodies~~".

offices opening the mysteries of your Creation and make us partakers of undefiled knowledge whereunto we move you both in power & presence whose works shall be a song of Honour, and the praise of your God in your Creation Amen.

Janua Meridienalis Reserata

or the Key opening and giving[814] Entrance into the Region, Angle, or division of the South.

Invocation or Key, moving & calling forth to visible appearance the 6 Angelical Seniors of the South Aaetpio, Adocoet, Alendood, Aapedoce, Arinnaquu, Anodoin, by the great and mighty name EDELPERNA.

O Ye glorious Angels or Angelical Seniors, Celestially dignified Aaetpio, Adocoet, Alendood, Aapedoce, Arinnaquu, Anodoin, Serving before the great and mighty Angel, or Angelical monarch EDELPERNA, In the mansion, Region, Angle or division of the South, unto whom is given of the Highest, by office Scientiam, Rerum, Humanarum et Judicium, And to declare, show forth, & reveal the same unto mankind living on Earth, whensoever you shall be called or moved thereunto by visible appearance & verbal converse. We the servants of the most high God, do Invocate, adjure, move & call you forth, to visible appearance, friendly society, and verbal converse with us, All, or some one, or any of you, O all ye Celestially dignified Angels or Benevolent Angelical Seniors of the South Aaetpio, Adocoet, Alendood, Aapedoce, Arinnaquu, Anodoin, In by and through, this mighty powerful, great & Royal name EDELPERNA, and the most Imperial Efficacy and virtue thereof, Move therefore we say, O all ye Benevolent Angels or Angelical Seniors of the South Aaetpio, Adocoet, Alendood, Aapedoce, Arinnaquu, Anodoin, And in this Royal & mighty name EDELPERNA, either some one, or all, or any of you, Descend, appear, and visibly show your selves unto the sight of our Eyes, in this Crystal Glass or otherwise out of the same, visibly here before us, as the pleasure of the Highest, and you his messengers of divine grace, shall seem best and most fit or requisite for us both now, & at all times hereafter, speaking plainly & showing forth unto us, by verbal converse, whatsoever is given you by office, to declare, discover, & make known, for the benefit of his servants the sons of men, Move therefore we say, and by the signal virtue & power of all aforesaid, Descend, appear, and some one, or all, or any of you, visibly show your selves here before us, and be friendly unto us,

---

[814] S2: "given".

Open the mysteries of your creation, & make us partakers of undefiled knowledge, whereunto we move you, both in power and presence, whose works shall be a song of Honour, and the praise of your God in your Creation Amen.

Invocation or Key, moving & calling forth to visible appearance, the four Angels or Angelical powers of the Air, Celestially dignified Dopa, Opad, Pado, Adop, by the great name of God Bedopa, governing & set over the first Lesser Angle or Quarter of the great Quadrangle or Table of the South.

O Ye Benevolent Angels or Angelical powers of the Air Celestially dignified Dopa, Opad, Pado, Adop, serving your God Bedopa, as governing & set over the first Lesser Angle or division, of the Region, or greater Angle of the South, unto whom is given of the Highest by office the true knowledge of the knitting together of natures and also as well the destruction of nature and of things that may perish, as of conjoining and knitting them together, And to declare, show forth, and reveal [815] the same unto mankind living on Earth, whensoever you shall be called or moved thereunto, by visible appearance, & verbal converse. We the servants of the most high God, do Invocate, adjure, move & call forth to visible appearance, friendly society and verbal converse with us, all, or some one, or any of you, O all ye Benevolent Angels or Angelical powers of the Air, Celestially dignified, set over the first Quarter part of the South Angle Dopa, Opad, Pado, Adop, In by and through, this great & powerful name of your God Bedopa, and the signal virtue thereof, Move therefore we say O ye Benevolent Angels or Angelical powers of the Air, Celestially dignified & placed in orders as aforesaid Dopa, Opad, Pado, Adop, And in this powerful name of your God Bedopa, either some one, or all, or any of you, Descend, appear, & visibly show your selves unto the sight of our Eyes, in this Crystal Glass or otherwise out of the same, visibly here before us, as the pleasure of the Highest & you his messengers of divine grace & permission, shall seem best and most fit or requisite for us, both now & at all times hereafter, speaking plainly & showing forth unto us, by verbal converse, whatsoever is given you by office to declare, discover, and make known, for the benefit of his servants the sons of men, Move therefore, we say and by the signal virtue & power of all aforesaid, Descend, appear and some one, or all, or any of you, visibly show your selves here before us, & be friendly unto us, open the

---

[815] S2: "&".

mysteries of your Creation, & make us partakers of undefiled knowledge, whereunto we move you, both in power and presence, whose works shall be a song of Honour, and the praise of your God in your Creation Amen.

Invocation or Key, moving & calling forth to visible appearance, the four Angelical powers of Light or dignified spirits of the Air Opemen, Apeste, Scio, Vasge, by the great name of God Noalmar, and also to do, what they are commanded (according to their offices) by the name of God Oloag, serving & set under the first Lesser Angle, or Quarter part of the greater Quadrangle or Table of the South.

O Ye Angels of Light or dignified Spirits of the Air Opemen, Apeste, Scio, Vasge, serving in orders under Superior Angelical powers your most high God, by his great name Noalmar, and doing all his commandments by his great name Oloag, as being set under, & servient spirits in the first Lesser Angle, or division of the Region or greater Angle of the South, unto which is given of the Highest by office, The true knowledge of physick in all its parts, & the curing of all Diseases whatsoever, that are Incident to Human bodies, And to reveal, show forth, & give the same to mankind living on Earth, whensoever you shall be called, or moved thereunto by visible appearance and verbal converse. We the servants of the most high God, do Invocate, adjure move, & call forth to visible appearance, friendly society and verbal converse with us, all, or some one, or any of you, O all ye Angelical powers of Light, or dignified Spirits of the Air, set under, and serving, in the first Quarter part of the South Angle, Opemen, Apeste, Scio, Vasge, In by and through, this powerful and great name of your God Noalmar, And also do for us whatsoever we shall request and Command you, by this great name of your God Oloag, & by the signal virtues of them, Move therefore we say O all ye Benevolent powers or dignified Spirits of the Air, placed in order as aforesaid Opemen, Apeste, Scio, Vasge, Either some one, or all, or any of you, Descend, appear, & visibly show your selves unto the sight of our Eyes in this Crystal Glass or otherwise out of the same visibly here before us as the pleasure of the Highest shall seem best, and most fit or requisite for us both now and at all times hereafter, speaking plainly and showing forth unto us by verbal converse, whatsoever is given you by office to declare, discover, & make known for the benefit of his servants the sons of men, Move therefore we say, and by signal virtue and power of this great name of your God Noalmar, Descend, appear, and some one, or all, or any of you, visibly show your selves here before us, In manner & form as it shall please God, and you his messengers of Celestial grace accordingly as aforesaid, And in this great name of your God Oloag, be friendly unto us, and do for us, in whatsoever we shall command you, Effectually fulfilling all our desires according to your offices, Opening the mysteries of your Creation, and make us partakers of undefiled knowledge whereunto we move you both in power & presence, whose works shall be a song of Honour, and the praise of your God in your Creation Amen.

Invocation or Key, moving & calling forth to visible appearance, the four Angels, or Angelical powers of the Air, Celestially Dignified Anaa, Naaa[816], Aaan, Aana, by the great name of God Banaa, governing and set over the Second Lesser Angle or Quarter of the great Quadrangle or Table of the South.

O Ye Benevolent Angels or Angelical powers of the Air Celestially dignified Anaa, Naaa, Aaan, Aana, serving your God Banaa, as governing & set over the Second Lesser Angle or division of the Region or greater Angle of the South, unto whom is given of the Highest by office, the true knowledge of (* Moving from place to place [817],) the knitting together of natures, & also as well the destruction of nature and of things that may perish, as of conjoining & knitting them together[818], And to declare, show forth, and reveal the same unto mankind living on Earth, whensoever you shall be called or moved thereunto by visible appearance & verbal converse. We the servants of the most high God, do Invocate, adjure, move, & call forth to visible appearance, friendly society, & verbal converse with us, all, or some one, or any of you, O all ye Benevolent Angels or Angelical powers of the Air, Celestially dignified, set over the Second Quarter part of the South Angle Anaa, Naaa, Aaan, Aana, In by & through this great & powerful name of your God Banaa, and the signal virtue thereof, Move therefore we say, O ye Benevolent Angels or Angelical powers of the Air, Celestially dignified & placed in orders as aforesaid, Anaa, Naaa, Aaan, Aana, And in this powerful name of your God Banaa, Either some one, or all, or any of you, Descend, appear, and visibly show your selves unto the sight of our Eyes, in this Crystal Glass or

---

[816] S1: Gives this name as "Maaa", but this is clearly a copyist's error as it is "Naaa" in the following invocation.
[817] S2: Inserts "as into this or that Country at will & pleasure".
[818] S2: This section is crossed through, thus: "~~and the knitting together of natures and also as well the destruction of nature and of things that may perish, as of conjoining and knitting them together~~".

otherwise out of the same, visibly here before us, as the pleasure of the Highest, and you his messengers of divine grace & permission, shall seem best, & most fit, or requisite for us, both now & at all times hereafter, speaking plainly and showing forth unto us by verbal converse whatsoever is given you by office, to declare, discover, & make known for the Benefit of his servants the sons of men, Move therefore we say, and by the signal virtue and power of all aforesaid, Descend, appear, & some one, or all, or any of you, visibly show your selves here before us & be friendly unto us, Open the Mysteries of your Creation, and make us partakers of undefiled knowledge, whereunto we move you both in power and presence, whose works shall be a song of Honour, and the praise of your God in your Creation Amen.

Invocation or Key, moving & calling forth to visible appearance, the four Angelical powers of Light, or dignified spirits of the Air Gemenem, Ecope, Amox, Berape, by the great name of God Vadali, and also to do, what they are commanded (according to their Offices) by the name of God Obavi, serving & set under, the second Lesser Angle or Quarter part of the greater Quadrangle or Table of the South.

O Ye Angels of Light, or Dignified Spirits of the Air Gemenem, Ecope, Amox, Berape, serving in orders under Superior Angelical powers, your most high God, by his great name Vadali, and doing all his Commandments by his great name Obavi, as being set under, and servient Spirits, in the second Lesser Angle, or division of the Region or greater Angle of the South, unto whom is given of the Highest by office, the true knowledge of (* finding[819] & use of the Metals &c[820],) physick in all its parts, and the curing of all diseases whatsoever that are incident to Human bodies[821], And to reveal, show forth, and give the same to mankind living on Earth, whensoever you shall be called or moved thereunto by visible appearance, and verbal converse, We the servants of the most high God, do Invocate, adjure, & call forth to visible appearance, friendly society, & verbal converse with us, all, or some one, or any of you, O all ye Angelical powers of Light, or dignified Spirits of the Air, set under & serving, in the second Quarter part of the South Angle,

---

[819] S2: Inserts "out".
[820] S2: Omits "&c" and inserts "& the Congelation of Stones, Use & Virtue of all Stones".
[821] S2: This section is crossed out, thus: "physick in all its parts and the curing of all diseases whatsoever that are incident to Human Bodies".

Gemenem, Ecope, Amox, Berape, In, by, & through this powerful & great name of your God Vadali, And also do for us, whatsoever we shall request & command you, by this great name of your God Obavi, & by the signal virtues of them, Move therefore we say, O all ye Benevolent powers, or dignified Spirits of the Air, placed in orders as aforesaid Gemenem, Ecope, Amox, Berape, Either some one, or all, or any of you, Descend, appear, & visibly show your selves, unto the sight of our Eyes in this Crystal Glass or otherwise out of the same visibly here before us, as the pleasure of the Highest shall seem best, and most fit or requisite for us, both now, and at all times hereafter, speaking plainly, & showing forth unto us by verbal converse, whatsoever is given you by office to declare, discover, and make known, for the benefit of his servants the sons of men, Move therefore we say, and by the signal virtue & power of this great name of your God Vadali, Descend, appear, and some one, or all, or any of you, visibly show your selves here before us in manner and form as it shall please God and you his messengers of Celestial grace accordingly as aforesaid, And in this great name of your God Obavi, be friendly unto us, & do for us in whatsoever we shall command you, effectually fulfilling all our desires according to your offices, opening the mysteries of your Creation, & make us partakers of undefiled Knowledge[822] whereunto we move you both in power & presence, whose works shall be a Song of Honour, and the praise of your God in your Creation Amen.

Invocation, or Key, moving & calling forth to visible appearance, the four Angels or Angelical powers of the Air Celestially Dignified Pesac, Sacepe, Acepes, Cepesa, by the great name of God Bepesac, governing and set over the Third Lesser Angle or Quarter of the great Quadrangle or Table of the South.

O Ye Benevolent Angels or Angelical powers of the Air, Celestially dignified Pesac, Sacepe, Acepes, Cepesa, serving your God Bepesac, as governing and set over the Third Lesser Angle or division of the Region or greater Angle of the South, unto whom is given of the Highest by office, the true knowledge of (* All Mechanical Crafts whatsoever,) the knitting together of natures, and also as well the destruction of nature, and of things that may perish, as of

---

[822] S1: The word "knowledge" is repeated here.

conjoining and knitting them together [823], And to declare, show forth, and reveal the same unto mankind living on Earth, whensoever you shall be called or moved thereunto by visible appearance & verbal converse, We the servants of the most high God, do Invocate, adjure, move & call forth to visible appearance, friendly society, and verbal converse with us all, or some one, or any of you, O all ye Benevolent Angels or Angelical powers of the Air, Celestially dignified, set over the Third Quarter part of the South Angle Pesac, Sacepe, Acepes, Cepesa, In by and through, this great and powerful name of your God Bepesac, and the signal virtue thereof, Move therefore we say, O ye Benevolent Angels or Angelical powers of the Air Celestially dignified and placed in orders as aforesaid, Pesac, Sacepe, Acepes, Cepesa, And in this powerful name of your God Bepesac, either some one, or all, or any of you, Descend, appear, and visibly show your selves unto the sight of our Eyes, in this Crystal Glass or otherwise out of the same, visibly here before us, as the pleasure of the Highest, and you his messengers of divine grace & permission shall seem best, and most fit or requisite for us, both now and at all times hereafter, speaking plainly unto us, and showing forth by verbal converse, whatsoever is given you by office to declare, discover, and make known for the benefit of his servants the sons of men, Move therefore we say, & by the signal virtue & power of all aforesaid, Descend, appear, & some one, or all, or any of you, visibly show your selves here before us, and be friendly unto us, open the mysteries of your Creation and make us partakers of undefiled knowledge, whereunto we move you both in power & presence, whose works shall be a song of Honour, and the praise of your God in your Creation Amen.

Invocation or Key, moving and calling forth, to visible appearance, the four Angelical powers of Light or dignified spirits of the Air Datete, Diom, Oopezod, Vrgan, by the great name of God [824] Volexdo, and also to do what they are commanded (according to their offices) by the name of God Sioda, serving and set under the Third Lesser Angle or Quarter part of the great Quadrangle or Table of the South.

O Ye Angels of Light, or dignified Spirits of the Air Datete, Diom, Oopezod, Vrgan, serving in orders under superior Angelical powers,

---

[823] S2: This section is crossed through, thus: "~~the knitting together of natures, and also as well the destruction of nature and of things that may perish as of conjoining and knitting them together~~".
[824] S2: "* ~~Sioda~~".

your most high God, by his great name Volexdo, And doing all his Commandments by his great name Sioda, as (governing) or being set under, & servient Spirits, in the Third Lesser Angle, of the Region, or greater Angle of the South, unto which[825] is given of the Highest by office, the true knowledge of (* Transformation & transplantation,) physick in all its parts, and the curing of all diseases whatsoever that are Incident to human bodies[826], And to reveal, show forth & give the same, to mankind living on Earth, whensoever you shall be called[827] or moved thereunto by visible appearance and verbal converse, We the servants of the most high God, do Invocate, adjure, move, & call forth to visible appearance, friendly society & verbal converse with us, all, or some one, or any of you, O all ye Angelical powers of Light or dignified Spirits of the Air, set under, and serving in the Third Quarter part of the South Angle, Datete, Diom, Oopezod, Vrgan, In by and through, this powerful and great name of your God Volexdo, and also do for us, whatsoever we shall request and command you by this great name of your God Sioda, and by the signal virtues of them, Move therefore we say, O all ye Benevolent powers of the Air, Celestially dignified & placed in orders as aforesaid Datete, Diom, Oopezod, Vrgan, either some one, or all, or any of you, Descend, appear, & visibly show your selves unto the sight of our Eyes in this Crystal Glass or otherwise out of the same, visibly here before us, as the pleasure of the Highest, shall seem best, and most fit or requisite for us, both now, and at all times hereafter, speaking plainly, & showing forth unto us by verbal converse whatsoever is given you by office to declare, discover, and make known for the benefit of his servants the sons of men, Move therefore we say, & by the signal virtue and power of this great name of your God Volexdo, Descend, appear, and some one, or all, or any of you, visibly show your selves here before us, in manner & form as it shall please God, and you his messengers of Celestial grace, accordingly as aforesaid. And in this great name of your God Sioda, be friendly unto us, and do for us in whatsoever we shall command you, Effectually fulfilling all our desires according to your offices, Opening the mysteries of your Creation, and make us partakers of undefiled knowledge whereunto we move you, both in power and presence whose works shall be a song of Honour, and the praise of your God in your Creation Amen.

---

[825] S2: "whom".
[826] S2: This section is crossed through, thus: "~~physick in all its parts, and the curing of all diseases whatsoever that are incident to human bodies~~".
[827] S2: "~~or~~".

Invocation or Key, moving & calling forth, to visible appearance, the four Angels or Angelical powers of the Air Celestially Dignified Ziza, Izaz, Zazi, Aziz, by the great name of God BEZIZA, governing & set over the fourth Lesser Angle or Quarter of the great Quadrangle or Table of the South.

O Ye Benevolent Angels or Angelical powers of the Air Celestially dignified Ziza, Izaz, Zazi, Aziz, serving your God Beziza, as governing & set over the fourth Lesser Angle or division of the Region or greater Angle of the South, unto whom is given of the Highest by office, the true knowledge of (* The secrets of men Knowing,) the knitting together of natures, and also as well the destruction of nature and of things that may perish as of conjoining and knitting them together[828], And to declare, show forth, & reveal the same unto mankind living on Earth, whensoever you shall be called or moved thereunto, by visible appearance & verbal converse. We the servants of the most high God, do Invocate, adjure, move & call forth to visible appearance, friendly society & verbal converse with us, all, or some one, or any of you, O all ye Benevolent Angels, or Angelical powers of the Air, Celestially dignified, set over the fourth Quarter part of the South Angle, Ziza, Izaz, Zazi, Aziz, In by and through, this great & powerful name of your God Beziza, and the signal virtue thereof, Move therefore, we say, O ye Benevolent Angels or Angelical powers of the Air, Celestially dignified, and placed in orders as aforesaid, Ziza, Izaz, Zazi, Aziz, And in this powerful name of your God Beziza, either some one, or all, or any of you, Descend, appear, & visibly show your selves unto the sight of our Eyes in this Crystal Glass or otherwise out of the same visibly here before us, as the pleasure of the Highest & you his messengers of divine grace & permission, shall seem best and most fit or requisite for us, both now, and at all times hereafter, speaking plainly and showing forth unto us by verbal converse, whatsoever is given you by office, to declare, discover, & make known for the benefit of his servants the sons of men, Move therefore we say, & by the signal virtue and power of all aforesaid, Descend, appear, and some one, or all, or any of you, visibly show your selves here before us, & be friendly unto us, open the mysteries of your Creation, and make us partakers of undefiled Knowledge whereunto we move you both in power and presence, whose works shall be a song of Honour and the praise of your God in your Creation Amen.

---

[828] S2: This section is crossed through, thus: "~~the knitting together of natures and also as well the destruction of nature and of things that may perish as of conjoining and knitting them together~~".

Invocation or Key, moving and calling forth to visible appearance, the four Angelical powers of Light or dignified spirits of the Air Adre, Sispe, Pali, Acar, by the great name of God Arzodionar, and also to do, what they are commanded (according to their offices) by the name of God Narzefem, serving and set under, the fourth Lesser Angle or Quarter part of the greater Quadrangle or Table of the South.

O Ye Angels of Light or dignified Spirits of the Air Adre, Sispe, Pali, Acar, serving in orders under superior Angelical powers, your most high God by his great name Arzodionar, and doing all his Commandments by his great name Narzefem, as being set under, & servient spirits, in the fourth Lesser Angle, or division of the Region or greater Angle of the South, unto whom is given of the Highest by office, the true knowledge (* Of all Elemental creatures &c[829],) of physick in all its parts, and the curing of all diseases whatsoever that are Incident to Human bodies[830], and to reveal, show forth and give the same to mankind living on Earth, whensoever you shall be called or moved thereunto by visible appearance & verbal converse. We the servants of the most high God, do Invocate, adjure, move, and call forth to visible appearance, friendly society and verbal converse with us, all or some one, or any of you, O all ye Angelical powers of the Air or dignified Spirits of Light, set under and serving in the fourth Quarter part of the South Angle, Adre, Sispe, Pali, Acar, In by and through this powerful & great name of your God Arzodionar, And also to do for us, whatsoever we shall request and command you by this great name of your God Narzefem, and by the signal virtues of them, Move therefore we say: O all ye Benevolent powers, or dignified Spirits of the Air, placed in orders as aforesaid Adre, Sispe, Pali, Acar, Either some one, or all, or any of you, Descend, appear, and visibly show your selves unto the sight of our Eyes in this Crystal Glass or otherwise out of the same, visibly here before us, as the pleasure of the Highest shall seem best and most fit or requisite for us, both now and at all times hereafter, speaking plainly and showing forth unto us by verbal converse, whatsoever is given you by office to declare, discover & make known for the benefit of his servants the sons of men, Move therefore, we say, and

---

[829] S2: Omits "&c" and inserts "amongst us, how many kinds & their use in the Creation, as they are severally placed in the 4 Elements Air, Water, Earth, & Fire".
[830] S2: This section is crossed out, thus: "~~of physick in all its parts, and the curing of all diseases whatsoever that are incident to human bodies~~".

by the signal virtue and power of this great name of your God Arzodionar, Descend appear, and some one, or all, or any of you, visibly show your selves here before us, in manner and form as it shall please God and you his messengers of Celestial grace accordingly as aforesaid, And in this great name of your God Narzefem, be friendly unto us, and do for us in whatsoever we shall command you, Effectually fulfilling all our desires according to your offices, opening the mysteries of your Creation, and make us partakers of undefiled Knowledge, whereunto we move you both in power and presence, whose works shall be a Song of Honour, and the praise of your God in your Creation, Amen.

[This is the end of Sloane MS 307. The following text is taken from Sloane MS 3821]

Humble Supplication to Almighty God[831]

       Enter not into Judgement with thy Servant O God, neither in thine Anger take vengeance on our Iniquities, nor chastise us in thy heavy displeasure, but spare us O Lord, be merciful unto us, pardon & forgive us all our sins, & confirm us in thy holy Spirit.

The Lord bless us, & keep us.

The Lord make his face shine upon us; & be gracious unto us.

The Lord lift up his Countenance upon us, and give us peace.

Our Father which art in Heaven, hallowed by thy Name, thy Kingdom come, thy Will be done in Earth, as it is in Heaven, give us this day our daily bread, & forgive us our Trespasses, as we forgive them that trespass against us, & lead us not into Temptation, but deliver us from Evil; for thine is the Kingdome, the power & the glory, for ever & ever, Amen.

O Lord arise, help us & deliver us, for thy Names sake.

O God we have heard with our Ears, & our fathers have declared unto us, the noble, great & wonderful works, that thou hast done in their days, & in the old time before them.

We are thy people & the Sheep of thy Flock, therefore graciously hear us our humble supplications, O God, & grant our Petitions, & let thy mercy be shewed upon us, as our trust is in thee.

Glory be to the Father, & to the Son, & to the Holy Ghost; as it was in the beginning, is now and ever shall be, world without end, Amen.

O Lord shew thy mercy upon us,
And grant us thy Salvation.
From our enemies defend us O God,
And graciously look upon our Afflictions;
Pitifully behold the Sorrows of our hearts
And mercifully forgive us our Transgressions;
O Lord deal not with us after our sins,
Neither reward us after our Iniquities,

---

[831] This prayer and the one following are in the hand of Elias Ashmole, from Sloane MS 3821, folio 188-193. They were obviously intended to be used before skrying sessions.

O God make clean our hearts within us,
And take not thy holy Spirit from us,
Favourably with mercy hear our Prayers,
And let our Cry come unto thee.

Glory be to the Father, & to the Son, & to the holy Ghost;
As it was in the beginning, is now & ever shall be, world without
end, Amen.

Almighty God, who hatest nothing that thou hast made, & dost
forgive the Sins of all them that be penitent; Create & make in us,
new & contrite hearts, that we by unfeigned Repentance, lamenting
our Sins, & acknowledging our wretchedness, may obtain of thee
God of all mercy, perfect remission & forgiveness; & grant O Lord,
that we which for our evil deeds are rightly punished, by the
Comfort of thy Grace, may mercifully be relieved, through Jesus
Christ our Lord Amen.

O God merciful Father, that despiseth not the sighing of a contrite
heart, nor the desires of those that be sorrowful, mercifully assist &
accept these our prayers, & supplications, which we make before
thee, in all our troubles & adversities, whensoever they oppress us;
& defend us against all assaults of our Enemies whatsoever, that we
surely trusting in thy defence, may not fear the power of any
adversaries; & so dispose our ways O Lord, that among all the
changes & chances of this mortal life, we may ever be defended, by
thy most gracious & ready help, relief, succour & protection; &
grant O merciful God, that those Evils, which the craft & subtlety of
the Devil, or man worketh against us, may be confounded &
brought to nothing; and that we thy servants, being mercifully
defended, by thy mighty power may incessantly give praise &
thanks unto you, to the glory of thy holy Name, Amen.

Almighty God, who hast prepared, for all those that unfeignedly put
their trust in thee, such good things as do pass the understanding
of man; mercifully distil into our hearts, the Oil of Celestial
Inspiration, that we may be endowed with true Wisdom, & have a
right Judgement in all things, & may both prescribe & know what
things we ought to do, & also to be capable presently to effect the
same; & that these things which for our unworthiness we dare not,
& for our blindness we cannot ask, vouchsafe graciously to bestow
upon us, through Jesus Christ our Lord, Amen.

Almighty God, which art always more ready to hear, than we are to
pray, & art wont to guide, more than we can desire or deserve, we

humbly beseech thee, mercifully to have compassion upon our Infirmities; & for the glory of thy names sake, turn us from us all those Evils that we most righteously have deserved, and grant that in all our troubles, we may put our whole trust & confidence in thy mercy; & that the working of thy Grace, may in all things direct & rule our hearts, & drive away all filthy & unclean pollutions from this place, forgiving us those things whereof our Consciences are afraid, & giving unto us, that which our unworthiness dare not presume to ask, through the mercy[?] of Jesus Christ our Saviour & redeemer, Amen.

Almighty God, who hast promised to hear the petitions of them that ask in thy Son's Name, we humbly beseech thee mercifully to incline thy gracious ear, unto these our unfeigned supplications, which in all obedience we ever penitently make unto thee, & grant that those things which we have faithfully begged of thee, we may by thy fatherly goodness & permission fully obtain, to the setting forth of thy honour & glory, & the relief of our necessities, through Jesus Christ our Lord Amen.

O Lord from whom all holy desires, all good Counsels & all just works do proceed, give unto us thy humble servants, here obediently present in thy holy fear, on the Knees of humility & obedience, that grace which your world cannot give, that we may always enjoy & be comforted in thy merciful benignities, bless, guide keep protect & defend us from all evils, graciously illuminate us with true Wisdom, & fill us with thy spiritual benedictory & heavenly grace, that we may live in thy fear, & die in thy favour, & after this life, to live with thee in thine everlasting Kingdom, unto whom, & with thy Son Jesus Christ, & the Holy Ghost, be all honour glory praise & thanksgiving for ever & ever, Amen.

Enoch Prayer

O Almighty, Immortal, Immense, Incomprehensible, & most high God & Lord of Hosts, Jehovah, the only Creator of Heaven & Earth, & all things contained therein, who in thy wonderful & great work of the Creation, hast miraculously [ap]pointed out many Hierarchies, of sacred Celestial Angels & blessed Intelligences, and placed them in a most admirable order above the fiery Region; & also many other Hierarchies & Orders dignified, Elemental Ministering Spirits, or Angelical powers of Light, under the same &c: and hast appointed them all to serve thee, & obey thy commands, in every & each of their several & respective places, natures, orders & offices; & by thy gracious & divine permission, to move descend & visibly appear, unto the sons of men dwelling on Earth, whensoever they shall Invocate or call them forth, to their conduct, comfort & benefit, O thou omnipotent & perpetual full flowing fountain of eternal life, light, majesty, power, glory, goodness, clemency & paternal bounty, & of all wisdom & true knowledge, both Celestial & Terrestrial, descending by certain Rivers[?] of mercy, immediately by the holy Ghost, unto more choice & peculiar vessels of honour, & by emanations of divine Grace, immediately by the sacred Celestial Angels or blessed Intelligences to the ministering Angels, or spiritual Messengers, and medium of Light, in & by thee subjected but dignified, both Celestial & Elemental, of several & respective degrees, names, natures, orders & offices, by whose Angelical Inspiration & instruction, thou dost fatherly and freely, open the secrets of thy own self unto Man, thereby showing forth, the mystery of true Science & sapience, with its benefits & comforts, to be obtained & received in mundane affairs, & temporal Concerns &c: O most high God & father of heaven, thou knows the foundation of our fragility, our imperfect- ions, & the darkness & weakness of our inward parts, how can we therefore speak unto them, that speak not after the voice of Man; or worthily call on thy name, considering that our imagination is variable & fruitless, & unknown to our selves: shall the Sands seem to imitate the Mountains, or can the small rivers, entertain the wonderful & unknown ways, can the vessels of fear, fragility, or that [which] is of a determinate proportion, pass up themselves, heave up their hands, or gather the Sun into their Bosoms, O Lord it cannot be. Our imaginations are great, we are less than sand; Lord thy good Angels scold us for, our proportions are not alike, our senses agreeth not, yet notwithstanding we are comforted for that we have all one God, all one beginning from thee, that we respect thee as a Creator; therefore will we call upon thy name, & in these will we become mighty; thou shalt light us, & we shall become Seers; we will see thy Creatures, & ever will magnify thee amongst them; those that come unto thee have the same gate, and through the same gate, defendeth such as thou sendest: we therefore humbly beseech thee, O Almighty & most merciful God, graciously to permit thy Celestial ministering Angels, & also the Elemental dignified Powers, or Messengers [of] spiritual of Light, to dwell with us & we with them, to rejoice with us & we with them, to minister unto us, that we may magnify thy great & glorious name, & by thy most gracious merciful & divine permission; that as thou art their Light & comfortest them; so they in thee will be our Light & Comfort. Lord they prescribe not Laws unto thee, so it is not meet that we should prescribe Laws unto them. What it pleaseth thee to offer, they receive; so what it pleaseth them to offer unto us, will we also thankfully receive. Behold Lord, if we shall call upon them in thy Name, be it unto us in mercy as unto thy Servants. O Lord, is there any[832] that measureth the Heavens that is mortal, how therefore can the Heavens enter into man's Imagination, thy Creatures are the glory of thy Countenance, whereby thou glorifiest all things, which glory excelleth, & is far above our understanding. Behold O Lord, how shall we therefore ascend into the Heavens; the Air will not carry us, bur resisteth our Folly, we fall down, because we are of the Earth, therefore O thou very light & true comfort, that canst and mayest & dost command the Heavens, hear us, & have mercy upon us, & grant our requests, which we humbly make unto thee, & that thou wouldst be so graciously glorified (by thy divine permission) to send all those Celestial & Elemental dignified Angelical powers of light, that we shall call upon by Orders Names & Offices, to appear visibly unto us in this crystal Stone or Glass Receptacle[833] standing here before us, & that in & through the same, they may transmit their true & real presence in appearance unto the sight of our Eyes, & their voices unto our Ears, that we may plainly see them & audibly hear them speak unto us, & verbally to converse & commune with us, & to inform instruct, show forth & teach us all such knowledge & Arcanum in nature, as shall be required by us, & necessary for us, & so be friendly unto us, & do for us as for thy servants, both now at this time present, & at all other times, whensoever, & wheresoever we shall move & call them forth, for instruction, relief, comfort & assistance, in whatsoever shall be necessary for us, &c: Enlighten therefore our Eyes O heavenly God, & open thou our Ears, that we may see thy

---

[832] S2: The word "thing" is crossed out in the text here.

[833] This classic phrase guarantees that the prayer was meant for use in invocation and skrying.

spiritual creatures, & have them speak unto us, quicken, illuminate & confirm in us, & unto us, our serious discretions, judgements understandings, memories & utterances, that we may be true & perfect Seers, Hearers & Witnesses of such things, which mediately by the ministry of thy sacred Celestial Angels & blessed Intelligences, & other elemental dignified Spirits or Messengers spiritual of Light, shall be manifested declared & showed forth unto us, both now & at all times whensoever necessity shall require their favourable & familiar society community and assistance, and now O all you sacred Celestial Angles & blessed Intelligences Ministers and true Light of understanding, & O you all Dignified Elemental Ministering Spirits or Angelical Powers of Light, governing this earthly fabric, & the Elements wherein we live, be friendly unto us, & do for us, as for the servants of the highest. And we further humbly beseech thee (O[834] God) herewith to guide our tongues Reasons Senses & Judgements, & give us eloquent utterances, gravity of speech, quickness of understanding, prudence in managing, temperance in pursuing, thankfulness in receiving, & grace in using all such Instructions Institutions, matters things or affairs, of what concern soever, that shall be revealed, showed forth or given by Angelical Ministry unto us, that all may be converted O Lord to thy honour & glory, & to our worldly comfort, & benefit.

Make us O Lord humble & obedient, without contradiction, proven [?] without quarrelling, chaste without corruption, patient without murmuring, merry without dissolution, sad without dejection, ripe[?] without unpleasantness, fearful without desperation, true without doubtfulness of heart, doing good things without presumption. Give us O Lord watchful hearts, that no envious or evil cogitations may lead us away from thee, give us noble & upright hearts, that no unworthy affection nor sinister intention may draw us downwards, give us invincible hearts, that no tribulation may overcome us, give us understanding truly to know thee, diligence to seek thee, evidence to find thee, conversation to please thee, perseverance faithfully to expect thee, & assured confidence to embrace thee, & after this life to live with thee, in thy everlasting Kingdom, where there is certain security, serene Eternity, eternal felicity, & most happy tranquillity, O merciful God, we humbly beseech thee to grant these our humble Supplications & petitions, which we unfainedly make unto thee. Behold O Lord be it unto us, as in mercy it pleaseth thee, & thy holy ministering Angels, we require nothing but thee & through thee & to thy honour, & glory. Amen.

---

[834] S2: The word "Lord" is crossed out here.

Appendix 1 – Angel Functions Table[835]

1   The knitting together
of Nature and also as
well the Destruction
of Nature, & of things
that may perish; as of
the Conjoining &
knitting them to-   lyeth
gether &c: lyeth &c: •   in the   {• first   {East
2. The   moving   from   four   {*second   {Lesser   {West   {Greater
place to place, as into   Angels   {⬚ third   {Angle   {North   {Quadr-
this or that Country,   set   {Δ fourth   {of the   {South   { angle
at will & pleasure,   over
lyeth &c: *   the
3. The knowledge of
Mechanicall Crafte
whatsoever, lyeth &c⬚
4. The   secrets   of   Men
knowing, lyeth &c: Δ

*Likewise the Offices of the subservient Angels in every of the
Lesser Angles are as followeth.*

1   The knowledge of
Physick in all its
parts, & the curing of
all diseases that are
incident to human
bodies. lyeth &c: •
2. The knowledge,
funding & use of   Lyeth
Metals, the   in   the
Congelation of Stones   4
& the virtue of all   Angels   {• first   {East
Stones, lyeth &c: *   serving   {*second   {Lesser   {West   {Greater
3. The knowledge of   to the   {⬚ third   {Angle   {North   {Quadr
Transformation,   {Δ fourth   {of the   {South   { -angle
Transplantation,
lyeth &c: ⬚
4. The knowledge of all
Elemental Creatures
amongst us, how
many kinds & their
use in the Creation, as
they are severally placed
in the 4 Elements, Air,
Water, Earth & Fire,
lyeth &c: Δ

---

[835] A note in Elias Ashmole's handwriting in the manuscript showing angel functions.

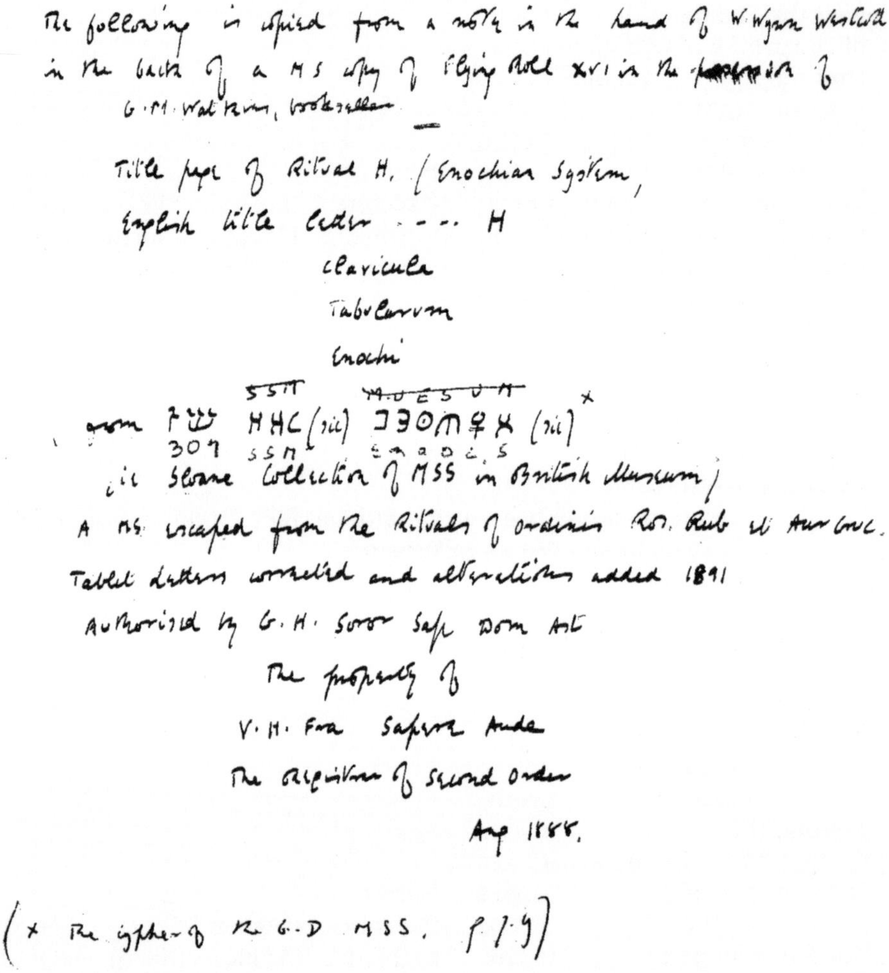

[Reproduction of handwritten note]

> The following is copied from a note in the hand of W Wynn Westcott in the back of a MS copy of Flying Roll XVI in the possession of G. M. Watkins, bookseller —
>
> Title page of Ritual H. (Enochian System,
>
> English title letter - - -- H
>
> Clavicula
>
> Tabularum
>
> Enochi
>
> from [symbols] HHC (ii) ƆƆOMΨX (ii)
>
> (in Sloane Collection of MSS in British Museum)
>
> A MS escaped from the Rituals of ordinis Ros. Rub. et Aur. Cruc.
>
> Tablet letters corrected and alterations added 1891
>
> Authorised by G. H. Soror Sapi Dom Ast
>
> The property of
>
> V. H. Fra Sapere Aude
>
> The acquisition of second Order
>
> Aug 1888.
>
> (× The cypher of the G. D. MSS. p. 1. 9)

A note in the back of the Golden Dawn Flying Roll XVI, *Book H,* in Gerald Yorke's handwriting.

268

Appendix 2 - Golden Dawn Book H: Clavicula Tabularum Enochi

From the front pages of Gardner's copy of *Book H*[836] it is clear that Wynn Westcott had seen and transcribed some of the material in Sloane MS 307 before August 1888, the date given in the document and that this material was subsequently copied from Gardner's copy seven years later. This early Golden Dawn paper from the collection of the late Gerald Yorke contains his note:

'The following is copied from a note in the hand of W. Wynn Westcott in the back of an MS copy of Flying Roll[837] XVI in possession of G[eoffrey] M. Watkins, bookseller.[838]

Title page of Ritual H. (Enochian System,
English title letter ---- H
Clavicula
Tabularum
Enochi

[Hebrew 'ShZ' and Golden Dawn cipher which is clearly translated by Yorke on opposite page]
i.e. Sloane Collection of MSS in British Museum[839]
A MS escaped from the Rituals of Ordinis Ros[ae] Rub[ae] et Aur[ae] Cru[cis]. Tablet Letters corrected and alterations added 1891.
Authorised by G[reatly] H[onoured] Soror Sap[iens] Dom[inabitur] Ast[ris].[840]

The property of
V[ery] H[onoured] Fra[ter] Sapere Aude[841]
The Registrar of [the] Second Order[842]
Aug[ust] 1888.
5=6 Taken from the Notebook of F. L. Gardner. Dated 5 June 1895.

The note on the title page is in Golden Dawn cipher characters, and says 'Sloane MS 307', confirming its source. Unfortunately for Golden Dawn members, less than 10% of the manuscript was transcribed, the rest being unavailable till now.

---

[836] Golden Dawn papers were designated with letters.
[837] Flying Rolls were the additional papers prepared for use by the Golden dawn for members in the higher grades. These papers were in part published by Francis King in his book *Astral Projection, Ritual Magic, and Alchemy,* Aquarian, 1971.
[838] Geoffrey Watkins was the founder of Watkins occult bookshop at Cecil Court, London, one of the two enduring occult booksellers in London, the other being the Atlantis bookshop, at 49a Museum Street.
[839] Now the British Library.
[840] Fräulein Sprengel.
[841] Wynn Westcott.
[842] Of the Golden Dawn.

H

Clavicula

Tabularum

Enochi

Escaped from the Order, mw = " 307 , s s ᴹ
ꜱ ꞇ ᴡ " א א @
ꜱ ɳ ᵃ ᵒ ᵉ ꜱ
) ꜰ ᴏ ᴄ ᖴ א

(5°) = [6°]

Cover Page of F. L. Gardner's copy of *Book H* showing the G.D. code for
'Sloane MSS' written backwards, and the Hebrew ShZ disguising '307'.

Appendix 3 – Angel Magic from Alan Bennett's Magical Diary

This reproduction of the Golden Dawn *Book H* is included for its historical value, as there is so little of Alan Bennett's material extant. It is interesting to note that the style has actually been changed to a deliberately *faux* antique style that is not reflected in the original manuscripts, or in F L Gardner's copy of *Book H*.[843]

Of the Opening and Exemplyfing of the Enochian Tablets

Here we have four Tables or Quadrangles which are but one generall Table, yette divided into foure partes, East, West, North and South. In the Center between these four Tablets is another little Tablet joined conveienlie to them alle, and which serveth to unite ye severall partes of ym together, accordinge as they are to be diversely referred, as shall be shewed hereafter.

Each single Quadrangular Table contayneth Twelve Squares athwarte by Thirteene Squares downwards: the two middle lines downwards that be of black letters enclosed between two black ruled lynes, and standing cross wise in ye middle of ye two middle perpendicular or upright Lynes make upp ye Name of ye Mity Angelicall Kynge; and Three Names of Godde: displayed in ye banners Regall which are borne before hym, beying ye armes of ye ensine, and ye Names of Sixe Angelicall Senyors governing in that Angle or Quarters of ye Compasse wch they are sette over. In every lesser Angle of every Table stande also black letters enclosed within black ruled lynes crosswise in ye forme of ye Crosse, out of wc are collected ye Names of Godde yt calle for the and make constrained those Angells and Spirits, both goode and bade yt are to bee gathered out of that particular Lesser Angle, belonging and serving to that Quarterlie Angle or Table.

---

[843] Alan Bennett copied the original form in one of his Golden Dawn notebooks between 1892 and 1894. This transcript was made from his MS in 1955. Errors have been kept in the script and the 'antique' style has been maintained exactly as the original.

2nd   3rd

The Names of the Six Great						F	A					
Angelic Seniors are drawne from						i	d					
the Centrall crosse						a	r					
of ye Table of Air						X	o					
in this way from the						a	t			Ahaozpi		4th Senior
center read backward.	o	R	o	i	b	A	H	A	o	z	p	i
Abioro, the first						u	i					
Senior. Habioro, same						t	p					
with 7 letters						o	o					
						T	t					
						a	g					
						r	a					

Autotar 6th.   5th Hipotga

The name of this Great Angelical and Mighty Angel, or King of ye East BATAIVAH upon whom all the Angels and Spirits of the Four Lesser Angles attend and give obedience, calleth forth the fore-recited Six Seniors, whose offices are to give Scientium Rerum Humanorum et Judicium according to the nature of their parts.

Now for the Sixteen Servient Angels next in order under the Six seniors in the eastern Quadrangle. Their names may be collected and composed out of each lesser Angle attendant on the greater Angle thus: - In the uppermost Lesser Angle on the left of this Quadrangle there is a small Cross of black letters whose perpendicular lyne goeth upwards from the black transverse line who goeth athwart the whole Quadrangle, upward to the top of the said lesser Angle, and containeth six letters from the Top downwards, which are I,d,o,i,g,o, making the name of God Idoigo the which is used to call forth ye subsequent good Angels, who are attendant next in order under those Sixteen Angels next succeeding the Six Seniors according to their graduation.

The Transverse line going athwart that line, making therewith the forme of ye Crosse is of five letters, and they make the Name of Godde Ardza: now those benevolent Angels which are called forth by the Name Idoigo are to be commended as to what they shall do by the Name Ardza.

This example is the form of the black letters as they stand crosswise in the uppermost Lower Angle of the Quadrangle: over this upper black transverse line are the four red letters r, z, l, a, leaving but the black letter of the Name of Godde Idoigo

r	Z	i	l	a	844
a	r	d	z	A	
		o			
		i			
		g			
		o			

and it maketh the name Urzla, wh[ich] is the substance of the Name of the first of those sixteen Angels spoken of, bearing rule under the Six Seniors in the eastern Quadrangle. Then take away the first of these four red letters and make it the last, and you will have the Name Zlar: which is to be pronounced Zodelar, for Z extended is to be pronounced zoD and this maketh the Name of the second of the aforesaid sixteen angels. Again make the first letter of the second Name the last of the Third, and the letters will be l a r z which maketh the name of the Third Angel Larzod. And in the same process is obtained the Name of the fourth Angel, Arzodel (? Arzoda T) and these four are the Superior Angels bearing rule under the Six Seniores in this first lesser Angle, serving to the Greater Eastern Quadrangle. And in the same manner that the names of these aforesaid four Angels are gathered from this lesser Angle, as are gathered the remaining Twelve Names from the other three lesser Angles.

Then the Names of the Angels subservient (? T) to these are read across the upright black cross, so that these lesser Angels are Cezodenes Totet Sias Epemande (? T). And the same rules are to be constantly applied.

Now as to the small Table, called the Tablet of Union: it sheweth how to join particular letters such as are contained therein to several Names and letters in each of the lesser Angles contained in each of the greater Angles of the Table in general for the collecting and making up of other particular for each proper and select material and intricate purpose as is to be exemplified.

The first line containeth the Letters E X A R P, which serves to bind together the Letters of the Great Table of the east. Observe that the name that stretchest from the Left to the Right must also stretch from the right to the left: observe also that the letters joining those names which may be put before the Names of the four Angels sitting

---

844 Note by copyist. Letters with a stop after them are red letters. Such letters should be enclosed in a square.

over each of every lesser angle, as well from the Right as from the Left, is the Name of God whereby those angels are called and do appear, as for example, the first letter of the first line of this small Tablet is e: The Name of the first Angel sitting over the first lesser Angle of the Eastern Quadrangle is Vrzla. Take away the letter V, being the first letter (added for to pronounce that name) and add instead the E of EXARP and you have Ersla erZla which is the Name of Godde wh governeth and calleth forth that Angel Urzodela, and also the other three Angels that are set over the first lesser Angle of the east Quadrangle. The Name of the first Angel sitting over the second lesser Angle is Utepa: then by adding the afore said letter e, there is obtained the Name Eutepa wh is the Name of God governing those four Angels sitting over the second lesser Angle of the east Quadrangle by which they are called forth and appear.

The Name of the first angel sitting over the third lesser Angle is CENBAR and therefore the Name ECENBAR governeth the four great Angles of that lesser Angle.

Similarly the Name of the first Angel sitting over the Fourth lesser angle is XEGEZODD, thence is obtained the Name EXEGEZOD wh is the Name of Godde governing the Angels of the Fourth Lesser Angle. And thus are gathered the four great Names of God governing those sixteen Angels bearing rule under the Six Angelical Seniors in this Eastern Quadrangle, and whereby they are called forth and do appear.

There are now left of the Word Exarp only the letters X a r p. Every name sounding of Three letters beginning out of the first line and out of these four letters are formed (sic T) the name of a devil or Angel of Evil: as well from the right as from the Left, excepting the lines containing the Names of the four great presiding Angels of each lesser Angle.

These latter are not thus to be made use of, as they contain not any participation in evil. For example. The four lines below the transverse bar of the small cross in the first lesser Quadrangle give the four names of certain subservient Angels as hath already been shewn. To any two contiguous of these letters add one of the letters X A R P from the Tablet of Union name Exarp: thus is formed the name of an evil spirit. Thus the first letters that can be so taken are C Z with which the aforesaid letter X maketh the name of the Evil Demon Xcez. And the next two letters are N S which with X maketh the name of the evil demon Xenes. Either of these names read backward maketh the name of another evil demon spirit

Zodecex, or Senex.[845]

The next letters below C Z are T.o and the next letter in the Tablet of Union is A, whence is made up the Name of the demon Ato but if added from right to left it will make another devil called Aot (sic T). And so on.

Having thus shewn the manner in which many of the Names may thus be collected and formed out of the Letters of the Mystic Tablets, we shall now proceed to exemplify in what manner the Angels Archangels and evil Spirits of these tablets may be called forth into visible appearance.

By the Three secret Names of God which are borne upon the Banners of the East
Oro Ibah Aozpi
shalt thou govern the Great King of the easte, whose Name is Bataivah. And this name of the King governeth the Six Seniores: it is by this Name that they are to be called forth to visible appearance.

The Names of god Erzla, Eutepa, Ecenbar, Exegezod govern respectively the fur angels placed over the four lesser angles of the Tablet of the East.

Then there is the middle black upright or perpendicular line in this first lesser Angle, subservient to the Quadrangle of the east, which maketh the name Idoigo, which ruleth the four subservient Angels that are under the black line athwart the lesser angle: by this name Idoigo shall these lesser Angels be called forth, and before its Power do they appear, and by the name Ardza they perform that which they are commanded, the like method is to be observed with the four lesser Angels of the angles of all the Quadrangles.

Now as to the evil Spirits before-mentioned these are governed by the Name of God which governeth the Angels subservientes: from part of whose names are the demons builded up. But to command and govern and invoke these Angels, it is necessary to pronounce the said names backwards. For example: In the first lesser Angle of the ~~Great Quadrature~~ Eastern Quadrangle the Sixteen Spirits are governed by the name Idoigo backwards, that is by the name

---

[845] This is an interesting correction from 'demon' to 'spirit.' Alan Bennett here added the note "these are not right, see next paragraph."

Oziodi, and by this Name are they to be called forth. And by the Name ~~Ardz~~ Ardza backwards that is Azrda, will they do as they are commanded. And similarly with all the groups of Sixteen evil Spirits in all the lesser Angles. With all these beings, the repetition of these Names is sufficient to invoke and govern them.

Now as to the general use and signification of the tables and of the Offices of the Angels and Spirits etc, and other remarkable observations: these Tables contain all human knowledge. They stretch to the knowledge of Solomon for out of that knowledge springeth physic: the findings and use of metals and the Virtues of them: congelations and virtues of stones (they are all of one Materium). The knowledge of all Elemental creatures amongst us, how many kinds there are, and for what use they were created.

Those that live in the Air, Water, Earth by themselves and of the property of Fire which is the secret of all things, but of those more particularly. The knitting together of Natures. ~~(Note in original: "By these Tables may be known the several Treasures of the waters, and the unknown caves of the North etc.)~~ The moving from place to place, as from this country unto that at pleasure lyeth in

4 Angels	First	lesser	East	
placed	second	Angle	West	Great Quadrangle
over the	third	of the	North	
	fourth		South	

The knowledge of all mechanical crafts whatever. The secrets of the knowledge of Men. And also the destruction of Nature and of things that may perish as of the enjoying and knitting them together etc. ~~Likewise the offices of the subservient angels in each of the lesser Angles are as followeth.~~[846]

Likewise the offices of the subservient Angels in each of the lesser Angles as followeth. The knowledge of physic in all its branches: the knowledge and finding and use of Metalls, the congelation of

---

[846] (Note in original: - "By these Tables may be known the several Treasures of the Waters, and the unknown caves of the Earth etc. As for example the subservient Angels in the Second Lesser Angle of every great Tablet and also the ministering servient Angels under them give the knowledge of the Finding and use of the Metals. The Benevolent Angels of that Order will offer the Passages of Earth unto the ~~Entrane~~ Entrance of the sons of Men (chiefly of serving) so that by the benevolent assistance of the Angels of Light they may plainly see and discover what treasure there are in the Earth. Both as to the natural Mines of the earth, and all manner of Treasure Trove.)

stones: Transformation, transplantation: the knowledge of all elemental creatures amongst us how many kinds there are of them and their use in creation as they are severally placed in the four elements Air Water Earth and Fire.

lyeth in	first		East	
The Four	second	lesser	West	Quadrangle.
Angels	third	Angle	North	
serving to the	fourth	of the	South	

Let the Philosopher prepare a book of very fine paper or Parchment and write very clearly therein the Invocations of the Names of God, and secondly of the Angels by the Names of God. Four days after the book is written the Magician must only call up the Names of God or rather the Lord of Hosts from the four Angles of the Compass. And fourteen days after he shall invoke the Angels by petition and by the tablet Names of God to which they are subservient. The fifteenth day he shall clothe himself in a white linen vestment and so cometh the Apparition of that Angelic Host. And afterwards it irks not to have the retirement, vesture book or special place etc.

In order to drive away an Evil Spirit guarding Treasure etc say "Begone, thou art a hindrance destruction, and of the place of darkness etc – that (treasure etc) is provided for the use of Man: thou art vanquished, thy time is fully expired, therefore I say, depart to thy orders Jeovah Jeovaschah - and lo! I saw you to the End".[847]

---

[847] The following note is added in the hand of Aleister Crowley:
Note. In 1st key "Vooan spoken with them that fall". Thus 1st key used in invoking the X or other letter from tablet of Spirit with the demonic names. Probably therefore each name should be invoked letter by letter. Thus for Xns 1. Key I for X, 2 for n (airy file but fiery rank) Key 9. 3 for s (Watery file fiery rank) Key 12. Also Key 3 Air of Air for synthesis. This first of all (or after Key I) while inverted pentagrams used appropriately.

Appendix 4 – Table of the Kings, Seniors and Angels

East

3 Great Names of God	Oro Ibah Aozpi
Governing the King	Bataiva
Governing the 6 Seniors	Habioro, Aaoxaif, Hetermorda, Ahaozpi, Hipotga, Autotar
Name of God	Erzla
Governs the 4 Angels set over the first lesser Angle	Vrzla, Zlar, Larzod, Arzel
Divine Names governing, calling forth & constraining	Idoigo, Ardza
Names of 4 Angels serving to the first lesser Angle	Cezodenes, Totet, Sias, Efermende
Name of God	Eutepa
Governs the 4 Angels set over the second lesser Angle	Vtepa, Tepau, Paute, Autep
Divine Names governing, calling forth & constraining	Haeza, Palam
Names of 4 Angels serving to the second lesser Angle	OYube, Paoc, Vrbeneh, Diri
Name of God	Ecenbar
Governs the 4 Angels set over the third lesser Angle	Cenbar, Enbarc, Barcen, Vrcenbre
Divine Names governing, calling forth & constraining	Aiaoai, Oiiit
Names of 4 Angels serving to the third lesser Angle	Abemo, Naco, Ocenem, Shael
Name of God	Eexgezod
Governs the 4 Angels set over the fourth lesser Angle	Exgezod, Gezodex, Zodexge, Dexgezod
Divine Names governing, calling forth & constraining	Aovararzod, Moar
Names of 4 Angels serving to the fourth lesser Angle	Acca, Enpeat, Otoi, Pemox

West

3 Great Names of God	Empeh Arsel Gaiol
Governing the King	Raagios
Governing the 6 Seniors	Lefarahpem, Saiinou, Laoaxarp, Selgaiol, Ligdisa, Soaixente
Name of God	HeTaad
Governs the 4 Angels set over the first lesser Angle	Taad, Aadet, Adeta, Detaa
Divine Names governing, calling forth & constraining	Obegoca, Aabeco
Names of 4 Angels serving to the first lesser Angle	Paax, Toco, Enheded, Saix
Name of God	HeTedim
Governs the 4 Angels set over the second lesser Angle	Tedim, Dimet, Imted, Emtedi
Divine Names governing, calling forth & constraining	Nelapar, Omebeb
Names of 4 Angels serving to the second lesser Angle	Magem, Leoc, Vsyl, Vrvoi
Name of God	HeMagel
Governs the 4 Angels set over the third lesser Angle	Magel, Agelem, Gelema, Lemage
Divine Names governing, calling forth & constraining	Maladi, Olaad
Names of 4 Angels serving to the third lesser Angle	Paco, Endezen, Fipo, Exarih
Name of God	Henlarex
Governs the 4 Angels set over the fourth lesser Angle	Enlarex, Larexen, Rexenel, Xenelar
Divine Names governing, calling forth & constraining	Jaaasde, Atapa
Names of 4 Angels serving to the fourth lesser Angle	Expeceh, Vasa, Dapi, Reniel

North

3 Great Names of God	Emor Dial Hectega
Governing the King	Jezodhehca
Governing the 6 Seniors	Laidrom, Aczinor, Elzinopo, Alhectega, Elhiansa, Acemliceve
Name of God	Enboza
Governs the 4 Angels set over the first lesser Angle	Boza, Ozab, Zabo, Aboz
Divine Names governing, calling forth & constraining	Angepoi, Vnenax
Names of 4 Angels serving to the first lesser Angle	Aira, Ormen, Reseni, Jzodenar
Name of God	Enphra
Governs the 4 Angels set over the second lesser Angle	Phra, Harap, Rapeh, Aphar
Divine Names governing, calling forth & constraining	Anacem, Sonden
Names of 4 Angels serving to the second lesser Angle	Omgege, Gebal, Relemu, Jahel
Name of God	Næoan
Governs the 4 Angels set over the third lesser Angle	Æoan, Oanæ, Anæo, Næoa
Divine Names governing, calling forth & constraining	Cebalpet, Arbizod
Names of 4 Angels serving to the third lesser Angle	Opena, Dopa, Rexao, Axir
Name of God	Niaom
Governs the 4 Angels set over the fourth lesser Angle	Iaom, Aomi, Omia, Miao
Divine Names governing, calling forth & constraining	Espemenir, Hpizol
Names of 4 Angels serving to the fourth lesser Angle	Mesael, Jaba, Jezexpe, Estim

South

3 Great Names of God	Oip Teaa Pedoce
Governing the King	Edelperna
Governing the 6 Seniors	Aaetpio, Adoeoet, Alendood, Aapedoce, Arinnaquu, Anodoin
Name of God	Bedopa
Governs the 4 Angels set over the first lesser Angle	Dopa, Opad, Pado, Adop
Divine Names governing, calling forth & constraining	Noalmar, Oloag
Names of 4 Angels serving to the first lesser Angle	Opemen, Apeste, Scio, Vasge
Name of God	Banaa
Governs the 4 Angels set over the second lesser Angle	Anaa, Naaa, Aaan, Aana
Divine Names governing, calling forth & constraining	Vadali, Obavi
Names of 4 Angels serving to the second lesser Angle	Gemenem, Ecope, Amox, Berape
Name of God	Bepesac
Governs the 4 Angels set over the third lesser Angle	Pesac, Sacepe, Acepes, Cepesa
Divine Names governing, calling forth & constraining	Volexdo, Sioda
Names of 4 Angels serving to the third lesser Angle	Datete, Diom, Oopezod, Vrgan
Name of God	Beziza
Governs the 4 Angels set over the fourth lesser Angle	Ziza, Jzazod, Zazi, Azizod
Divine Names governing, calling forth & constraining	Arzodionar, Narzefem
Names of 4 Angels serving to the fourth lesser Angle	Adre, Sispe, Pali, Acar

Practical Angel Magic

Bibliography

When trying to understand the magical work of John Dee, it is essential to look at it from *his* point of view, a point of view rather removed from our own. The problem with all Dee bibliographies is that they are always drawn up from the point of view of the location of the manuscript in the present day library collections in which they reside (such as the Sloane manuscripts in the British Library).

This really tells you nothing about the contents of the manuscript. These manuscript numbers are simply the order in which Sir Hans Sloane's collection of manuscripts (for example) was catalogued, or shelved.

All commentators writing about Dee also refer to his manuscripts by their library shelf number, for example 'Sloane MS 3188'. This is fine for identification, but it is obviously not the way Dee would have looked at them, and certainly not the name Dee would have used to identify them.

To help attempt to reconstruct Dee's mindset we have below identified Dee's main works by their original title, given to them by Dee. By doing this the relationship between the different manuscripts falls into place. Of course the full library shelf mark details are given also to help you refer to them.

In addition we have rendered the manuscript titles into English so that a modern audience who are not Latin orientated will have no difficulty understanding Dee's titles. The Latin will also be provided for the sake of scholarly completeness, and for those who want to look for another or better translation.

We refer to Dee's manuscripts by the name he used for them, for example, "The First Book of Mysteries" (*Liber Mysteriorum Primus*) or "The 48 Angelic Keys" (*48 Claves Angelicae*) or "The Sevenfold Mystery" (*De Heptarchia Mystica*). In that way the listing is not hindered by continually trying to remember what is contained in a manuscript entitled 'Sloane MS 3191' for instance.

Although the Latin titles sound more impressive, we use English titles for ease of apprehension. Although Dee was fluent in Latin, by Dee's period in the late sixteenth century, Latin was often only used to provide impressive sounding titles for works that had in fact been originally composed in English.

We will not include Dee's books on navigation, geography, astronomy, alchemy, or the politics of the founding of the British Empire, which are well covered elsewhere. Dee's books on angel magic and similar pursuits divide into 3 classes:

1   His day-to-day diaries, much like an appointments diary that we might still use.

2   His spiritual or magical diaries, in which he meticulously recorded the scrying experiments. These contain word by word accounts of the material transmitted to him via his three main scryers Edward Kelly, Bartholomew Hickman, and Barnabas Saul, from angels, spirits, and other 'spiritual creatures' and denizens of the unseen world. Unfortunately, he destroyed some of these, especially those ranging from 1569 to 1581, believing them to be false transmissions.

3   His finished self-contained books of magical practice, derived from what he learned in these scrying experiments.

This is very much the way Dee saw his life divided, and these books and manuscripts he treated accordingly.

His day-to day diaries were openly kept, and later published as of antiquarian interest some time after his death by Haliwell, Crossley, and Bailey. Unfortunately these were in fact partly edited to remove some of the material of most interest. A modern edition of his diaries by Fenton remedies some of these omissions.

His spiritual/magical diaries from 28 May 1583 to May 1587 (with some gaps) where published by Meric Casaubon in 1659, and caused quite a stir, as well as helping to blacken and diminish Dee's reputation. These manuscripts were originally kept in the library of Sir Thomas Cotton, having been apparently at one stage rescued by him from burial in a field in Mortlake.

The balance of the spiritual/magical diaries from 22 December 1581 till 23 May 1583, were not published till almost 400 years after his death. The most complete version of these were edited by Joseph Peterson and published by Adam McLean in 1985, and again by Weiser in 2003.

In fact some of these diaries were also completely destroyed, especially a period referred to by Meric Casaubon as the 'Great

Chasme' in Dee's records. These spiritual diaries offer you the chance to judge the validity, quality and method of Dee's 'angelic transmission.'

His most secret works however, were the finished volumes of magical technique, in effect his grimoires, although he would not have described them in that way, his books giving instructions for practice. These were carefully written out in a fair hand, much more carefully than either of the other two categories of manuscript. In addition they were secreted in the secret drawer in the bottom of the chest where they laid hidden for more than 50 years after Dee's death. The story of this chest has been told in the Introduction. They were so carefully hidden by Dee, that even though the chest belonged at one time to an expert in chest construction, he never guessed at their existence. These works, about which Dee was so particular, are the distillation of Dee's system, and offer you the chance to understand and practice Dee's magic as he himself did.

Manuscript Source Material

Dee's manuscripts, some written by him, some copied for him by Kelly, and some later transcribed by Elias Ashmole, are the core of Dee's legacy of research into angel magic.

1   His Daily Diaries:

Bodleian Ashmole MS 423, art 122. 1543-1566.
Bodleian Ashmole MS 487-8. 1577-1600 & 1586-1601.
Published by Bailey (1880), Halliwell [1842], Crossley [1851] and Fenton (1998). [848]

2   His Spiritual or Magical Diaries:

"The Five Books of Mysteries" - *Mysteriorum Libri Quinque*:
BL Sloane MS 3188. Copied by Ashmole in BL Sloane MS 3677. 1581- 1583. Published by Peterson (2003)

"The Sixth and Holy Book of Mysteries" – *Liber Mysteriorum Sextus et Sanctus:* [with *Libri Mysteriorum VI*]
BL Sloane MS 3190, Cotton Appendix XLVI. 1583–1587 & 1607.
Published by Casaubon (1659 and 1974).

"A Missing Action with Spirits" - *Praefatio Latina in Actionem:*
Bodleian Ashmole 1790, art 1. 1586. Published by Josten (1965).

3   His Grimoires of Magical Practice:

"The Sevenfold Mystery" - *De Heptarchia Mystica (Collectaneorum Liber Primus):* BL Sloane MS 3191, art. 3. 1582.
Compendium Heptarchiae Mysticae: BL Add MS 36,674, fol. 167rff. Published by Turner (1983).

"The 48 Angelic Keys" - *48 Claves Angelicae*:
BL Sloane MS 3191[849], art. 1. Published by Turner (1989) p.30-47.

"The Book of Knowledge, Help and Victory on Earth" *Liber Scientiae, Auxilii & Victoriae Terrestris*:
BL Sloane MS 3191, art. 2. Published by Turner (1989) p.48-58.

---

[848] See printed books for full details of the published versions of each manuscript on page 288.

[849] Copied by Elias Ashmole in BL Sloane MS 3678.

A Book of Supplications and Invocations (Table of Invocations to the Good Angels) – *Tabula Bonorum Angelorum Invocationes:*
BL Sloane MS 3191, art. 4. Published by Turner (1989) p.59-79.

The Book of Enoch or The Book of Speech from God – *Liber Logaeth:*
BL Sloane MS 3189, Sloane MS 2599. Bodleian Ashmole MS 422, art 2. An unpublished book of large Enochian tables.

4   The 17th Century Development of Dee's Angel Magic:

"The Key to the Tables of Enoch" - *Clavicula Tabularum Enochi:*
BL Sloane MS 307, Sloane MS 3821.
Bodleian Rawlinson D. 1067, Rawlinson D. 1363.
Published in this present book.

Printed Source Material

Bailey, John E. *[Dee's] Diary for the years 1595-1601.* 1880.

Casaubon, Meric (ed). *A True and Faithful Relation of what passed for many Yeers between Dr John Dee...and some Spirits.* London, 1659 and reprinted Askin Publishers, London, 1974. The text of the later *Libri Mysteriorum.*

Crossley, James [ed]. *Autobiographical Tracts of Dr. John Dee, Warden of the College of Manchester.* Chetham Society Publications, Vol. XXIV. Manchester, 1851.

Dee, John. *Mathematicall Preface* to *The Elements of Geometrie of the most auncient Philosopher Euclide of Megara.* Translated by Sir Henry Billingsley, London, 1570. Also edited by Thomas Rudd, London, 1651.

Fenton, Edward [ed]. *The Diaries of John Dee.* Charlbury, Oxon., 1998. A better edition than the earlier Halliwell & Bailey editions, but still not complete.

Halliwell, James O. *The Private Diary of Dr John Dee.* London, 1842.

Josten, C. H. 'A Translation of John Dee's 'Monas Hieroglyphica.' Antwerp, 1564, with an Introduction and Annotations," *Ambix* 12, 1964. One of Dee's most obscure works uniting philosophy, symbolism, geometry and alchemy, of which he was very proud.

Josten, C. H. 'An Unknown Chapter in the Life of John Dee', *Journal of the Warburg and Courtauld Institutes,* Vol. 28, London, 1965. A missing fragment of the *Libri Mysteriorum.*

Peterson, Joseph (ed). *John Dee's Five Books of Mystery.* Weiser Books, York Beach, 2003. Most important. The text of the early *Libri Mysteriorum.*

Turner, Robert (ed). *The Heptarchia Mystica of John Dee.* Aquarian Press, Wellingborough, 1986. One of Dee's complete grimoires.

Turner, Robert. *Elizabethan Magic, the Art and the Magus.* Element Books, Shaftesbury, 1989. Pages 1-80. Contains a very useful transcription of Sloane MS 3191 added to other less relevant material.

Secondary Printed Sources

Agrippa, H. C. *Three Books of Occult Philosophy.* Translated by James Freake. Edited by Donald Tyson. Llewellyn, St Paul, 1993.

Agrippa, H. C. *Fourth Book of Occult Philosophy.* Askin Publishers, London, 1978. It includes *Of Occult Philosophy* by Agrippa plus the *Arbatel* and the *Heptameron* by Peter de Abano. New complete reset modern edition available from Nicolas Hays 2005.

Calder, I. R. F. *John Dee studied as an English Neoplatonist,* Ph.D thesis. 2 vols. London, University of London, 1952.

Clulee, Nicholas H. *John Dee's Natural Philosophy: Between Science and Religion.* New York, 1988. The standard work on Dee's philosophy.

Clulee, Nicholas H. *"Astrology, Magic, and Optics: Facets of John Dee's Early Natural Philosophy",* in *Renaissance Quarterly* 30, 1977.

Clulee, Nicholas H. "John Dee and the Paracelsians", in *Reading the Book of Nature: The other side of the Scientific Revolution,* ed. Allen G. Debus and Michael T. Walton. Kirksville, 1998, pp.111-132.

Deacon, Richard. *John Dee.* London, 1968. A little over the top in relation to Dee's spying activities.

Fanger, Claire [ed]. *Conjuring Spirits: Texts and Traditions of Medieval Ritual Magic.* Pennsylvania State UP & Sutton Publishing, 1998. Magic in History Series.

French, Peter J. *John Dee: the World of an Elizabethan Magus.* London, 1972. The standard life with an excellent bibliography.

Gilbert, R.A. [ed]. *The Magical Mason: Forgotten Hermetic Writings of William Wynn Westcott, Physician and Magus.* Aquarian, Wellingborough, 1983.

Harkness, Deborah E. "Alchemy and Eschatology: Exploring the connections between John Dee and Isaac Newton", in *Newton and Religion,* ed. James E. Force and Richard H. Popkin. Dordrecht, 1999.

Harkness, Deborah E. "Managing an experimental household: The

Dees of Mortlake and the practice of Natural Philosophy", *Isis* 88, 1997.

Harkness, Deborah E. *"Shows in the Showstone: A Theater of Alchemy and Apocalypse in the Angel Conversations of John Dee (1527-1608/9)"*, *Renaissance Quarterly*, 49, 1996.

Harkness, Deborah E. *John Dee's Conversations with Angels: Cabala, Alchemy, and the End of Nature.* Cambridge, 1999. [The most recent and perhaps most scholarly work on his angel magic.]

Howe, Ellic (ed). *The Alchemist of the Golden Dawn: The Letters of the Revd W.A.Ayton to F.L.Gardner and Others 1886-1905*, Aquarian Press, Wellingborough, 1985.

Howe, Ellic. *The Magicians of the Golden Dawn: A Documentary History of a Magical Order 1887-1923*, Aquarian Press, Wellingborough, 1972.

Kieckhefer, Richard. *Forbidden Rites, A Necromancer's Manual of the Fifteenth Century.* Sutton, Stroud, 1997. A slightly misleading title, as the subject is evocation, not raising the dead. Mostly in Latin.

King, Francis. *Astral Projection, Ritual Magic, and Alchemy: Golden Dawn Material by S.L.MacGregor Mathers and Others"*, Aquarian, Wellingborough, 1971.

Knoespel, Kenneth J. "The Narrative Matter of Mathematics: John Dee's preface to the 'Elements' of Euclid of Megara (1570)", *Philological Quarterly* 66, 1987.

Laycock, Donald with Skinner, Stephen. *The Complete Enochian Dictionary.* Askin, London, 1978.

Poole, Robert *"John Dee and the English Calendar: science, religion and empire"*, a paper preparatory to his book, *Time's Alteration: Calendar Reform in Early Modern England.* London, 1998.

Roberts, Julian and Andrew G. Watson, [eds]. *John Dee's Library Catalogue.* London, 1990.

Rose, P. "Commandino, John Dee, and the 'De superficierum divisionibus' of Machometus Bagdedinus", *Isis* 63, 1972.

Runyon, Carroll 'Poke'. *The Book of Solomon's Magick.* CHS,

Siverado, 2003. Interesting insights into the nature and use of the Goetic triangle and mirror.

Sherman, William H. "John Dee's *Brytannicae Republicae Synopsis*: A Reader's Guide to the Elizabethan Commonwealth", *Journal of Medieval and Renaissance Studies* 20.1990.

Sherman, William H. *John Dee: The Politics of Reading and Writing in the English Renaissance.* Amherst, 1995.

Slights, William W.E. "The Cosmopolitics of Reading: Navigating the margins of John Dee's 'General and Rare Memorials' ", in *Margins of the Text*, ed. D.C. Greetham, Ann Arbor, 1997.

Smith, Charlotte Fell. John Dee (1527-1608), London, 1909.

Thomas, Keith. *Religion and the Decline of Magic.* Penguin, London, 1973. An excellent study.

Traister, Barbara Howard. *The Notorious Astrological Physician of London: Works and Days of Simon Forman.* University of Chicago Press, Chicago & London, 2001.

Trattner, Walter I. "God and Expansion in Elizabethan England: John Dee, 1527-1583", *Journal of the History of Ideas* 25, 1964.

Walton, Michael T. "The Geometrical Kabbalahs of John Dee and Johannes Kepler: the Hebrew tradition and the mathematical study of Nature" in Michael T. Walton and Phyllis J. Walton. *Experiencing Nature: proceedings of a conference in honor of Allen G Debus.* Dordrecht, 1997.

Walton, Michael T. "John Dee's 'Monas Hieroglyphica': Geometrical Cabala", *Ambix* 23, 1976.

Woolley, Benjamin. *The Queen's Conjuror: The Science and Magic of Dr. John Dee, Adviser to Queen Elizabeth I.* New York, 2001. A readable biography, including some of the latest scholarship.

Yewbrey, Graham. "A redated manuscript of John Dee", *Bulletin of the Institute of Historical Research* 50. 1977.

Zetterberg, J. P. "Hermetic Geocentricity : John Dee's Celestial Egg", *Isis* 70, 1979.

Index